# THE SOVIET STUDY OF INTERNATIONAL RELATIONS

## SOVIET AND EAST EUROPEAN STUDIES



The National Association for Soviet and East European Studies exists for the purpose of promoting study and research on the social sciences as they relate to the Soviet Union and the countries of Eastern Europe. The Monograph Series is intended to promote the publication of works presenting substantial and original research in the economics, politics, sociology and modern history of the USSR and Eastern Europe.

## SOVIET AND EAST EUROPEAN STUDIES

Rudolf Bićanić *Economic Policy in Socialist Yugoslavia*
Galia Golan *Yom Kippur and After: The Soviet Union and the Middle East Crisis*
Maureen Perrie *The Agrarian Policy of the Russian Socialist-Revolutionary Party from its Origins through the Revolutions of 1905–1907*
Paul Vyšný *Neo-Slavism and the Czechs 1898–1914*
Gabriel Gorodetsky *The Precarious Truce: Anglo-Soviet Relations 1924–1927*
James Riordan *Sport in Soviet Society: Development of Sport and Physical Education in Russia and the USSR*
Gregory Walker *Soviet Book Publishing Policy*
Felicity Ann O'Dell *Socialisation through Children's Literature: The Soviet Example*
T. H. Rigby *Lenin's Government: Sovnarkom 1917–1922*
Stella Alexander *Church and State in Yugoslavia since 1945*
M. Cave *Computers and Economic Planning: The Soviet Experience*
Jozef M. Van Brabant *Socialist Economic Integration: Aspects of Contemporary Economic Problems in Eastern Europe*
R. F. Leslie ed. *The History of Poland since 1863*
M. R. Myant *Socialism and Democracy in Czechoslovakia 1945–1948*
Blair A. Ruble *Soviet Trade Unions: Their Development in the 1970s*
Angela Stent *From Embargo to Ostpolitik: The Political Economy of West German–Soviet Relations 1955–1980*
William J. Conyngham *The Modernisation of Soviet Industrial Management*
Jean Woodall *The Socialist Corporation and Technocratic Power*
Israel Getzler *Kronstadt 1917–1921: The Fate of a Soviet Democracy*
David A. Dyker *The Process of Investment in the Soviet Union*
S. A. Smith *Red Petrograd: Revolution in the Factories 1917–1918*
Saul Estrin *Self-Management: Economic Theories and Yugoslav Practice*
Ray Taras *Ideology in a Socialist State*
Silvana Malle *The Economic Organization of War Communism 1918–1921*
S. G. Wheatcroft and R. W. Davies *Materials for a Balance of the Soviet National Economy 1928–1930*
Mark Harrison *Soviet Planning in Peace and War 1938–1945*
James McAdams *East Germany and Detente: Building Authority after the Wall*
J. Arch Getty *Origins of the Great Purges: The Soviet Communist Party Reconsidered 1933–1938*
Tadeusz Swietochowski *Russian Azerbaijan 1905–1920: The Shaping of National Identity*
David S. Mason *Public Opinion and Political Change in Poland 1980–1982*
Nigel Swain *Collective Farms Which Work?*
Stephen White *The Origins of Detente: The Genoa Conference and Soviet–Western Relations 1921–1922*
Ellen Jones and Fred W. Grupp *Modernization, Value Change and Fertility in the Soviet Union*
Catherine Andreyev *Vlasov and the Russian Liberation Movement: Soviet Reality and Emigre Theories*
Anita J. Prazmowska *Britain, Poland and the Eastern Front, 1939*
Allen Lynch *The Soviet Study of International Relations*
David Granick *Job Rights in the Soviet Union: Their Consequences*
Jozef M. Van Brabant *Adjustment, Structural Change and Economic Efficiency: Aspects of Monetary Cooperation in Eastern Europe*
Susan Bridger *Women in the Soviet Countryside: Women's Roles in Rural Development in the USSR*
Benjamin Pinkus *The Jews of the Soviet Union: The History of a National Minority*

# THE SOVIET STUDY OF INTERNATIONAL RELATIONS

ALLEN LYNCH

*Deputy Director of Studies, Institute for East–West Security Studies, New York*



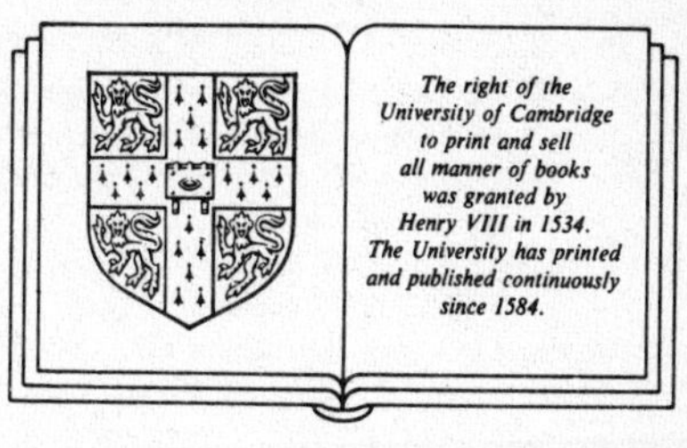


CAMBRIDGE UNIVERSITY PRESS

CAMBRIDGE

NEW YORK NEW ROCHELLE

MELBOURNE SYDNEY

Published by the Press Syndicate of the University of Cambridge
The Pitt Building, Trumpington Street, Cambridge CB2 1RP
32 East 57th Street, New York, NY 10022, USA
10 Stamford Road, Oakleigh, Melbourne 3166, Australia



First published 1987

Printed in Great Britain at the University Press, Cambridge

*British Library cataloguing in publication data*

Lynch, Allen
The Soviet study of international relations.–(Soviet and East European studies)
1. Soviet Union – Foreign relations – 1953–1975 2. Soviet Union – Foreign relations – 1975–
I. Title II. Series
327.47 DK274

*Library of Congress cataloguing in publication data*

Lynch, Allen, 1955–
The Soviet study of international relations.
(Soviet and East European studies)
Bibliography
Includes index.
1. Soviet Union – Foreign relations – 1975–
2. International relations. I. Title. II. Series.
JX1555.L96 1987 327′.0947 87-790

ISBN 0 521 33055 6

VN

*For Robert Legvold and*
*Adam Ulam, exemplars*

# Contents

# Foreword

There are many signs and declarations that the Soviet Union under Secretary General Mikhail Gorbachev intends to enter into a new era in terms of both reforms at home and new initiatives abroad. The two are obviously interlinked: the extent and success of the former will in many ways determine the credibility and persuasiveness of the latter. Nobody, not even Gorbachev himself, knows whether the Soviet system is capable of the kind of internal and economic reforms that will make her, above and beyond the military realm, a genuine world power. One thing, however, is clear: Gorbachev and his supporters have recognized that military power alone is not sufficient anymore – if it ever was – to justify their country's claim to global status and to respond to the many challenges and demands of the outside world that require everything except a military answer. They now acknowledge global interdependence and the fact that the Soviet Union is not exempt from but inextricably tied to it.

It would indeed be a revolution in Soviet foreign policy if the Soviet Union accepted such linkage to, and responsibilities for, the present international order which, ever since her creation in 1917, she has rejected as immoral and whose doom she has predicted. To be sure, by her own ideological standards she cannot officially renounce her ultimate objective, world revolution. Hence, her world outlook and her foreign policy remain conditioned at least in theory by what has long been recognized as an outdated worldview. It is this ideological straitjacket which has made the adjustments to reality and the ensuing changes in actual policy so difficult and slow.

Rare are the fields in which this is more true than in that of international relations, where the mission of the Soviet Union as the "Rome" of communist ideology and her prestige as a world power are at stake. Whoever, as scientist or academic, dares to venture into this inner sanctum of Kremlin authority, has to read cautiously and circumspectedly. Little wonder that under these circumstances it took a long time until international relations and the Soviet Union's place in them became accepted as an area of research and self-reflection. It took even longer until a minimum of debate – dare we say: controversy – on some foreign policy issues was tolerated.

One should have thought that this long process and its significance for Soviet policy making would have stirred the interest of many Western scholars. To follow how the Soviet colleagues see and interpret the outside world, what conclusions they draw from major events and trends on the international stage for their own country, and how they gradually shift in their appraisal of the nature and future of modern "capitalism," is indeed worth serious and sustained study. And yet, surprisingly and sadly enough, there are very few scholars who have done so in any systematic way. Innumerable books exist on Soviet foreign policy as such, and so do scores of analyses on the evolution and changes of Soviet strategy. But there are all too few studies on the work of Soviet political scientists and the way they perceive and interpret contemporary international relations. As a result, "we know little about how Soviet foreign-policy intellectuals view the structure and tendencies of contemporary world politics."

The most notable exception to this has so far been William Zimmerman's study on *Soviet Perspectives on International Relations 1956–1967* covering the Khrushcev and early Brezhnev periods. It is now, after fifteen years, followed by a second study of no doubt equal value and interest. Dr Allen Lynch's book (from which we have quoted the above sentence) is both a sequel to that of Zimmerman and a highly successful effort to "cumulate" the hypotheses which Zimmerman put forward. They now find themselves re-examined, updated and enriched in the light of almost twenty more years of Soviet research activities and writings on the subject.

It is a most timely book. The author, currently Deputy Director of Studies at the Institute for East–West Security Studies, New York, shows in this well researched and documented overview that there has been much more advancement and greater differentiation in Soviet thinking on international politics than most people in the West realize. These Soviet scholars have laid the groundwork for a more sober and sophisticated evaluation of world politics and its present and future direction. Lynch concludes that a greater realism prevails today in their writings, as a result of their attributing more weight to subjective factors in the historical process and thus moving away from the determinism of Leninist doctrine; they have also begun to recognize the underlying stability of capitalism in the West and the relative decline in the influence of the two superpowers in their respective alliances. But inasmuch as they maintain that, in spite of the changes, the world remains dominated by conflicts of interests and deep ideological antagonisms, they stay within the fundamental teachings of Marxism–Leninism.

How much of these findings have penetrated the Kremlin leaders is difficult to judge. The fact is, however, that a number of things that Gorbachev has said since coming to power, and that were restated, albeit in more veiled terms, in the revised program of the Communist Party of the Soviet Union, are not very far from what the scholars have written. The least one can say is that, within a system as closed as the Soviet, there has been an osmosis and interaction between science and politics that may signal some greater influence of the former and somewhat more openness on part of the latter.

This study by Allen Lynch gives us thus a highly interesting and no less welcome insight into an important sector of Soviet policy thinking and Soviet policy making and the relationship between the two. In substantive terms it reveals a process of gradual disillusionment of Soviet expectations about both the chances of world revolution and the limits of Soviet power – a process of adjusting the high prognostications of ideology to the sober facts of reality. But Lynch also leaves no doubt that this process does not go beyond the line where it would put into question the foundations of official doctrine and hence the Soviet system and its legitimacy themselves. That some adjustments and modifications of the Soviet worldview are under way and find their reflection in present Soviet foreign policy under Gorbachev is, however, evident. It is the great merit of Allen Lynch's excellent study to show us their scope but also their limits and, in so doing, provide us with the necessary guidance that helps us to recognize their importance and gauge their future direction.

*Geneva, November 1986* CURT GASTEYGER

# Acknowledgements

I would like to thank the Russian Research Center of Harvard University for having made its facilities and resources available to me as a visitor from the Russian Institute of Columbia University in 1980/81, and in particular Ms Susan Gardos, the Center's librarian, for her gracious cooperation at every stage of the research. I would also like to thank the Albert Gallatin Fellowship Fund of the Feris Foundation, and its very able President, Mr William D. Carter, for their generous support during the 1981/82 year at the Graduate Institute of International Studies, Geneva, where the first version of this book was written. Finally, I would like to thank Mr Peter Kaufman of the Institute for East–West Security Studies for his meticulous readings of the manuscript in various forms for substance, style and correct form.

# Introduction

Whatever the political fate of the new General Secretary of the Soviet Communist Party and his program, it is clear that the current transition in political leadership in the Soviet Union is going far beyond a shift in personnel and involves the displacement of an entire generation of Soviet leaders even now fading from the scene with a younger, less experienced but in certain ways better prepared generation of Soviet politicians and their advisors. What, if any, changes might we expect in the thinking of this new Soviet leadership about the outside world? In truth, we really do not know. In the United States at least, few in either governmental circles or political science departments take what Soviet political analysts have to say about the broader world very seriously. Except for William Zimmerman's pathbreaking study of the Khrushchev period, we know little about how Soviet foreign policy intellectuals view the structure and tendencies of contemporary world politics.[1]

Yet one would expect some changes of consequence to have taken place in the Soviet vision of the contemporary world, and not simply because of a change of political generations. Many of the conditions affecting the conduct of Soviet foreign policy, including both Soviet capabilities themselves and the structure of international relations in recent decades, have also changed, at times quite dramatically. Conceivably the ideological imprint of Marxism–Leninism on the Soviet political mentality is so strong that the Soviet vision of international relations has stood fast before the challenges posed by the contemporary world. But that would first have to be determined. A simple comparison of Nikita Khrushchev's bombastic pronouncements about the imminent triumph of communism with the late Soviet leader Konstantin Chernenko's admission in 1984 that contemporary capitalism "still possesses quite substantial and far from exhausted reserves for development,"[2] suggests something of the changes that have affected the Soviet outlook on the world over the last several decades. The 1986 Soviet Communist Party Program, the first since Khrushchev's rather utopian program of 1961, explicitly refers to "the accumulated experience and the scientific interpretation of changes . . . in the world arena" since then. These changes, and changes in interpretation, the new program states, "makes it possible to define more precisely and more specifically . . . the tasks of international policy under the new historical conditions."[3] Clearly, something of interest is taking place in the Soviet sense of international tendencies in recent years.

Traditionally, our conception of the Soviet view of international relations has rested on Lenin's theory of imperialism as expressed in his work *Imperialism: The Highest Stage of Capitalism*. Lenin there develops a model of international relations in which the international behavior of states is explained through the simple projection of the alleged internal contradictions of capitalism onto a crisis-prone, world capitalist system. It is the driving internal dynamic of capitalism, requiring foreign markets for surplus production, which determines the issue of war and peace in our day. Class relations are key; national interests are definitely subordinate. There is no qualitative distinction in this view between internal and international politics. International relations are essentially the product of the various socio-economic systems organized as separate states. Consequently, one cannot speak of international relations as an independent field of analysis. It is, rather, a subordinate branch of political economy.

A whole series of substantive conclusions follows from such a model of world politics. Among the most important is the proposition that the existence of (doomed) "capitalist" states throughout the world assures the inevitability of world war. Conversely, war between "socialist" states, which have abolished the anarchy of the market and thereby the mainspring of modern warfare, is a manifest impossibility. Yet surely the survival and even prosperity of the advanced capitalist states; the advent of the atomic and then hydrogen bombs; the eventual emergence of a hostile (communist) Chinese state along the Soviet border – all must have shaken certain assumptions of this Leninist model for Soviet leaders and analysts of world affairs. Zimmerman's work indicated that this was indeed so. The question remains, to what extent are Zimmerman's findings, largely restricted to the Khrushchev and early Brezhnev period, valid today? How enduring and how far-reaching have these changes in the Soviet vision of international relations been?

This book, then, seeks to establish the existence and trace the evolution of certain conceptions about international relations in the Soviet Union since the mid-1960s and assess their meaning, in Soviet terms, for Soviet understanding of the basic structure and processes of world politics. This is not, however, a venture in "Kremlinology." It does not try to identify patterns of influence among various Soviet leaders and their "protégé circles" in this or that research institute on international affairs or elsewhere. Were that to be done, the enterprise would still fall short of the Kremlinological criterion, for the Soviet outlook on international relations, the focus of our attention here, does not necessarily imply any specific set of conclusions about Soviet foreign policy, which is the proper concern of the policy analyst.

This is not to say that there is no relation at all between analysis and policy in the Soviet Union. Indeed, it would be most surprising if there were not. In few other countries is the link between public policy and public analysis, especially in the sensitive area of foreign policy, as strong as in the Soviet Union. Soviet publicists themselves make a virtue out of this bond. Yet one of the most significant developments in Soviet society over recent decades, amply supported by the literature under investigation and the research of others,[4] has been the emergence of a series of "within-system" debates, or discussions about the course Soviet society should be taking. Consequently, one can no longer assume a direct link between one analyst's views and state policy. The character of the analysis may be related to a particular policy preference, and in the case of certain individuals – such as Georgi Arbatov or the late Nikolai Inozemtsev[5] – the connection to higher policy may at times not be too difficult to discern. But in general the attempt to deduce Soviet policy or the views of the leadership from this or that analysis of various Soviet foreign policy intellectuals is an unrewarding exercise.

This book instead attempts to infer and construct a range of plausible conclusions that Soviet "political man" might draw about world politics on the basis of the available Soviet literature. It then examines the implications of those conclusions for certain fundamental Soviet attitudes toward international relations. Would a Soviet official or specialist feel that he had a firm grasp on, and was comfortable with, the state of international politics? Would he discern, on the basis of the literature in question, more, or less favorable trends? Would the Soviet Union be seen, consequently, as more, or less distinct compared to other states in the international system? Would it be felt to be more, or less capable of meeting its goals, as well as of generating a certain range and intensity of goals? Would it be possessed of more, or less confidence about its place and course in the world? In particular, what conclusions might be drawn, if, as the literature suggests:

the world is becoming increasingly multipolar;

the main adversary (the US) is fundamentally enduring and, furthermore, may not even represent the main threat (China);

the structure of socialist international relations is fixed for the forseeable future;

politics, and thus policies, are increasingly divorced from their supposedly economic and thus "objective" foundation, as a result of the increasing influence of the "subjective" element in social life;

therefore, the course of historical evolution is open, and so without a predictable "solution point" at any given moment in space and time;

international relations are increasingly regarded by analysts as a system, with the USSR now as one of a number of subsystemic elements, rather than as the center of a unique, and expanding, system of its own, both in the here-and-now and in the longer-term future.

The work begins with a brief discussion of the writings of Marx and Engels, Lenin, and Stalin concerning international relations, considering their thoughts on the subject as a standard of comparison for later Soviet efforts in this field. This is followed by an examination of the ground-breaking efforts in the area of international relations begun after the twentieth Congress of the Soviet Communist Party in 1956. Though this has been well covered by Zimmerman, the analyses of the Soviet economist Yevgeniy Varga will be treated in some detail, focusing on his work on the political economy of contemporary capitalism and its implications for international relations. The debate over the possibility of a Soviet political science, initiated in 1965, is then examined with a view to determining the influence of the course and resolution of that debate, ultimately unfavorable for the advocates of an independent political science, on the prospects for the development of a Soviet study of international relations.

The subject proper of the book, that is, international relations as an object of research, is then broached. We begin with a consideration of the Soviet discussion on methodological approaches to the subject, touching on the implications of "interdisciplinary" (*kompleksnyy*) analysis and greater empiricism in the treatment of international relations. Discussions over the relative weight to be assigned to "objective" factors, rooted in the general laws of dialectical materialism and finding their clearest expression through economic forces, and "subjective" factors, reflecting the indeterminate aspect of reality, are then analyzed. The meaning of the term "creative Leninism" is examined to determine how Soviet theorists treat Lenin's pronouncements on international relations. This is followed by a treatment of Soviet analyses of some basic theoretical aspects of international relations, as well as Soviet views on international relations as a system. These areas of inquiry concern the fundamental nature, the essence of international relations as an object of analytical reflection. On this basis we shall examine more specific aspects of the Soviet treatment of international relations, focusing particularly on the structure of the international system, the idea of the "correlation of forces" as a standard for judging the state and evolutionary tendencies of both structure and system; the "new" correlation of forces said to have emerged in the 1970s and the emergence of an increasingly multipolar world order; the role of Soviet–American relations in the international system; and such critical subsystems as "inter-imperialist" (i.e., inter-Western) and "inter-socialist" relations, and international organization.

This work specifically seeks to test Zimmerman's finding that Soviet perspectives on international relations have tended to converge with many non-marxist American (and other Western) theories in their view of the basic structure of the international system.[6] Such a structure would be characterized by:

(a) *the primacy of states over classes*, and social forces in general, as the defining units of the structure: such an analysis would pay special attention to the hierarchy of states and the roles and responsibilities incumbent upon particular states at particular points in the hierarchy;

(b) *the primacy of the political sphere* (the "superstructure") over the economic sphere (the "base") in relations among states: hence, the centrality of international political relations within the field of international relations;

(c) *the "subjective" element* in political relations among states, represented by such intangible factors as leadership, accident, and chance, possesses a weight not necessarily inferior to the "objective" element, represented by such "tangible" elements as resource bases, military forces, *etc*.

(d) greater importance assigned to the determining qualities of the *structure of international relationships* as opposed to the qualities of the individual units.

All the while a counter-hypothesis has been kept in mind: that Soviet international relations theory is deficient in that "it confines the international aspect of social change to a one-directional projection of the alleged internal contradictions of capitalism onto a crisis-prone, world-capitalist system."[7] If so, then Soviet international relations theory would have changed little in its essentials from the assumptions contained in Lenin's *Imperialism*.

## A NOTE ON METHODOLOGY

Methodologically, the author employs traditional Sovietological tools of analysis in the book. The main body of material to be treated consists of social science literature published by the series of Soviet institutes, classified by region and function, studying international relations. These institutes include the Institute of the World Economy and International Relations, especially its section on Theory of International Relations, headed by Vladimir Gantman and containing a half-dozen or so individuals particularly interested in Western theories of international relations; and the Foreign Policy Departments of both this Institute and the Institute for US and Canadian Studies, which include analysts who treat and publish on theoretical aspects of international relations.

The identity of individual writers and publishers will also be established, where possible, in an effort to assign relative weights of official approbation to various works. A volume published by *Politizdat*, for example, the publishing house of the Central Committee of the Communist Party, with a run of 50,000 or more copies per volume, receives the official imprimatur more decisively than a book intended primarily for academic audiences, with a run of 5,000 or less. Works by such individuals as Vladimir Petrovsky, now a Deputy Foreign Minister, or Georgi Shakhnazarov, deputy chief of the Central Committee department responsible for liaison with ruling foreign communist parties as well as head of the Soviet Political Sciences Association, have obvious import in shaping both the tenor of discourse and the bounds of the acceptable in Soviet theorizing on international relations. Special importance will be given to analyzing the book reviews which regularly appear in Soviet historical, philosophical, and social science journals that are devoted to examining both individual Western theorists, and indeed entire schools of Western theory of international relations, as well as exclusively Soviet works on the subject.

As far as treatment of these materials is concerned, it is assumed that, following Donald Zagoria, "differences over strategy are frequently expressed on the level of theory."[8] The significance of much of the material to be analyzed often lies in how and to what degree it departs from precedent. Some of the interpretive clues, as suggested by Zagoria, include: divergent emphasis given to the same point, omission, distortion, selective reporting or interpretation, a highly differentiated pattern of response, and a sudden change in routine formulations. Such an approach would enable us to examine in the field of international relations theory what Ronald Hill has argued of Soviet political science as a whole: that "a characteristic feature of Soviet political science is its discriminating use of concepts and vocabulary developed in Western political analysis including, indeed, whole approaches."[9]

# I

# The background: Marx, Lenin, Stalin and the theory of international relations

> It seems that I have left out a section of Lenin's fundamental thoughts about the approach to the program and they are worth recalling.
>
> Mikhail Gorbachev*

## MARX AND ENGELS

At first glance one is struck by the dearth of substantive references to Marx and Engels in contemporary Soviet writing on international relations. True, Marx and Engels are often enough hailed as offering the first genuinely systemic view of society and the world, but little beyond this is said in indication of Marx and Engels' actual contribution to the study of relations among states. Such silence, though, is hardly surprising, since in fact neither Marx nor Engels devoted any sustained attention to international relations, though they frequently wrote of world politics, which could encompass the role of classes, and the various diplomatic constellations and maneuvers of the day.[1] It is interesting to note, however, that most of what Marx in particular had to say about international relations was concerned with relations among states, on the whole diplomatic, military, and colonial affairs. Like other historians of the nineteenth century, Marx and Engels saw through the prism of great power politics, and not in the perspective of a "*Europe des nations.*" And, as in the case of Lenin, whose authority *is* constantly invoked in Soviet writings on international relations, the materialist conception of history, despite its stress on economic determinism, is modified by the role they attribute to voluntary human activity, especially where revolutionary action is concerned. "Thanks to this 'corrective',"

* Aside by Soviet General Secretary Mikhail Gorbachev in his Political Report to the 27th Soviet Party Congress, 25 February 1986.

Molnar notes, "international politics displays [for Marx and Engels] a certain autonomy in relation to economic forces."[2] This "corrective," it should be added, also prepared the ground for Lenin's decisive contribution, i.e., the salvaging of Marxism "through the concept of social practice which becomes the decisive verificatory criterion of theory," or Marxism–Leninism.[3] While objective forces, above all the social and political consequences of the state of the means of production in relation to the "mode," or organization of production, continued to determine the nature of a given historical epoch, the actual course of events depended on the conscious intervention of men in the historical process. That the efficacy of such intervention depended on the degree to which the objective "laws" of a period were subjectively apprehended (in the sense of "freedom as recognition of necessity") in no way effaced the decisiveness of the human element. The introduction of this subjective element, with its consequent enhancement of the influence of the political and ideological "superstructure" on the economic "base," imparts a certain flexibility to Soviet thinking on international relations which is concealed by notions of a rigidly deterministic Soviet ideology.

Although it is true that Marx never formulated a theory of international relations, he did help "to 'unveil' one aspect of international relations that was completely ignored in his time. He had the merit," writes Marcel Merle:

> of bringing out the interdependence of phenomena – economic and political, internal and external – and to discern, behind the apparent incoherence of the facts, the inexorable march toward the globalization of international relations. If he had not necessarily discovered the actual motor of social evolution, he at least formulated a hypothesis which explains a portion of the facts and which remains one of the possible outcomes of an uncertain future.[4]

The Marxist hypothesis states, of course, that the contradiction between the means and the mode of production under capitalism leads to a dynamic surge on the part of capitalism to expand in an effort to resolve this fundamental tension – new markets, in particular, would enable capitalists to dispose of otherwise surplus production. This expansionist drive, which cannot be understood simply in terms of the system of sovereign states but which must incorporate the increasingly internationalist perspective of the holders of "capital," leads to the globalization of the capitalist system whereupon, the labour–capital conflict having become insoluble, capitalism self-destructs and the reign of socialism is ushered in.[5]

In this way Marx's theory breaks totally with traditional approaches of understanding international relations. Whereas traditionally states, possessing juridical sovereignty and standing over the nations they ruled, were considered the focal point of international relations, Marx argued for what today might be called a "transnational" perspective, concentrating especially on the increasingly internationalist character of the forces of production. Indeed, in this regard Marx's analysis was quite consistent with that of the liberal Manchester School critique in favor of free trade. Marx simply carried that critique further. He viewed the state as subject to the influence of the very economic forces it had so recently set in motion. Where others took the interstate order as given, and were preoccupied with ways of assuring its "stability" (or its subordination to a hegemonic power), Marx viewed the state system as a temporary phase in the transition from feudalism to socialism *via* "bourgeois", and initially national capitalism. The international aspect is thus central to Marx's revolutionary vision. And the validity of his view of international relations, as well as of revolution itself, collapses if his predictions on the self-destruction of capitalism are not fulfilled. It is this insufficiency of the critique, "its relative failure . . . to account for contemporary international realities"[6] through its underestimation of the independent vitality of the political, national, and technological forces which makes international relations the area of greatest confrontation between Marx and his ideological successors.

In its pure, theoretical form, then, Marx's critique of international relations subordinates political struggle to the imputed requirements of the capitalist system and is strictly determinist. Yet, in examining specific aspects of the international politics of his day, such as the foreign policy of Tsarist Russia or capitalist Britain, Marx was not, in a sense, a "Marxist". In his journalistic writings for the *New York Herald*, for example, Marx focused, as the Romanian Marxist sociologist Silviu Brucan has said:

> on such factors as the mutual influence between the forces of revolution and those of counter-revolution; the rivalries between the big powers; Prussia's aspiration to become a major power and the opposition it encountered from Russia and Austria; the revival of old European antagonisms generated by the struggle for territories, strategic positions, and commercial routes and markets, and for influence in the Middle East; and the role played in that general ambience by the nationalist ideologies of various European countries.[7]

Marx noted, for example, that the Second French Republic often had the same foreign policy as the France of King Louis Philippe, thus recognizing the imperatives that geopolitical position imposed upon states.

In his discussion of colonialism, whose cruelties were justified, in Marx's mind, by its historical effect of breaking down traditional socio-economic structures and paving the way for the universalization of the capitalist system, Marx often gave ample consideration to the influence exerted by non-economic factors.[8] He conceded that profits derived from colonialism could be of a purely private, and not national, character, and that the total cost of colonial enterprises could be negative (just as the Manchester liberals argued, to continue the parallel).[9] In an article written for the *New York Herald* Marx gave an analysis of Persian–Afghan political antagonisms "founded on diversity of race, blended with historical reminiscences, kept alive by frontier quarrels and rival claims . . . sanctioned by religious antagonism."[10]

It is in his writings on the Euro-centric international balance of power, however, focusing above all on the position of Imperial Russia, that Marx's attitude to contemporary international relations most closely resembles the classical, state-centric approach that is best epitomized in the work of Leopold von Ranke. Though Marx's concern, indeed obsession, with Russian foreign policy was ultimately tied to his general conception of revolution, and the obstacle that was posed by a powerful, reactionary Russia, his analysis of the play of power interests preserves a certain autonomy in relation to his revolutionary theories. Most immediately concerned with the organization of the revolution in Germany, and hence in the consolidation of the historically "progressive" German bourgeoisie (as well as proletariat), Marx was a fervent advocate of a unified Germany. The precise nature of the unification, whether carried out by the Frankfurt liberals or under Prussian auspices, was a secondary consideration.[11] Consequently, Marx developed an analysis of the European balance of power that was tied to his interest in a strong Germany (as a "civilized" country) and that came to resemble very closely a "power-politics" approach, hinging directly on the relationship between Prussia, Poland, and Russia. In terms of content, Marx's writings on the subject are filled with a passionate analysis of political intrigues; methodologically, there is very little reference to social and economic forces.

For Marx, Prussia would necessarily remain subordinate to Russia, the bastion of reaction, in the absence of an independent Poland as buffer and check upon Russian policy. Since the Polish question was, for Marx, the German question, containment of Russian power became, in some sense, the indispensable precondition for the liberation of the revolutionary forces in Europe. The Russian suppression of the Hungarian revolution in 1849 naturally weighed heavily on Marx's mind. Yet Marx also saw that the prospects for Russian foreign policy were intimately tied to British foreign policy and its relation to the "Orient," which extended from the Balkans through the Middle East to include Afghanistan and India. Anglo-Russian rivalry thus came to occupy a critical place in Marx's preoccupations with international politics.

There is no neat way to separate these concerns from each other in Marx's thought. Each impinged on the others. Topics of particular interest, though, were the events of the revolutions of 1848–9 and the Russian threat to Europe and German politics; the Crimean War; the foreign policies of Napoleon III in Italy, Mexico, and Western Europe, with the Franco-Prussian War of 1870–1 as the culminating point; and the American Civil War. It was Marx and Engels' view of Russia, Poland, and Germany, as we have said, which occupied the center of their attention on international politics; international politics, in turn, had become essential to their revolutionary outlook. And yet, it

> represents an entirely new revolutionary conception compared to *The Communist Manifesto*. Foreign policy, the struggle among nations, takes precedence over class struggle, even only temporarily. States become invested with a role that only classes could fulfill in the *Manifesto*. They embody in some sense the revolution. Instead of being absorbed by the revolution, it is international politics which absorbs, envelops, and implements social struggles. And it is German foreign policy which bears, more than any other, this new mission.[12]

Thus Engels supported German claims on Schleswig, in the name of civilization *versus* "barbarism," and the law of historical development (and which would lead, as Molnar notes, to the "Brezhnev Doctrine" *via* the colonization of Asiatic countries).

In their analysis of the Crimean War, which really represents their first analysis of international politics *per se*, Marx and Engels transformed the very meaning of revolution in their unqualified, indeed enthusiastic support for the British and French position. Whereas 1848–9 presented a revolution without war, the Crimean War of 1853–6 posed the problem of war without revolution, yet war with revolutionary import nonetheless. In their unstinting opposition to Tsarist Russia, which they regarded as an inherently expansionist power whose "natural" frontiers would extend from Stettin to Trieste unchecked, Marx and Engels clearly hoped more for some change in the balance of power than in revolution or revolutionary war, as in 1848–9. The very meaning of revolution was changed – it no longer connoted insurrection as much as the "process" or "march" of history. In this way power politics was fitted into the Marxian revolutionary framework. Any action was justified toward undermining Russian power, including the encouragement of Serbian and Romanian nationalism as bulwarks against it.

To sum up, we note that, on the one hand Marx, whose first concern was revolution, was interested in the world as a whole rather than in international relations as such. His global vision encompassed class-conflict, not the conflict among states. For Marx, the "horizontal division [of the world] into states is only a surface projection of the basic conflict between classes and serves only to conceal the real struggle underneath."[13] Although, as we have suggested, the "base-superstructure" relationship is dynamic, the superstructure, i.e., the realm of the political, can never substantially modify the irresistible economic currents. Hence, there are no essential distinctions among "capitalist" states. International antagonism is absolutely dependent on domestic strife. Thus Marx posits, to the extent that he explicitly treats the subject at all, a reductionist theoretical vision of international relations. The nature of international relations, of the international system, is to be understood in terms of the nature of its constituent units. This, of course, represents Marx's fundamental position on the subject and is his major legacy to history with respect to it.

Yet diplomacy eventually assumes capital importance for Marx and Engels. They integrated the study of diplomacy with their conception of revolutionary action and historical factors in an attempt to grasp and advance the movement of history. An event of international politics could have direct repercussions on the revolutionary cause through changes in the existing equilibrium of interstate power, economic change, change in the structure of the international order, etc. To this extent, their view of international relations possesses a certain independence as a field of analysis. The tension between the class-oriented, economics-grounded, determinist analysis of the *Manifesto* and the state-focused, politically-oriented, open-ended critique of international power would continue to inform the attitudes of Marx and Engels' ideological heirs in the Soviet Union from Lenin's time to the present day.

### LENIN: "IMPERIALISM"

To the extent that the Soviet Union is credited with a theory of international relations at all, one is thrown back to Lenin's critique of "imperialism." It is curious critique, for it combines, in its purest form, a reductionist interpretation of international relations with a voluntarist vision of revolution. War, and by extension interstate tension and conflict, is an inevitable corollary of the division of society into classes and can hence be abolished only with the abolition of classes. International relations are thus conceived as a deterministic projection of the contradictions of capitalism onto a crisis-ridden world capitalist system. The study of the topic is, in this view, fundamentally a problem of global political economy. The "problem of studying imperialism," Lenin's student Bukharin wrote in 1915, "its economic characteristics, and its future, reduces itself to the problem of analyzing the tendencies in the development of the world economy, and of the probable changes in its inner structure."[14] It is thus that we associate with Lenin the most prominent features of traditional Soviet theory of international relations: the primacy of "objective," economic factors; the law of uneven capitalist development as the generator of the driving tensions of international relations; the classification of states, following Marx and Engels, into oppressor and oppressed; the inevitability of war in a class-riven international society; the inseparability of the survival of socialism from the successful advent of the world revolution.

Lenin's analysis, most clearly expressed in *Imperialism. The Highest Stage of Capitalism*, focused on the dynamics of the internal contradictions of capitalism to explain international political behavior. World politics, in this view, is merely the field for the resolution of these contradictions. The economic factor is dominant; it is the character of the individual units which defines the essence of the international "system of states." It was thus necessary for the student of international politics to acquire a thorough mastery of "the fundamental economic question, *viz.*, the economic essence of imperialism, for unless this is studied, it will be impossible to understand and appraise modern war and modern politics."[15]

For Lenin the term "imperialism" acquired a peculiar meaning. Traditionally conceived of as a particular kind of power relationship between at least two political units, imperialism became for Lenin a condition, and an essentially economic condition at that. Now imperialism was the highest stage of capitalism. The progressive concentration of production, foreseen by Marx, had led to the transformation of competitive capitalism, which was considered an historically progressive force, into "monopolistic, finance" capitalism, viewed by Lenin as both parasitic and dangerous.[16] The fusion of banking and industrial capital, which Lenin noted particularly in the somewhat exceptional case of Germany, led to the creation about 1900 of a narrow financial oligarchy, both national and international, which held the economic life of whole countries between its hands. "Finance capital is such . . . a decisive force in all economic and international relations," Lenin wrote, "that it is capable of subordinating to itself, and actually does subordinate to itself, even states enjoying complete political independence." Faced with the necessity of disposing of surplus capital that was incapable of being profitably invested in the home market, this new "imperialism" intended to continue the division of the globe by the great capitalist powers to secure markets for goods and outlets for capital. "The more capitalism develops," wrote Lenin, "the more the need for new materials arises, the more bitter competition becomes, and the more feverishly the hunt for raw materials proceeds all over the world, the more desperate becomes the struggle for the acquisition of colonies." These five elements – monopolization; the merging of bank capital with industrial capital and the consequent emergence of a powerful financial oligarchy; the export of capital, which is critical to the system's survival, as distinct from the export of commodities; the rise of *international* monopolies which divide the world amongst themselves; and the completion of the territorial division of the world – constitute the core of the Leninist critique of imperialism.[17]

How does this structural analysis, though, lead to an explanation of international political behavior, especially of war? How is it that imperialism necessarily generates war, and ultimately world war, as Lenin held? How, in short, is Lenin's skeletal analysis fleshed out, as it were? Lenin advances the thesis of the uneven development of capitalism, a kind of power-disequilibrium analysis, to explain the phenomenon of war. "Is there," Lenin asks, "*under capitalism*, any means of remedying the disparity between the development of productive forces on the one side, and the division of the colonies and 'spheres of influence' by finance capital on the other side – other than by resorting to war?" The answer is emphatically no. In spite of the increasingly internationalist character of capital, there is no basis under capitalism for permanent alliances, such as negotiated spheres-of-influence arrangements. Such alliances, in Lenin's view, were based on calculations of strength – economic, financial, military – and the strength of the participants does not change in equal measure because of the uneven development of capitalism. In particular, the changes in the relative standing of the capitalist powers that would take place in the "scramble" for colonial dominion would reinforce the inequalities in levels of development among capitalist states, intensifying still further the struggle for colonies and necessarily implying the resort to force. Such alliances, Lenin concluded, are therefore inevitably nothing more than truces in the periods between wars.[18] In this "anarchical" *milieu* (though one of an admittedly distorted market-kind rather than an international–political one, properly speaking) characteristic of contemporary imperialism, "there is nothing else that periodically restores the disturbed equilibrium [a product of the uneven development of capitalism] than crises in industry and war in politics." "There is and there can be no other way of testing the real strength of a capitalist state," Lenin concluded, "than that of war."[19]

War, then, is produced by conflicts of interest, heightened by differing levels of economic, and thus political and military development, that are endemic to the capitalist mode of production. If capitalism were to be abolished, as it necessarily would be, and replaced by socialism, wars would cease. "We understand," Lenin declared, "the inevitable connection which relates wars to the class struggles within a country . . . that it is impossible to suppress wars without suppressing classes and without installing socialism."[20]

Thus Lenin, like the Marx of *The Communist Manifesto*, presents an economically determinist view of international relations, in which the explanatory source of international behavior is located in the nature of the constituent units of the international "system." That is, capitalist states must produce war, socialist states will not. The state system is secondary to the global social system; in a sense, as the Soviet theorist Vladimir Gantman wrote in 1969, the international social system (capitalism vs. socialism) "runs deeper" than the interstate system (the US vs. the USSR).[21]

We know, however, that Lenin's opinions were ultimately far from categorical on these issues. Arguing that inasmuch as knowledge is a reflection, or copy, of reality, and that the only true test of knowledge is practice, Lenin opened the way to the introduction, and even the primacy, of the "subjective" element. The October Revolution itself is inconceivable without this conviction on Lenin's part. The test of practice, ironically, would later modify another of Lenin's central propositions, that concerning the necessity of world revolution (or at least revolution in Germany) for the survival of socialism.

Though Lenin conceded the theoretical possibility of "socialism in one country" as early as August 1915, he clearly had the triumph of socialism in one of the advanced capitalist countries in mind.[22] "The task of the proletariat in Russia," Lenin argued, "is to complete the bourgeois–democratic revolution in Russia *in order* to kindle the socialist revolution in Europe." The pervasive internationalism of Lenin's pre-revolutionary outlook is reflected in article 20 of the Soviet Constitution of 1918. All foreign workers residing in the territory of the Russian Republic possessed Soviet citizenship because of their *class* affiliation. (Strictly speaking, of course, the contemporary Soviet Union is not a state but a federation of soviet republics.) The later assertion of the thesis of socialism-in-one-country, foreshadowed even in the Soviet debate on the Treaty of Brest-Litovsk of March 1918, is all the more striking.

The development of the concept of "peaceful cohabitation" with the capitalist world may be seen as another rent in the classical Leninist critique. In his closing speech to the Tenth All-Russia Party Congress in late May 1921, Lenin held that a rough "equilibrium" prevailed between revolutionary Russia and the capitalist world. He did not speak of "coexistence" (*sosushchestvovaniye*), though he had already introduced the word "cohabitation" (*sozhitel'stvo*), in an interview with a Western journalist on 18 February 1920, "as a Soviet *aim*." Lenin argued before the Congress that "we are now exercising our main influence on the international revolution through our economic policy [i.e., of cultivating state-to-state contacts with the capitalist world]."[23]

Thus, as with Marx and Engels, there is a genuine problem in determining the "real" Lenin. Lenin's prodigious output, reflecting his experiences as theorist and statesman, only magnifies this difficulty. One can, with little hindrance, search and find the appropriate citations for almost any point one wishes to make. Indeed, an entire department of the Central Committee of the Soviet Communist Party is devoted to providing exactly such a service for Soviet leaders and journalists.[24] The point is simply that Lenin too, through a voluminous and often contradictory output and a view of international relations that evolved from an apocalyptic one envisaging, and expecting, the end of international relations itself to one that was considerably less deterministic and sure of itself, does not represent for contemporary Soviet theorists on international relations the last word on the subject. This does not mean that Lenin is not terribly important, certainly in the normative sense and probably in setting the bounds to the discourse as well. It does suggest, though, that Lenin's writings, which unlike Marx and Engels' did explicitly consider international relations as such, are subject to and indeed experience "creative" interpretation on the part of respected and influential Soviet theorists on the subject.[25]

## STALIN: "SOCIALISM IN ONE COUNTRY"

Curiously enough it was Stalin, for all of his strident dogmatism and general ignorance of the outside world, who in effect laid the foundation for the eventual development of international relations as a self-conscious area of study in the Soviet Union, though he annihilated or terrorized many of its practitioners in the process. While it is true, as Barghoorn put it, that Stalin had "followed Lenin's conception of international relations as essentially a struggle between Soviet Russia and her foreign supporters and a capitalist camp usually wracked by contradictions," he was nevertheless "the first Marxist writer to formulate a theory of international relations that would not explicitly incorporate a theory of the end of international relations and in so doing started a process that continues to the present day."[26] The concept of "socialism in one country," by distinguishing the complete, or domestic victory of socialism from the final, or worldwide victory of communism, superseded Lenin's perception of international relations as above all a field for the class struggle and substituted for it Stalin's conception of international relations as "a subject around which the struggle for power raged . . . [C]ontroversial issues in the domestic environment were [thus] all to a greater or lesser extent reflections or derivations of international developments and relationships."[27] The idea of the Soviet state was itself transformed with this conception of international relations. No longer, at least not primarily, focused outward toward and expanding into and incorporating a vulnerable and receptive international environment, the Soviet state was to turn inward, to be sealed off as a "healed area," as Kubalkova and Cruickshank suggest, permanently isolated from the rest of the diseased capitalist body. This Stalinist corollary, as it were, to Lenin's critique of imperialism, decisively affected future Soviet attitudes toward the question of international relations. It fused the sense of moral outrage at the current international order with the novel Marxist idea that international relations would persist into the indefinite future. To be sure, this was never explicitly broached by Stalin and indeed, many of his statements on, for example, the inevitability of war and the economic wellsprings of foreign policy tend to contradict the assertions just made. Yet, the assumption of a world where Soviet Russia could survive, however precariously, into the indefinite future, combined with the conviction that it was the power-political relations among the great states that really counted, implied the existence of a discipline of international relations that was no longer the mere handmaiden of the class struggle and the orthodox categories of Soviet political economy. Indeed, by actually subordinating the class element, by in effect containing the revolutionary proletariat in the developed countries and ignoring the underdeveloped world, "Stalin's focus would seem to be on that part of the triangle that remains – the capitalist states . . ., a most un-marxist theory of inter-*state* relations."[28] The clear implication of this analysis is that the foreign relations of the Soviet Union are essentially a derivation of interstate relations, rather than of the socio-economic character of the socialist order in the Soviet Union. These relations, in turn, are subsumed under a "two-camp doctrine," according to which the main contradiction of the current historical period is that between capitalism and socialism. In fact, the protagonists in this struggle are states, in the first instance the United States and the Soviet Union, each leading its own alliance system of states with sympathetic socio-economic structures.

Stalin's influence, then, on the Soviet study of international relations in the Soviet Union must be reckoned as considerable. Though preserving the traditional Marxist notion of the irreconcilable hostility between the forces of socialism and those of capitalism, Stalin grafted onto this edifice a conception of international relations that was fundamentally political, rather than economic, that preserved the voluntarist thrust of much of Lenin's later writings, and that implicitly refuted the old idea of international relations as a closed system, and thus with a predictable solution point at any given moment in space or time.[29] It must, though, be conceded that the preservation and elaboration of the two-camp image has tended to obscure some of Stalin's innovations in the area of international relations as well as the extent to which current Soviet undertakings in this field, however unorthodox at first glance, have their roots in the deeper Soviet past.

## STALIN'S DISPUTE WITH VARGA

Much of the difficulty in perceiving the extent to which the idea of international relations as something more than an exercise in political economy had already been implanted in Stalin's time lies in the debate, more precisely in the repression following the debate, that took place in the immediate postwar period between, in effect Stalin, and the economist Yevgeniy Varga over the prospects for the survival of capitalism. More narrowly, the debate focused on whether the capitalist economies could avoid an immediate postwar depression in light of their wartime experience with a substantial amount of state intervention, i.e., planning, in the economy, something which traditionally Marxism held to be impossible. One must be careful here and avoid the attribution of perfect theoretical consistency to Stalin. On the one hand he did prepare the ground, however inadvertently, for a systemic interpretation of international relations with the idea of socialism-in-one-country. This was an idea, furthermore, which reconciled itself to the long-term existence of international relations. Much of Stalin's later postwar discourse, though, is dedicated to demonstrating the imminent collapse of capitalism (and by extension international relations) and the inevitability of war among *capitalist* countries because of their economic competition.[30] Thus the course of the Varga controversy, in which Varga was compelled to recant his views affirming the probability of the medium-term survival of capitalism, has often been interpreted as aligning Varga, the forerunner of a more sophisticated Soviet study of economics and international relations, against Stalin, the dogmatic defender of the orthodox Bolshevik conception of these subjects. As we have tried to indicate, this is only partially true. To be sure, many of Stalin's notions were crude and mechanically deterministic. But they did not preclude the possibility of studying international relations in terms other than those of the class struggle. The Varga dispute should be viewed first as a policy debate about the conduct of relations with the West as well as an even more veiled debate about the degree of sophistication and empirical input that the Soviet model of international relations – incorporating both elements of the class struggle and the struggle of nations – was to possess.

It is interesting to read contemporary Soviet evaluations of Varga's work, for they indicate that the underlying postulates of this prominent Soviet economist, once compelled to publicly recant his strongly held and carefully formulated views, have long been treated as accepted dogma by the Soviet academic establishment.[31] In essence, Varga maintained three points: that as a consequence of the wartime experience with government intervention in the economy, capitalism would stabilize itself, at least for ten years; that the nature of the political systems in the Western capitalist democracies, especially Great Britain and the United States, was such that socialist reforms could be introduced without violence; and that war, both among capitalist states and between capitalism and socialism, was not inevitable.[32] The counter-thesis, advanced by Stalin and decisively established with the 1952 publication of his *Economic Problems of Socialism in the USSR*, held that, on the contrary, capitalist collapse was imminent and that war among capitalist states was more likely than war between capitalism and socialism – in short, a substantial reversion to the traditional Bolshevik critique of imperialism. In light of the later appropriation of many of Varga's ideas by a number of contemporary Soviet analysts of international relations, to the point where something like a Varga revival may be observed among Soviet economists, it may prove instructive to treat Varga's main points in greater detail.

As if to draw attention to the originality, in Soviet terms, of the views to be presented, Varga prefaced his 1946 work, "Changes in the Economy of Capitalism as a Result of the Second World War," by emphasizing the difficulty of the material, and that "some parts" should be read twice and "carefully thought about." "Deep and complex changes," Varga began, had occurred in the societies of the belligerent capitalist countries. Most important of all, the difficulties in realizing profit had been eased as a consequence of the state's systematic intervention in the economy. The bourgeois state had thus come to represent "the interests of the entire bourgeoisie as a class," in the process creating the entirely new phenomenon of "military-monopoly-state capitalism," posing the possibility of a partly stable economy, at least in the near future. This probable stabilization of the more advanced capitalist economies was assisted by an unprecedented concentration and centralization of capital, a great increase in labor productivity, and the prospects for the peaceful application of atomic energy. The improved productive capacity of the United States in particular provided it with the foundation for good economic progress in the short term. Such economic development could be relatively stable inasmuch as the capitalist governments were now seriously committed to "capitalist" planning, both on the domestic and the international levels. Indeed, Varga's embrace of the Keynesian analysis in his treatment of the capitalist economies is quite categorical. Hence, it would be wrong to assume a repetition of the economic catastrophe that eventually followed the First World War. Conditions had changed too much for that.[33]

The political implications of Varga's analysis were clear. The capitalist countries would continue to exist for the foreseeable future and in fact would even progress. War would not be the inevitable handmaiden of revolution.[34] The question became, then, what form would relations among states, in particular among capitalist states themselves, and among capitalist and socialist states, assume? In addressing this delicate question, Varga was careful to draw a sharp distinction between the character of the polities of the leading capitalist states and those of the fascist countries. He suggested that "bourgeois" democracy contained a considerable portion of the real thing, thereby providing avenues of influence for the substantial elements of public opinion in the advanced capitalist countries that were in favor of improved relations with the Soviet Union.[35] Relations of tension, not to mention of war, were by no means a foregone conclusion. Prospects for the peaceful development of relations between the USSR and the West, including no doubt the export of capital in one form or another to the Soviet Union for reconstruction purposes, would be reinforced by the geopolitical imperative of inter-allied cooperation to suppress the resurgence of fascism. Therefore,

> Relations of the capitalist countries with the Soviet Union will not be like those of the prewar period . . . [T]he [capitalist] governments, considering the forces of democracy and with the proof in the Second World War of the military might of the Soviet Union, will not lightly decide to embark on a military confrontation. Before the new international organization for the preservation of peace,

Varga concluded,

> stands the task of not permitting different contradictions from spilling over into military struggle.[36]

After the death of Stalin, Varga returned to the theses developed in his 1946 book and applied them to the international conditions of the late

1950s to early 1960s. This work revolved around two fundamental notions: the "third" stage in the general crisis of capitalism, and the implications both of this stage of capitalist development and of nuclear weapons for the nature and conduct of international relations.

The concept of the third stage in the crisis of capitalism represented a further development of the implications of Varga's 1946 book and effectively removed the issue of the collapse of capitalism from the historical present to an ever distant and receding future. Indeed, the thrust of Varga's later, post-Stalin work, already implicit in 1946, was aimed at pinpointing the changes that capitalism had undergone in the course of the twentieth century.[37] A number of previously held dogmas were therein refuted. The Second World War, for example, represented the last period in which inter-imperialist contradictions were stronger than the contradictions between the two systems, capitalism and socialism. It was recognized that the existence, and perhaps even some of the policies, of a powerful Soviet-led bloc contributed, in a decisive way, to the greater harmony that characterized inter-capitalist relations in the postwar world. Varga drew attention to the prolonged period, over a decade long, of capitalist economic growth on the basis of a "one-time extraordinary widening of the capitalist market and the absence of a world crisis of overproduction until 1957–8" and concluded that this implied a relatively stable and prosperous future for the capitalist economies. No tendency toward a levelling off of industrial production, in contrast to the pre-war period, was discernible. Hence, and this was the point which had created so much trouble for him a decade earlier, government intervention in the capitalist economy could, did, and would continue to constitute an efficient tool for economic stabilization. The external changes wrought by decolonization hardly affected the matter. Although Varga explained this partly by recourse to the theory of "neocolonialism," according to which the former metropoles perpetuated their imperial positions through the maintenance of informal, but no less effective, economic empires, primary emphasis was squarely placed on the ability of the capitalist countries to exploit their domestic markets more intensively. It was also unfair to allege that the capitalist economies could not exist without vast military expenditures. On the contrary. "[P]olitical problems," Varga wrote, "are much more difficult for imperialism than economic ones."[38]

The political implications of this analysis were hardly encouraging for committed revolutionaries. Though the material preconditions for socialism and communism in the capitalist world were growing, "monopoly-capital" had experienced considerable success in spreading counter-revolutionary ideology among the masses. Combined with the pernicious influence of social democrats and the Catholic Church (i.e., Christian Democracy), these efforts had resulted in the setting in of a certain degree of passivity among the working masses. Furthermore, this was no mere "subjective" trend. The changing composition of the capitalist proletariat in favor of service employees, a fact of "great political significance," added an objective foundation to the counter-revolutionary spirit of the Western working class.

All of these remarkable new phenomena taken together, Varga said, constituted the essence of a new, third stage in the developmental crisis of capitalism, characterized above all by the growth of "state-monopoly capitalism." This has occurred, in addition, in peaceful conditions. Although there was a possibility of a global, nuclear war by accident, the struggle between the two systems did not necessarily have to assume a military form. "Time," Varga wrote, with an intimation that perhaps time alone would prove sufficient, "works for socialism, for communism!" Concerning the end of capitalism, Varga would only aver that the twentieth century was the last century of capitalism. And even that foggy prediction was qualified with the proviso that: "The exceptional complexity of the situation of the historical transition from capitalism to socialism does not permit a more concrete prognosis."[39] Later work, including a volume published posthumously in 1965, essentially extended this scheme.[40] His main theses were defended and elaborated upon by his successor at the Institute of the World Economy and International Relations, A.A. Arzumanyan.[41] Varga's theses continue to occupy an important place in the work of contemporary Soviet analysts of international relations. However unorthodox their contributions may seem, their basic viewpoint, like Varga's, remains Marxist, but, as Jerry Hough has noted, "it is a Marxism that fully accepts Varga's judgements about the ability of capitalism to survive for a long time."[42]

Varga's name has come to symbolize, for Soviet economists and analysts of international relations, the principles of greater professional latitude in their work and the application of strict empirical criteria to political analysis. One of the most influential Soviet students of international relations has maintained that Varga's ideas are useful not only for studying such international and transnational phenomena as the scientific–technical revolution and economic integration, but also for the analysis of the contemporary political economy of the United States.[43] The initiation of the Soviet study of international relations, so ably documented by William Zimmerman,[44] not to mention its development in the post-Khrushchev period, almost certainly would have been a far more arduous task had it not been for the pioneering efforts of Yevgeniy Varga.

# 2

# The development of Soviet political studies

. . . but genuinely profound research presupposes the raising of questions, the answers to which are not known in advance.

Fyodor Burlatskiy*

Varga's contribution to the development of the social sciences in the Soviet Union goes beyond the challenge he posed to the Stalinist conception of the capitalist world. Varga also challenged the entire Stalinist methodology for analyzing politics and society. In one of his very last works, an introductory piece to "Essays on the Political Economy of Capitalism," Varga attempts to develop his conception of the methodology proper to the Soviet study of "political economy." He begins by challenging what he calls "mindless dogmatism," having obviously in mind the hoary Soviet tradition of justificatory social science, and opposes to it the idea of "a concrete scientific analysis of historical factors . . ."[1] He sees his subject, political economy, as one without a sharp distinction between the political and the economic spheres. He indicates that he has been concerned with the "new" aspects of the political economy of capitalism and hence presents a "new" analysis of the subject. The time-encrusted dicta of Marx and Lenin are clearly insufficient for this task.[2]

Varga then proceeds to an examination of the character of laws in social research. Laws of nature, he argues, which are distinguished by their objective character, their independence of human will and consciousness, can in no way be compared to laws of society, with their distinctively human, and hence dynamic and unpredictable quality. Laws in general, and there *can* be laws of society, Varga says, must be sharply delineated from hypotheses intended to order knowledge. A

* Political-sociologist Fyodor Burlatskiy, *Pravda*, 10 January 1965, p. 4.

law is not a mere reflection of separate processes; on the contrary, a law can only be an *adequate* reflection of regularly repeating processes in nature and society. Now in political economy, Varga observes, hypotheses play an important role. Changes in the means of production (one understands by this also changes in the field of technology, such as nuclear weapons) introduce new elements, modifying the laws of socio-economic systems. The same holds true for the general crisis of capitalism. A creative social science, one not necessarily bound by the strictures of the general laws of Marxism–Leninism, is required in order to assess the true meaning of these changes.[3]

Varga turns next to an effort to carve out a special place for such "creative" social science by rigorously delimiting the sphere of application of the incontestable, general laws of dialectical materialism. The basic laws of the "*diamat*," according to Varga, possess an ontological rather than a phenomenological character. These include, for example: (a) the law of the transformation of quantity into quality, and *vice versa*, (b) the law of the union of opposites, and (c) the law of the negation of a negation. These hold true because both nature and society operate dialectically.[4] Note, however, that these "laws" include nothing of substance about the actual behavior of capitalism, or any other socio-economic structure for that matter, in the world.

Varga thus criticizes Stalin, held to be greatly deficient in his view of dialectical materialism in attributing to the existential world of society laws that could only be valid on the most general level of nature. Indeed, the laws of nature and society, "in spite of their identical dialectical development, are essentially distinct from each other."[5] Economic laws, for example, "act in a constantly changing situation." This applies equally to the other social sciences. "Laws of society are, therefore, tendencies . . . There is no difference between [such] a law and a tendency." A law of society can only be represented as a tendency because, unlike in the natural sciences, the social sciences present no opportunity for genuine experiment and proof. Applied to political economy, these observations imply that "the class struggle within capitalist society occurs in each separate case in different and constantly changing conditions. One cannot possibly predict these changes, as is possible in nature . . . The laws of society are the result of the activity of people, though not of their conscious will."[6]

In effect Varga is here trying to liberate social science scholarship from the stultifying oversight of the party ideologist while attempting to preserve, and indeed strengthen, its proper concern with the law-like activities of society. Yet even here distinctions count. No general "law," such as the "crisis of capitalism," "can contain all, or even all the important laws of capitalism . . . Any effort to extract from any kind of fundamental law other, less general laws [i.e., laws applying properly to the social sciences], *as is often done by us*, contradicts Marxism." Fundamental laws "should be presented as rational abstractions, indeed delineating the general . . . and no more!" In fact, there is only one basic law of capitalism, that of the contradiction between the social mode of production and the private mode of accumulation, which, leading to periodic crises, lays the foundation for the collapse of capitalism through a proletarian revolution.[7]

There are, in addition, two specific laws of "imperialism", i.e., the exchange of free competition for protection and regulation by the state, and the partition of the world into essentially proletarian and bourgeois countries, which also paves the way for the socialist revolution.[8] Any other statements purporting to represent generally valid and fundamental laws of Marxism–Leninism are not tenable, according to Varga. The rest of the domain, which remains vast indeed, is open to the kind of critical sociological analysis that Varga had been advocating. Thus Varga must be seen as a doubly critical and influential presence in the development of the Soviet study of politics and international relations: his contributions in the area of the substantive study of contemporary capitalism as well as his keen methodological essay in favor of a greater empirical emphasis to Soviet research constitute an important cornerstone of Soviet social science, as Soviet scholars readily acknowledge.

Certainly, if we examine the work of Soviet academics on politics over the past decade we discover a conceptual universe far removed from the sterile, deterministic dogmatism of the Stalin period. Yuriy Krasin, in a 1977 essay for the Soviet Political Sciences Association, offers an instructive kind of definition of politics. He refers to "politics . . . [as] an area which involves the relations between classes in respect of state power." In a spirit reminiscent of Varga's vigorous defense of methodological empiricism, Krasin argues that "single term solutions are, as a rule, impossible in the field of politics." The indeterminacy of the political realm, the existential activity of which is not subject to the universally valid "fundamental" laws of dialectical materialism, leads to the inclusion of the subjective, and even of the irrational element (Krasin speaks of the importance of the politician's intuition, his political acumen) into the analysis. This analysis, furthermore, in order to assist a truly scientifically grounded policy, must be "built on facts that are open to precise and objective verification."[9] That is to say, the center of such a science is to be occupied by "the concrete analysis of a concrete situation," i.e., by empirical analysis. This is so because "no abstract truth exists; the truth is always concrete . . . [Furthermore]

> the principles of dialectical logic acquire exclusive importance in the area of politics, since political reality is marked by particular complexity, contradictoriness, and dynamism. In this sense, according to Lenin, politics bears a stronger resemblance to algebra than to arithmetic, to higher mathematics than to elementary mathematics.[10]

Politics must hence encompass a "complex object–subject dialectics," according to which "objective" tendencies are qualified by "the actions of the subject of political activity." This "dialectics" is further complicated by the fact that a purely class analysis, no matter how sophisticated, is simply inadequate to the task of genuine political criticism. "Political thinking," Krasin writes, "is affected not only by overall class interests but also by the specific interests of the social strata and groups that belong to such strata, or stand in an intermediate position." This dispersion of political power (in any polity, we are led to believe) constitutes a very "complex" phenomenon, "which gives a certain independence to a politics based on maneuvering between major social forces that are comparatively evenly matched."[11] The liberation of the political "superstructure" is thereby accomplished.

In concluding this revision of a number of tenacious Soviet dogmas about the relationship between politics and economics, between objective and subjective forces, Krasin invokes the somewhat idiosyncratic but influential authority of Aleksandr Bovin in his own defense. "Politics," Bovin wrote,

> deals with a practically infinite variety of facts and events, with highly changeable and contradictory processes, and with the clash of different interests and wills. The enormous difficulty of grasping all of the links and the stormy dynamism of social relations creates a certain instability in the ground on which the politician has to construct all of his calculations . . . There is always tremendous room here for assumptions and appraisals of probability, so that an important role is here attached to the ability to grasp intuitively the overall direction taken by processes.[12]

One may debate whether this represents a "Marxist" interpretation of politics or not. It is, though, certainly a Soviet one, or at least compatible with a Soviet framework, and falls within the bounds of established political discourse in the contemporary Soviet Union. It seems incontestable, however, that the kind of interpretation of the nature of things political that is offered by Krasin, and upheld by Bovin, is a long way from the argument propounded in Stalin's *Economic Problems of Socialism in the USSR*. It is an interpretation that is less deterministic, particularly on the influence of economic forces on politics, less bound by a strict class analysis in its recognition of the influential role of non-class "intermediate" groups and strata, and persuaded of the primacy (or at least the equivalency, i.e., with respect to economics) of the political, in "capitalist" no less than in "socialist" polities. Hence, many of the tendencies first pointed out by Zimmerman on the phenomenological level (asking whether United States foreign policy is really dominated by Wall Street, for example) have penetrated to the methodological level (questioning the nature of political activity, and the implications of the answers to this questioning for grasping the general relationships between polity and economy).

The approach just outlined is clearly inspired by a conviction as to the insufficiency of historical determinism, most of all one based overwhelmingly on economic variables, for the comprehension of the political.[13] Politics is simply too complex, dynamic, and unpredictable for it to be subordinated to the dictates of traditional Soviet political economy. As far as Western political systems are concerned, Varga's contention that the state represents the entire bourgeoisie (and, by implication, society) seems to have become generally accepted by Soviet political scientists; as has his accompanying argument that, therefore, the analysis "of the class nature of political power in bourgeois society cannot be confined to showing the predominance of the bourgeoisie."[14] Economic and class relations, then, may explain the *kind* of system that prevails in a given country or region, but it is entirely inadequate, by itself, to explain the functioning of the system itself, i.e., of its political process. The goal, for Soviet political studies, would be "to move from the investigation of norms to more thorough research on the structure of political relations."[15] Stated in more authoritative terms, it is necessary to overcome "the elements of the scholastic and the commentary approach [i.e., reacting to events as they happen, in accordance with the prevailing line] to the formulation and elaboration of fundamental problems in Marxist philosophic science . . ."[16]

In sum, we see a Soviet study of politics that is increasingly attentive, methodologically and substantively, to the existential world of political behavior. The study of politics, in a way that goes beyond even what Varga had proposed, is to be understood as a kind of discipline in itself.[17] The categories of political economy, with their concentration on the economically and particularly class-dependent nature of the political, are viewed as inadequate to the task of grasping the essence of politics in the contemporary world. This world is distinguished by a multiplicity of power centers, both among and within polities, and a dispersion of the ability to exert influence on the course of politics, and policy. Classes, as well as formal, juridically established state entities, are to be seen as located *among* a number of "actors" capable of affecting the political process. And, it is this political process, rather than the formal organs of authority or the correlation of class forces alone, which shapes the political character of the system under examination. "Subjective" elements are to be treated on the same level as "objective" ones; indeed, with the effective emancipation of the political "superstructure" from the economic base, they may at times occupy a superior level of analysis.

One should not, however, be misled into interpreting the increasing use of non-Marxist terminology and perspectives by Soviet political theorists as an indication of convergence with Western patterns of political thinking. For the Marxist–Leninist, dialectical–materialist world view "may be quite receptive to many concepts and theories which are employed by Western political scientists" as long as they "can be integrated into a general class model of society." The integration of these concepts "may be justified on the grounds of need for a greater sophistication of the model, but not in terms of a rejection of the entire model."[18] The history of the development of the Soviet social sciences, including the post-Stalin period, has been distinguished by the close tie between these sciences and the practical political concerns of the state. What has changed since the death of Stalin is the full and open recognition by the Soviet leadership of the need to exploit systematically the accumulated expertise of the academic community. The experience of Stalin's campaign against international studies, for example, which had "proved so successful that by 1956 recruitment into the social sciences in general, and into international studies in particular, had dwindled to near zero," has been taken as an exemplary negative object lesson.[19]

# 3

# Approaches to international relations

## INTRODUCTION

Most observers, both Soviet and Western, see the year 1956, the year of the twentieth Soviet Party Congress and Khrushchev's "secret speech" denouncing Stalin's "crimes" against the Party, as the critical turning point in Soviet thinking on international relations.[1] Two ideological revisions – the breaking of the capitalist encirclement by the Soviet Union, and the non-inevitability of general war, were of special significance. They openly suggested that, as had been implicit in Stalin's critique of socialism-in-one-country, henceforth the revolutionary transformation of the world would be effected through international relations.[2] States had now become protagonists in the class conflict. The increased importance that relations among nation-states were held to have for the future of socialism required going beyond the "rather mechanistic transplant of theses regarding internal relations and laws of society to external, intersocietal relations."[3] From this date ensues the proliferation of Soviet research institutes devoted to the systematic study of international relations, a consequence of the transformation of international relations into a legitimate area of inquiry below the apex of the Party–government apparatus.[4] From 1962 on international relations as such begins to emerge as a self-conscious discipline. Vladimir Gantman, for example, now head of the Theory of International Relations section of the Institute of the World Economy and International Relations, objected to one writer's denial of the possibility of setting up a science of international relations and asserted in reply that such a science does exist as an autonomous discipline of study.[5] Divergences between the analyses of specialists, which stressed the importance of a methodology appropriate to the subject, and more general commentary, began to appear. This was not yet a dominant pattern by October 1964, when Nikita Khrushchev, whose name is associated with many of the changes connected to the emergence of new Soviet perspectives on international relations, was ousted from office.[6] The purpose of this section is to determine whether, and to what extent, the trends identified in the 1956–64 period have continued.

These trends, in summary, included: first, the view of international relations as an arena populated by a plurality of corporate actors, with states (as opposed to the two camps) as dominant; second, increasing attention paid to the role of institutions as sources of foreign-policy conduct; third, recognition of the non-inevitability of world war in the nuclear age, which tends to undermine the Soviet view of international relations as a closed system, i.e., comprehensible by a general theory which posits a predictable solution at every point. Too many critical elements are in the hands of others; the idea of general war as the handmaiden of revolution is thereby negated. Finally, there appeared to be a marked tendency for Soviet perspectives on international relations to converge with much American analysis on (a) the course of international relations as indeterminate; (b) the basic (state) structure of the modern international system; (c) recognition of the role of internal politics in American foreign policy; and (d) preoccupation with the political significance of technology (especially weapons technology) and the constraints thereby imposed on the behavior of states in the atomic age.[7]

Unfortunately, there has been relatively little study in the West of Marxist concepts of international relations, particularly Soviet Marxist ones, as well as a general lack of interest in contemporary Soviet Marxist–Leninist thinking as a whole. Such depreciation of Soviet efforts is especially true in the field of international relations, though not, perhaps, without some justification. The Romanian Marxist sociologist Silviu Brucan, for example, pointed out in 1971 that Marxist studies on international relations were "rather scarce."[8] Other theorists have contended that there "is not, strictly speaking, a marxist theory that is structured and explicitly formulated."[9] Proceeding from the assumption that the Soviet conception of international relations is directly based on the Marxist–Leninist analysis of social relations, most Western theorists have tended to dismiss Soviet thinking on the subject as inclined "toward mono-causal explanation, based on the socio-economic variable, the quasi-exclusive importance of which represents a serious obstacle to theoretical efforts . . ."[10]

"How," it is often asked, "can one explain the intricacies of [contemporary] power politics exclusively in class terms?"[11] Brucan adduces the Soviet–Yugoslav conflict of 1948 as an example: it is not explicable in class terms, since the same class structure prevails in both countries; references to a "cult of personality" will not do, since if Stalin had led a *small* country, nothing could have happened. Consequently, Soviet writing on international relations, which in the past has resembled rather closely the descriptions just cited, is frequently dismissed as misleading, if not irrelevant. Even the authors of a recent Polish work on "continuity and change" in international relations virtually ignore the Soviet work that has been done in the field.[12]

Is the Soviet analysis of international relations, despite all of the modifications since 1956, and indeed since Varga, essentially a vertical, class-oriented paradigm? Or, has it instead become a model of "*realpolitik*", retaining for appearances sake the ideological trappings of the Bolshevik past but in no way to be distinguished from countless non-Marxist Western theories of international relations. The question is not an easy one. The Marxist idea itself resists the concept of international relations, with its central feature of horizontal group diversity. For, as R.N. Berki notes, there is "a clear moral argument in Marxian thought against group diversity as such . . ."[13] Marxian, and, traditionally, Soviet thought, have always held questions of international relations and conflict to be secondary and derivative in nature, once removed "from relations and conflicts that are really significant." Indeed, "the whole paraphernalia of horizontal diversity", according to traditional Marxist and Soviet ideas, are supposed to "derive from the one basic vertical conflict between classes." The issue revolves about the extent to which the intrusion of strategic considerations, relating to the correlation between means and ends, and the appearance of political realism in the wake of success (i.e., equating the original ideas with the viewpoint and interests of a particular country), compels Soviet theorists to reexamine the meaning of the Marxist intellectual heritage for international relations in the atomic age.[14]

## THE EARLY BREZHNEV PERIOD

Certainly the Soviets have not been reluctant to concede insufficiencies in their traditional treatment of international relations. Anastas

Mikoyan's remark at the Twentieth Party Congress in 1956, in which he observed that while "the whole East has awakened," the Institute of Eastern Studies of the Academy of Sciences "was still dozing," is only the most famous of these.[15] The influential Leonid Ilychov, then chairman of the Ideological Commission of the Central Committee and since 1965 Deputy Minister of Foreign Affairs, observed in the early 1960s that the contemporary state of Soviet studies on international relations left much to be desired and criticized Soviet scholars for focusing so exclusively on "historical" themes that contemporary analysis was being seriously slighted. Bourgeois social scientists, he lamented, were far more active in the study of contemporary international relations than were Soviet scholars, reason enough to improve the state of the art.[16] Despite the undoubted progression of Soviet studies of international relations since 1956, complaints abound about the excessively historical or economic focus of Soviet work in this field, to the detriment of a more precise conceptual grasp of the subject.[17]

Striking the theme of the necessity for theoretical clarity is hardly a novel one in the Soviet tradition. Yet the intrusion of this note into the Soviet social sciences has been taken to signify ideological uniformity in the face either of the threat posed by bourgeois concepts or of changes in the intellectual atmosphere. If one recalls the language and atmosphere of the Varga controversy and its legacy, it is clear that this particular call to theoretical clarity was designed to hinder the autonomous development of any area of study by keeping it especially close to the breast of Party policy and ideological orthodoxy. Generally, this theme is tied to the "fundamental" elements of Marxism–Leninism, such as the laws of dialectical materialism. What interests us, rather, are efforts to develop theories and concepts with more particular application than such ideas as the transformation of quantity into quality, the unity of opposites, etc. Such efforts, which do not go to the core of the ruling ideology, in this way attain greater latitude for the analyst than would be the case were he to introduce fundamental concepts. It is in this sense that the emphasis by Soviet researchers on the importance of theory should be understood.[18] Such approaches, which tend to be receptive to the work of Western students of international relations (to the extent that they can be characterized as strictly "technical"), are to be encountered with increasing frequency throughout the Brezhnev years, and especially after 1969. The dictionary may prove a useful place to begin this examination of the conceptual development of contemporary Soviet theory of international relations.

The 1973 edition of the Soviet "Diplomatic Dictionary" devotes a special entry to "Theory of International Relations".[19] It is immediately apparent what the Soviet conception of such theory is not. It is not, as indicated by other "theories" listed in the "Dictionary", a theory of foreign policy, of foreign policy planning, of foreign economic forecasting, or decision-making and information processing. "International relations" itself, the *Dictionary* notes,

> are a specific form of social relations. They exist in the form of economic, political, legal, diplomatic, military, ideological, and other ties and mutual relations between nations, and between classes of social systems of different countries, in the first instance through the mediation of their political organs – of states, governments, parties, and other organs.[20]

International relations, then, are concerned first with relations among nations (only secondly, perhaps secondarily?, between social systems) and such relations are conducted by political entities, i.e., states and governments, though less formal political groupings such as parties may also have a role. The different spheres of international relations, such as the history of foreign policy, international economic relations, the theory and history of international law, military science, etc., are usually studied from the historical and area-studies points of view. The theory of international relations seeks to go beyond this traditional treatment of the subject and treat "not the concrete phenomena and events of international life," but rather to attempt

> to define the central interrelationship (*vzaimosvyaz'*) and mechanism of the development of events, the deep-rooted processes, the discovery of the sources of the development of the system of international relations as a whole. The theory of international relations is called upon to advance as a rigorously dialectical system of scientific categories, correctly reflecting the structure of the system of international relations, the basic elements, factors, moving forces and objective laws [phenomena – *zakonomernosti*] of its changes and development.[21]

The affinity of such a conception with the systems approach to international relations is suggestive. Indeed, from the Soviet perspective, Marx's entire theoretical edifice, with its emphasis on the primacy of the whole over its constituent parts, the primacy of relations over the terms related to them, and its insight that the structure is not apparent but rather hidden behind the phenomenon, is not only compatible with but *is* a structural–functional analysis, indeed, the first such analysis ever attempted.[22] Though Marx was not writing about international relations *per se*, the same cannot be said of Lenin, whose authority is often invoked to support the thesis that the Soviet Union has to come to terms with "a system of states." *Pravda* can thus comfortably invoke the authority of Marx for the proposition that, politically, the modern national state is located "within the framework of the system of states" (as opposed to the world market).[23] In this way the dialectically oriented systems approach of Marx is fused with the interstate bent of later Soviet analysis to form a uniquely Soviet view on international relations. It is a view which retains the moral outrage of Marx and Lenin about the iniquity of the existing international order while at the same time providing for a vision of *realpolitik* that transcends preoccupation with micropolitical detail in its concentration on the basic moving forces and structure of the "international system." By focusing on only one of these aspects we might come to the premature conclusion that either nothing in the Soviet perspective had changed or, on the contrary, that the Soviet outlook on international relations had been transformed beyond recognition. The matter is more difficult inasmuch as both the moral outrage and the more contemporary vision of *realpolitik* can and do comfortably coexist in the Soviet world view. The repudiation of the legitimacy of the international order has never precluded, indeed has at times ordained, the cold calculation of the balance of power in order to assure the survival and later expansion and consolidation, of the revolutionary base constituted by the Soviet Union. The balance of power, denounced by the early Bolsheviks as a "bourgeois" institution, finds its incarnation in no more pure or cynical form than in the way it was practised by the Soviet Union in the 1930s, leading to the "Molotov–von Ribbentrop" Non-Aggression Pact of 1939 and the fourth partition of Poland.

What, then, are the most important problems facing a Soviet theory of international relations? The "Dictionary of Diplomacy" envisages six main areas of concern: first, factor analysis, i.e., the meaning and role of different "factors" (in order – geographical, national, historical, economic, political, legal, moral, ideological, etc.) in international relations and in the foreign policies of states; second, the study of the patterns of interrelationships and interaction of these factors with one another; third, the criteria defining the role of different states in the world arena; fourth, the mechanisms and patterns of the formulation of foreign policy interests, goals, direction, and methods of the foreign policy of distinct classes, and the correlation of interests, goals, and means in foreign policy; fifth, the dynamics of alliances; and finally, "the general laws of change and development of the global system of international relations as a whole, and also of its laws of development in specific periods, the study of the problem of the interrelationships between objective and subjective factors in the sphere of international relations, etc." International relations theory is to be approached in a multidisciplinary way. The contributions of Marx, Engels, and Lenin to the subject are noted in a manner that provides maximum scholarly latitude to the theorist. Marx and Engels, for example, provided the methodological key to the study of international relations by their discovery of the influence of economic ties on political and ideological relations among and within societies. Nothing which could serve as an authoritative constraint on the analyst, though, is revealed about those views. Lenin's "enormous contribution" relates to the basic methodology and theory of the "science" of international relations; to comprehending international relations as a system; to the link between internal and foreign policy; to the laws of development of international relations in different historical periods, especially regarding relations between capitalist and socialist states; and to "the strategy, tactics, and principles of the foreign policy of the working class, its party, and the socialist state."[24] In this way the boundaries of the field of study are set without imposing insuperable obstacles to a relatively autonomous professional development, within those limits. How successful have Soviet specialists in international relations been, then, in the cultivation of their discipline since the fall of Khrushchev?

The post-1956 movement toward greater methodological self-awareness clearly survived the demise of Khrushchev in October 1964. To a certain extent the survival of these tendencies was encouraged by the power of the Soviet Union in an international system increasingly affected by its influence, though this is largely supposition. To the degree that the Soviet Union may be plausibly argued to exert an influence on its political environment that is at least as strong as that exerted upon it, the prospect for a more empirically oriented study of the world would appear to improve. That is, as the world becomes progressively less threatening, it would become easier for the professional analyst to subject it to academic diagnosis. The consequences of analytical error or doctrinal dispute, a likely by-product of greater freedom of professional expression, would be seen as less threatening to the system as a whole. In addition, while the international environment is construed as inherently less threatening, and indeed often ripe with opportunities, it is also understood to be an environment that is vastly more complex, requiring a higher level of analytical expertise than before, which tends to reinforce the movement toward greater empirical content, methodological self-consciousness, and professional latitude.

A point often stressed in the early Brezhnev period, at times by Brezhnev himself, was the importance of professional expertise and critical attitudes in the social sciences. A theme often pursued at lower levels of the hierarchy, especially in the academic world, concerned the need for "concrete sociological research," that is, work with a greater empirical content and devoted to the analysis of problems of day-to-day import for the Soviet state. An All-Union Symposium of Sociologists, meeting in mid-1966, drew attention to the gap existing between research in the areas of general sociological theory (historical materialism) and scientific communism, "and concrete sociological investigations." This was due, according to the summary of the symposium, to the absence of a system of professional preparation of "cadres" in the field of concrete sociological research.[25] Not surprisingly, the 1960s saw the proliferation of Soviet research institutes on international affairs, adding to the reconstituted Institute of the World Economy and International Relations (1956), the Institute of the USA and Canada, the Institute of Latin America, the Institute of Africa, and others.

Further evidence of the evolution of Soviet work in international relations is provided by the appearance of a number of articles in the late 1960s that either dealt with novel themes or treated familiar subjects in new ways. The theme of international conflict was a particularly popular one among Soviet analysts. Arguments to the effect that international relations do not represent a strict "zero-sum game," for example, begin to be heard for the first time in the Soviet literature.[26] The theme of "the sociology of international relations," clearly associated with the case for "concrete sociological research," was also broached in an effort to delineate an area of study that, while distinctly Soviet, is nevertheless something quite different from pre-Khrushchev attitudes toward international relations.[27] The "Leninist Science of International Relations" is defined in such a way as to liberate, once and for all, the study of international relations from a tight economic determinism based on a predominantly class analysis.[28] The underlying theme of all of these disparate writings, after Varga, is that the fundamental, and thereby most general precepts of

Marxism–Leninism are inadequate for the study of the existential world of international relations. Soviet "international-relationists," therefore, had to develop a conceptual apparatus of their own, one appropriate to the discipline. By the late 1960s, Soviet theorists had indeed begun to undertake this task.

In a 1966 discussion of the "sociology of international relations," Dmitri Yermolenko regarded international relations as a social process, studying "their general laws, and the social systems, institutions, classes, social groups and personalities taking part in them. It singles out the broadest and most complex problems and examines the most general methodological aspects of research into the objective and subjective factors of international relations." The category of conflict is central to such a sociology. In researching these problems, "some of the specific methods and technical means for research into various problems of international relations worked out by bourgeois scholars are undoubtedly worth looking into."[29] As examples, Yermolenko mentions psychological analysis as applied to specific instances of international tension: game theory, mathematical models, and, because of the difficulty of social experimentation, simulation. These methods are in no way to be dismissed out of hand, because although a bourgeois sociologist may be lured into defending reactionary policies, he "is free to act within the limits of the task set before him, producing his recommendations with varying degrees of reality." The quality of a particular bourgeois analysis would thus depend on the author's talent, knowledge, sense of honesty and independence. Yermolenko seems to be bidding to open up the Soviet study of international relations through the introduction of a multi-factoral analysis transcending categories of class and economics, and through greater receptivity to non-Soviet viewpoints. These are ideas that have not been universally embraced, especially outside of the academic world. Shalva Sanakoyev, properly speaking a journalist-commentator who can often be interpreted as speaking for the government, argued with some heat in 1969 that even "among democratic circles . . . we find views that run counter to the class approach . . . Moreover, there is a tendency to reduce the processes of historical development of the two oppos(ing) systems, and relations between them, virtually to diplomatic combinations," thereby confusing the qualitative differences between socialist and capitalist states, presumably by considering the category "state" superior to that of "class" as far as the analysis of international relations is concerned. "I think," concluded Sanakoyev, that "there is no need to refute [or study?] such 'theories'."[30] The evolution of Soviet international relations studies continues nevertheless, indicating that the leadership either has not decided how to resolve the apparent tension between its need for expertise and the toeing of the ideological line or is unconcerned by such tension, if it even perceives its existence.

Frequently, the call for the "opening-up" of international studies in the Soviet Union begins with an allusion to the unprecedented changes brought on by the advent of contemporary military technology. If nuclear weaponry has changed international relations, the study of international relations itself might stand in need of change. So, Yermolenko justifies his "sociology of international relations" by invoking the "qualitatively new stage" in the destructive power of modern weapons. V. Israelyan, writing in a similar vein in 1967, observed that scientific and technological progress and the consequent military–technical revolution had exerted such an influence on contemporary international relations that "it is impossible to understand or correctly assess the characteristic features of international relations in our time" without taking it into account. Note is simultaneously taken of the increasingly favorable trends in international relations. Taken together, stress on the qualitatively changed nature of international relations in the nuclear age and on the opportunities offered by this development, supports an author's call for a more sophisticated Soviet study of international relations.

Israelyan himself, in summarizing the main changes in recent international relations, mentioned, in addition to the influence of nuclear weapons, the mounting importance of the international sphere on the class struggle within nations (the reverse of the original Marxist paradigm); the "rise of the masses," as both influential determinant of government policy in the advanced capitalist countries and as resistor of Western "imperialism" (e.g., against American involvement in Vietnam); the increase in the number of states consequent upon decolonization, with a corresponding increase in the scope of international affairs; and an increase in activity transcending the traditional boundaries of the nation-state. "For the first time in the history of the world," Israelyan concludes, "exploiting states have ceased to determine the main directions and prospects of international development."[31]

The resulting fluidity of contemporary international relations makes the dialectical approach particularly apt. Such an approach, which according to Israelyan constitutes the essence of the "Leninist science of international relations," consists of two fundamental elements: (1) international relations are to be interpreted as a single, dynamic whole in which apparently discrete events are interconnected and mutually determine each other; (2) the insight that quantitative shifts can lead to qualitative transformations. While such a method takes due account of the influence of economic forces, the sphere of the political, i.e., the superstructure (which according to the Marx of the *Political Economy* is a passive, reactive element), and here Israelyan cites Lenin, exercises an "active" role in society. "It is well known," he writes, "that politics has a most direct influence on society and may either facilitate or retard its development."[32]

This "emancipation" of the polity, which occurs from time to time in a number of fields according to the particular motives of the author, entails a greater role for "subjective," relatively intangible factors and widens the gap between the applicability of the writings of Marx and Lenin, including the fundamental, general concepts of dialectical materialism, and the requirements of the subject matter in which these subjective elements are said to operate. The need for the professionally trained specialist, capable of applying educated intuition to a field that is recognized as increasingly complex and unpredictable, thereby increases.

In this view, the old categories of international analysis, based upon the simple projection of imperialist contradictions (themselves the direct reflection of predominantly economic and class bound forces) onto the whole world, no longer apply. International behavior can be neither deduced nor predicted just through knowledge of the "class character" of the states involved. "The world of the last quarter of the twentieth century," Nikolay Inozemtsev wrote in 1977, "is characterized by highly complex and often contradictory processes . . ." If one considers that each state has its own specific traits, in all spheres (political, economic, cultural, etc.), with a multiplicity of different classes and social groups in play, "it then becomes all the more obvious how complicated the world in which we live is."[33]

To be sure conflict, which has always occupied the center of the Soviet analysis of international relations, is explicable only in terms of the presence of "imperialism" in the world. Yet, as Yermolenko writes, while

> imperialist actions are in 'the final analysis' the prime cause of all modern contemporary conflicts . . ., these actions are refracted on many levels and

> pass through many stages. It is only by studying the ultimate and immediate causes responsible for international conflict, its nature and character, the forces opposing it, the circumstances which threaten to aggravate it and the methods of possible regulation or prevention of conflicts, that an analysis of international conflicts can be made.[34]

Such analyses appeared from time to time in the early Brezhnev period, but infrequently enough to justify Zimmerman's doubts as to whether the currents that he had identified toward the development of a Soviet discipline of international relations would survive the fall of Khrushchev. By the autumn of 1969, however, a turning point seemed to have been reached with the organization by the Institute of the World Economy and International Relations, under the direction of Vladimir V. Gantman, of a "round table" (*kruglyy stol*) conference of interested Soviet scholars on Problems of the Theory of International Relations.[35]

In its published form, the round table was justified by the necessity of "interdisciplinary" research, a consequence of "the increasing complexity of international relations, which are becoming a more important and dynamic factor influencing the course of world development."[36] In this respect, the variety of approaches that were advanced during the conference, ranging from the general methodology of historical materialism to the relevance of game theory for international relations, should not be surprising. Indeed, the diversity of perspectives reflected, it was claimed, different professional concerns.[37] In summarizing the results of the conference, the editors of *Mirovaya Ekonomika i Mezhdunarodyne Otnosheniya* drew attention to the main tasks facing the development of Soviet international relations theory:

> study of the subject, method and basic categories of the theory of international relations; of the system, structure and moving forces of contemporary international relations; of the foreign policy strategy of imperialism; the critique of bourgeois theories; development of the method of forecasting international relations, and definition of the borders and concrete methods of using mathematical tools in this field.[38]

Clearly this symposium reflected efforts at very high levels in the Soviet Union to actively foster the development of a kind of discipline of international relations, if only for the obvious purpose of a more reliable empirical foundation for the conduct of Soviet foreign policy.

In an essay for the symposium on Current Tasks of Theoretical Research, Nikolay Inozemtsev identified as one of the most important theoretical projects facing Marxism–Leninism "the researching of the basic moving forces, laws, and distinguishing characteristics of contemporary international relations." In this statement "international relations" stands by itself, neither associated with nor subordinated to the class struggle or the world revolutionary process. It represents an authentically distinct sphere of "scientific" inquiry. And yet, it is a most uncertain science, for (again we encounter this particular citation of Lenin), though indeed a science, politics resembles algebra more than arithmetic, higher mathematics more than lower. This is especially so with contemporary international relations because of its unusual complexity.[39] Similarly, Dmitri Tomashevskiy argued in a 1971 book for the establishment of "a new formula and the revision of familiar concepts," since "many new facts and phenomena no longer fit within the old framework . . ." He suggests that the *Communist Manifesto* was outdated by 1895, implying that the same might hold true for some of Lenin's theories. Tomashevskiy later recalls the difficulties of the early Bolsheviks, whose "vanguard found it hard to change from its thinking as an underground revolutionary party to the political realism of a government in power," as Georgi Chicherin, one of the first Soviet diplomats, said.[40] Chicherin's frustrations with the constraints imposed on the conduct of early Soviet foreign policy by excessive ideological zeal are well documented.[41] Those Soviet theorists who emphasize the continued validity of traditional concepts cite another remark by Chicherin to the effect that a radical distinction exists between the foreign policy of Soviet and Imperial Russia. This seems to have become an established tactic in a running debate on continuity and change in international relations, and, by extension, Soviet foreign policy.[42]

The complexity that is now said to inhere in international relations as an object of research demands new research tasks. The fundamental principles of the Marxist–Leninist revolutionary dialectic should be applied to the analysis of new, "concrete" political conditions in order to achieve a "more concrete assessment" of the correlation of both class factors, and factors that are unique to each particular historical situation. Such an approach would have a decidedly favorable application for Soviet foreign policy. It should be firmly based "on a new level of Marxist–Leninist social science – a complex theory of international relations, i.e., an interdisciplinary approach. This approach is to incorporate the study of bourgeois theories as well. Unfortunately, Inozemtsev noted, there has hitherto been no systematic Soviet treatment of such theories. The one essential point, in short, is that "information" is "an independent and highly essential factor" in the study of international relations. Soviet scholars must break away from the old habit of permitting the intrusion of normative concerns into actual analysis. One "must look at the world as it is," Inozemtsev concludes, "not as we wish it to be." Integrated into a single methodology, such an approach would fulfill the requirement for "an interdisciplinary [*kompleksnyy*] research of the system of international relations," that is to say, an approach based on a healthy degree of methodological eclecticism. "Creative Leninism" is the order of the day.[43]

Many of these themes were pursued by Vladimir Gantman in his essay for the symposium entitled, "The Place [of International Relations] in the System of the Social Sciences." Posing the question of whether research in international relations can answer to scientific criteria, Gantman responds that it can. To do so, research has to encompass the totality of international relations; it cannot remain fixed on aspects that are artificially isolated from the broader and qualitatively distinct pattern of relations characterizing the international system. The note of methodological eclecticism, first raised by Inozemtsev, is further developed by Gantman, who states that "the theoretical science of international relations is born from the interaction of processes of the integration and disintegration of sciences which are developing very strongly in our time." Bourgeois political science, though "fruitless" by nature, may contain specific applications for research that could prove of use in Soviet analyses of international relations. Following Inozemtsev, and before him Varga, Gantman makes a sharp distinction between the "theoretical (logical) and historical (genetic) aspects" of Marxist–Leninist research in the social sciences. Though necessarily interrelated, each aspect possesses its own characteristics and properties. In the case where, in analyzing "historical" (phenomenological) situations, the two aspects stand in an ambiguous relationship to the subject matter, the historical must be accorded superiority over the logical.[44] It is difficult to imagine, given the Soviet tradition, a more ringing affirmation of Varga's assertion of the fundamental irrelevancy of the general and universally valid precepts of dialectical materialism to the existential problems facing the Soviet state in the sphere of international relations. Seen from another angle, the "civil society" of international relations is to be accorded analytical primacy over the *a priori* dictates of ideology.

This approach to international relations should not be interpreted as a strictly utilitarian evolution on the part of Soviet "international-relationists" in response to demands received or anticipated from above. To a certain extent, of course, this is true. Yet one detects a somewhat different attitude toward the nature of international relations, and its implications for the Soviet state, than is revealed in any of the pre-1956 commentary, on any level, and in much of the work since then, especially in journalism (i.e., explicit propaganda directly reflecting the views of the highest leadership). Dmitri Tomashevskiy, for example, writing at the same time as the symposium on international relations theory but in a different journal, argued that whereas in domestic affairs contradictions become less acute as socialism advances (itself a direct repudiation of a central Stalinist thesis), in international relations the opposite obtains. "There," Tomashevskiy continues,

> socialist states have to deal not only with allied or neutral but also with hostile class forces, experienced adversaries, an intimate complex of intertwined class and national, at times also group, interests in the policy of foreign states; moreover, many of these interests, far from being controlled, cannot always be discerned, analyzed or taken into consideration.[45]

Once again, the implicit conclusion is that, since one can neither control nor know every important variable in an historical situation, it is fruitless to attempt to apply universally valid "laws" of historical development to them. One must become increasingly empirical while at the same time remaining conscious of the inherent limits of the best developed social science methodology as applied to international relations. Thus, Tomashevskiy concludes, referring to the "scientific–technical revolution", that, "In foreign policy, notwithstanding its intrinsically conservative forms, particularly rapid and striking changes have been taking place . . . It is increasingly important to make . . . a kind of 'adaptation' to this reality, while exerting the maximum possible active influence upon it."[46] In sum, there is something inherently resistant in international relations as an object of inquiry. How, as Stanley Hoffman put it, is one to develop a science of the intrinsically unpredictable?[47]

R. Kosolapov, in an essay for the "Theory" symposium entitled: "[International Relations] as an Object of Scientific Research," elaborated upon these themes in dealing with the distinctive qualities of international, as opposed to domestic political, relations. Unfortunately, Kosolapov notes, there has been no general theoretical analysis of international relations in the Soviet Union. Such an analysis was desperately needed because, although international relations retained their "secondary, derivative" nature (i.e., they are dependent on relations of production), foreign relations assume a fundamentally political character in their more developed stages. Previous categories of political economy are simply inadequate to the task of analyzing "the international relations of class relations," which are really inter-state (*mezhnatsional'nye*) relations.[48] For while the political functions of the state in the international sphere remain a continuation of the state's internal functions, there are, nevertheless, essential differences between the two spheres: the realm of international relations is a relatively autonomous one (whence the need for a relatively autonomous study of it); and, it is far more difficult to achieve class objectives – the very environment of international relations, distinguished by fewer possibilities and means of implementing class interests, demands a new set of analytical concepts. What is required is a "systems" approach, based upon consideration of the interaction of social relations within a country and the system of international relations.[49]

Others in the seminar spoke in a similar vein, drawing attention, in one case, to "objective processes of international integration," which tended to meld the roles of internal and foreign relations. The same author, in distinguishing among the different aspects of historical materialism *vis-à-vis* international relations (i.e., the general, which can serve as a point of departure, of orientation but which is insufficient, by itself, for analytical purposes; and the particular, which is appropriate for such purposes), complained that too often in the past the Marxist stricture of the primacy of the material over the ideological had been ignored in Soviet work on international relations. Misplaced normative preoccupations had thus hindered the effective comprehension of the subject which, in its analytical aspects at least, must be emancipated from such constrictions if it is to progress at all. In short, respect for the facts (the material) has too often been glossed over because of an indiscriminate adherence to the official line (the ideological) in the more properly analytical aspects of research.[50]

This direct challenge to the traditional Soviet-Marxist conception of international relations, in which those relations are depicted as a simple derivative of the internal socio-economic constitution of states, received its highest expression in the course of the symposium in a paper by A. Nikonov entitled, "International Relations and the Policies of States." International relations, according to Nikonov, form the environment in which the policies of states are executed. Both domestic and foreign policy are, to a considerable extent, dependent on this environment. Cognizant of the unorthodoxy of his approach, Nikonov is quick to qualify these assertions, noting that while it is incontestably true that one cannot speak of international relations as defining the policies of state, one can speak of the demonstrable impact of international relations on those policies. Having reversed the orthodox alignment of internal policy and international relations, Nikonov then proceeds to give a trans-class analysis of the factors to be studied in both spheres. Citing Lenin to the effect that politics represents relations "among nations, classes, and parties," Nikonov argues that the original, specific characteristics (*svoyebraziye*) of each state (as opposed to each class-type of state) play a great role in international relations. Finally, the dynamic, evolving character of contemporary international relations, exemplified in the first instance by the changing correlation of military forces in the world, has compelled a change in the behavior, though not the nature, of imperialism.[51] It follows that traditional categories of Soviet thought on international relations, which have been above all concerned to depict the *essential* qualities of "imperialism" and deducing practical consequences therefrom, are radically insufficient in a period when the essential character of imperialism remains unchanged but its actual behavior has been significantly transformed. The new Soviet study of international relations should thus concentrate on these behavioral aspects of the subject if it is not to miss "the trees for the forest."

The IMEMO symposium on international relations theory was apparently the first publicly coordinated effort by Soviet specialists in international relations to impart a self-consciously methodological tone to their "discipline," indeed, even to suggest that it might constitute a distinct realm of academic inquiry. In a sense the symposium gathered together the disparate strands of Soviet academic thought on international relations that had arisen and been sustained throughout the Khrushchev period, in an attempt to sum up what had hitherto been achieved and indicate what remained to be done. It represents an effort to establish a kind of minimum foundation for the subject, incorporating its distinguishing characteristics and fundamental concepts. The success of the symposium would be measured by subsequent conceptual developments, as Soviet theorists endeavored to consolidate and expand the standing and achievements of the discipline.

## TOWARD A SOVIET SOCIOLOGY OF INTERNATIONAL RELATIONS

The works of two Soviet academics, Yelena Modrzhinskaya, and especially Dmitri Yermolenko, stand out for their efforts to lay the basis for an empirically oriented study of international relations in the Soviet Union. Taking as their starting point many of the same issues raised by both the 1969 round table sponsored by the Institute of World Economy and International Relations (IMEMO) on the theory of international relations and by Tomashevskiy, these theorists affirmed the need to analyse international relations as an independent discipline and argued for a multi-factoral, interdisciplinary methodology. They term such an approach "a sociology of international relations."

In a 1970 article Modrzhinskaya asserted that, in spite of the influence of class forces, international relations should not be regarded in class-determinist terms. Though such "objective" forces indeed influenced the character of national foreign policies, they determined those policies only "in the long run." In an argument recalling Varga, Modrzhinskaya contended that the "general laws of the development of international relations do not reveal, of course, the whole of the concrete and historical intricacy of the international situation."[52] It is grossly inadequate to simply proceed from the major contradiction of an historical epoch (which *is* revealed by the general laws of dialectical and historical materialism) in an attempt to comprehend the behavioral complexities of any given international situation. Such understanding requires "concrete," or empirically supported analysis, with an adequate consideration of the influence of the "subjective" element. Fortunately, the "theory of Marxism–Leninism . . . provides the key to apt cognition and use of the subjective factor in the life of society." A properly Marxist theoretical analysis of international relations demands the "study of the *objective dialectics* of the epoch with all its concrete and historical peculiarities." Primary emphasis is to be attached to the specific and the unique, to that which has been so transformed that new efforts of conceptual understanding are required.

International relations cannot, consequently, be considered as the direct translation of domestic tensions, whatever their source, onto the world arena. States, the chief agents of these relations, are affected by the pattern of behavior, to a certain degree beyond their control, that constitutes the totality of the international system. As stated rather obliquely by Modrzhinskaya, the rise and development of the Soviet Union, a fundamentally new phenomenon, "is in a state of struggle and interaction with the old world, whose typical processes and trends are *affected*, however, by the external and internal *new objective conditions*." The analyst of international relations needs to examine "the structural and functional aspects" of the social processes underlying those relations.[53]

What, then, are the research tasks facing Soviet scholars? Modrzhinskaya divides them into five major categories: (1) the international relations of the socialist bloc; (2) the influence of the socialist countries on international relations as a whole; (3) foreign policy aspects of the developing countries; (4) the "complex and contradictory" international relations of capitalism; and (5) sociological aspects of war and peace.[54] Where the "Dictionary of Diplomacy," in its entry under "theory of international relations," indicates the kinds of criteria to be applied and the types of phenomena to be studied (alliances as such, foreign policy interests as such), Modrzhinskaya focuses on specific aspects of the international system. Her last category, which of the five most closely approximates a macropolitical approach, receives special attention. The cause of socialism, she argues, requiring peace, demands that particular attention be paid to "interstate" relations. Theoretical analysis of such relations is especially required since bourgeois opponents themselves are employing such analysis. These theories need to be carefully examined, with an eye toward extracting that which reflects truly objective processes. This is true, for example, of some Western psychosociological (behavioralist) theories of international relations which, "in spite of [their] obvious subjectivism . . . are based on the universality of human behavior."[55] Western structural–functionalist theories, on the other hand, as represented by the work of Ernst Haas, are to be rejected because of their putative emphasis on stability and balance. Modrzhinskaya does not elaborate, though it seems that approaches which take a certain structure as given, and then concentrate on examining how the structure maintains itself, through adaptation or otherwise, necessarily possess conservative political implications and are thus to be rejected. Invoking Lenin, she argues that "interaction" alone equals sterility of analysis, for it does not suggest possibilities for movement away from the existing order. Thus the demonstration of capitalist economic integration does not signify the end of inter-imperialist rivalry. Theories of international relations, if they are to possess any validity at all, should be capable of incorporating dynamic, evolutionary (and revolutionary, of course) processes. This is the essence of dialectical method. So, the major "sociological aspects of international relations" deal with processes rather than structures and focus on the conditions and patterns of development of relations. This is quite natural, since theories of balance, stability or equilibrium are clearly distasteful to those speaking for a power that is ideologically committed against the prevailing international order. These processes include: the relationship between foreign policy and the socio-economic system of society; the social character of contradictions in international life; ways and means of resolving international conflict; political integration; the types and dynamics of international relations, according to socio-economic system; and examination (and support) of the principle of peaceful coexistence.[56]

For Modrzhinskaya, then, international relations, considered essentially though not exclusively as interstate relations, are distinguished by a certain autonomy in relation to "deep", objective forces such as economics and class. The international behavior of the separate states is significantly affected by the structure of the totality of their relations. The importance of subjective factors imparts a certain dynamism as well as indeterminacy to international relations. Concepts based on equilibrium analysis are clearly inadequate for grasping this dynamism driving the international system. Such comprehension does require greater methodological discrimination among Soviet theorists than has previously been the case, though, including the careful critique, and even adaptation, of bourgeois approaches, as well as those, bourgeois and Soviet, originating in other disciplines of study. A truly sociological, i.e., empirically based and multi-disciplinary, Soviet science of international relations can develop only by incorporating these elements.

It was Dmitri Yermolenko, however, who later confronted most explicitly the status of international relations among the Soviet social sciences. As Vladimir Gantman observed in a review of Yermolenko's *chef d'oeuvre*, "Sociology and Problems of International Relations," Yermolenko raised the question of "the character of the theory of international relations as a scientific discipline and its place among other branches of Marxist-Leninist social science. Is the theory of international relations just one field of sociological knowledge or does it, as an autonomous branch of science, have more complicated relationships with many branches of the social sciences?"[57]

In a 1971 article, Yermolenko attempted to suggest the kind of methodology appropriate to the subject. He conceded that general explanatory laws arise on the basis of dialectical and historical materialism, such as the relation of the economic and the political, the correlation of internal and foreign policy, the basic moving forces, laws, distinguishing characteristics, and main tendencies of international relations. However, he observes, recent research has indicated the existence of an order of less general theoretical questions which constitute "the specialized (sociological) theory of international relations." These questions treat international relations as a social process, employing an interdisciplinary methodology and taking proper account of the complex, dialectical relationship between objective and subjective factors.[58] Yermolenko is, in fact, advocating a Soviet version of "middle-range analysis." Such an analysis would represent "the connecting link between the highest level – the theory of historical materialism – and foreign policy practice."[59] Yermolenko notes the interest of bourgeois scholars in these matters and urges the adoption of an attitude of critical eclecticism toward them. Soviet theorists, he urges, should "critically employ some partial achievements in the sphere of techniques of concrete research."[60] In fact, Yermolenko is rather well disposed to the "scientific" school of international relations in the West (as opposed to the "traditionalist" approach of political-historical analysis). The former, less concerned with asking broad, evaluative questions touching the core of political systems, is less threatening ideologically and can more easily be interpreted in technical terms.

Yermolenko offers a definition of international relations which, though transcending a purely class-economic analysis, threatens to be so broad that it indicates very little about the distinctive content of those relations. In this regard the similarity with the "Dictionary of Diplomacy" is striking. "International relations," he writes, "constitute the economic, political, legal, diplomatic, military, ideological, cultural, social-psychological, *et al.* ties among peoples, states, systems of states, classes, parties, organizations, and personalities acting in the international sphere." He soon makes clear, though, as is also suggested by the "Dictionary", that it is the state which is to be considered the main subject of international relations. While the activity of the state is ultimately determined by relations of production, the connection between production relations and the political activity of the state is not a strictly determinist one. "Elements of the superstructure of the corresponding states" have to be taken into account, such as the often serious divisions and struggles within the foreign-policy elite in capitalist states, and the impact of public opinion.[61] Though rooted in materialist dialectics, hence in socio-economic processes, the study of international relations must accord "a leading role", as another Soviet theorist put it, "to international political relations."[62] The political factor "can operate as the dominant and determinant factor in every sphere of international relations, as a force transforming both the overall political climate and the state of the global system of international relations."[63] Given the importance of the subjective element in political relations, it seems clear that international relations can no longer be viewed as a closed system, with predictable solution points for every problem. In different words, international relations are being transformed from a purely dependent variable into an increasingly independent one, while just the opposite has been happening with domestic affairs.[64] Within this framework, it is conflict that represents one of the most critical aspects of interstate behavior for the comprehension of international political relations.[65] Such conflict can be analyzed with the aid of quantitative methods. Game theory, for example, is an appropriate analytical tool if the participants are considered to be "free," while scenarios may be employed if the participants are held to be constrained by strict rules. In the end, however, "formalization cannot be separated from qualitative analysis."[66]

Interstate conflict, then, occupies the central position in Yermolenko's sociology of international relations. But such conflict should be examined in terms of a multi-level, sociological scheme of research, which includes: (1) a general analysis of the nature of international relations; (2) specialized research of the central categories of international relations (e.g., war and peace; foreign policy concepts, doctrines, and programs; principles of foreign policy); (3) specialized research of categories indicating the position of states in the international arena (e.g., class nature; state interests; power and force; economic, scientific-technical, and military potential; ties with other states); (4) specialized research of categories and problems associated with the practical conduct of foreign policy (e.g., foreign policy decision-making); and (5) forecasting. Many of these areas, Yermolenko writes, have, unfortunately, been insufficiently treated in the Soviet literature on international relations.[67] Proper account should be taken of the relative autonomy of superstructural relations (i.e., in this case, interstate political relations) in relation to the economic base. For interstate relations, which compose the essential core of international relations, "are a variety of social relations. They arise in a definite stage of human society when the interaction of social formations leads to a certain stability of interrelationships." International relations consequently assume the stature of a genuinely distinct sphere of human relations, substantially independent of the general laws of historical and dialectical materialism, as well as of the "deep" economic forces constituting the socio-economic base. And, it cannot be stressed too much, "relations in the international sphere are conducted not between peoples, but between states."[68]

International relations, then, as any great area of social life, possess a relative autonomy with respect to the objective laws of the socio-economic base. As with any social entity, international relations should be analyzed in relation to a variety of phenomena, including the relations between the components of the structure of society taken as an organic whole; the spheres of society (e.g., economics and politics); the existing relations between society as a whole and its separate spheres (e.g., foreign policy); and the existing relations within a particular sphere, which represent the interaction not simply of different spheres of a given social organism, but of various social "formations" (especially international relations).

International relations, however, assume a more general character than other spheres. It is distinguished by the interaction and interwovenness of relations among different social entities, and by the peculiarly interdependent, and unpredictable character, of the various factors in this milieu. This very complexity of the subject, reflected in the rise of a universal international relations involving, ultimately, all aspects of social life, has resulted in the absence of a single terminology for the subject *either* in the Soviet Union or in the West. The theorist is now faced with "a unified system of international relations."[69] In an extraordinary manifestation of disdain for traditional Soviet attitudes toward the subject, Yermolenko notes that "contemporary international relations now include economic as well as political and international-legal aspects." It follows that only those theories that view international relations "as a specific group of integrated phenomena" can successfully comprehend the nature of those relations in the contemporary world. It should concentrate on the two world systems of capitalist and socialist states and on the interaction not just between those systems but within them. Though recognizing "the significance of force as a central concept of the behavior of important states," attempts to reduce international relations to one or two determining factors, by "absolutizing the role of force," for example, are to be avoided.[70] Systems approaches, which Yermolenko claims have made important strides in the effort to solve problems in capitalist countries, hold special promise.[71] Indeed, "bourgeois authors have a whole series of interesting and important achievements." "A veritable reconsideration of traditional doctrines," based on *diktat* and force, has been taking place in the West. These developments, in conjunction with "changes in the international climate," "compel us to rethink the contemporary world situation anew."[72]

For Yermolenko, then, international relations defy explanation in terms of "key" variables, whether the class-oriented economic approach of traditional Soviet political economy or the power analysis of the American "realist" school. The complexity of the subject is in part defined and certainly magnified by the fact that international relations constitute an integral whole, or system. So, no one aspect can be explained *in vacuo*, apart from a consideration of all other aspects. The existence and interaction of the two class-based socio-economic systems, capitalism and socialism, create the main contradiction, or tension, of the system. Nevertheless, it is the behavior of states, in particular the most "important" states, and their proclivity for violent conflict, that occupies the center of the theorist's attention as he attempts to understand and explain the phenomenological reality of international relations. If he is to avoid the twin pitfalls of excessive generality, explaining the forest but not the actual trees in it, or preoccupation with minutiae devoid of any explanatory power, the theorist had best adopt a kind of "middle-range analysis," based upon a multi-disciplinary, or sociological approach.[73] Focusing "on the interdependence of nature and society," such an approach transcends historical and legal analysis and sees international relations as a coherent system in itself.[74]

In many ways Yermolenko's work, praised for its "scholarly and political analysis,"[75] represents the best statement by a Soviet specialist on international relations on the directions that research in the field should take if knowledge is to "cumulate." The analyses of several other Soviet theorists, however, of Georgi Shakhnazarov, President of the Soviet Political Sciences Association, and again Fedor Burlatskiy and A. Galkin, are instructive in completing this picture as Soviet views on international relations move toward an increasingly self-conscious methodological attitude toward their subject.

In a 1976 essay appearing in *Kommunist*, the leading theoretical journal of the Soviet Communist Party, Shakhnazarov, following Yermolenko, argued for "the necessity of an analysis of societies as systems." This is understood to include "international relations, *and* the struggle of different political forces in the world arena," which are "proper subjects of political analysis."[76] Burlatskiy and Galkin also approve of a political approach to international relations. They complain of "the insufficiency of the legal [i.e., institutional] approach when the element of force is the pivot of international relationships." Indeed, a systems analysis, based on an interdisciplinary approach, is needed in international relations more than in any other field of social studies. Though socialism has now become "a decisive factor in world development," the influence of external factors on socio-economic systems, a consequence especially of the scientific-technical revolution, "is greater than ever before."[77] Both groups of theorists agree on the utility of a critical consideration of bourgeois theories.[78]

Burlatskiy and Galkin warn that a politically focused, systems approach should not confine itself to "diplomatic activity."[79] Though the issue of recourse to force among sovereign states must lie at the center of any analysis of international relations, many of the forces that have contributed to the rise of the influence of external factors on states have also effected a partial transformation, or at least a broadening of the scope, of international relations. Shakhnazarov writes that, "World politics today is defined by the complex consequences of the struggle of socialism and capitalism, the mutual interaction of different social movements, and, together with this, of businesslike international cooperation."[80] To the extent that scientific–technical innovations in the military or economic fields increase the impact of the international sphere on domestic structures, those structures must adjust to the universal demands of the scientific–technical revolution. International relations, then, should be understood as an integral complex of interrelating elements, with the central tension obtaining in relations among nationally based systems and their surrounding environment. Impulses from the environment to the (sovereign, state-organized) system pass through many channels, ranging from the institutional structures of the official national foreign policy process to bureaucratic conflicts in those structures and to groups not actually in the ruling class but important from the point of view of preserving its rule ("attentive publics," it would seem). In this light, with attention drawn to a certain passivity of national structures in relation to the international environment, foreign policy decisions, which constitute the behavioral core of international relations, are seen to "occur in the context of risk, conflict, and indeterminacy." One of the most important aspects of the influence of the external factors composing the environment of international relations is not just the character of the advancing impulses but their intensity and the corresponding gravity of their possible consequences for the states involved.[81]

In this view, international relations make up a unique phenomenon among types of social relations – they are relations among sovereign political structures, none of which possesses a monopoly on the means of violence, and all of which are increasingly subject to the dictates of the system in which they find themselves enmeshed. This extends not just to their international political relations but also to the very prospects for successful domestic economic, social, and cultural development. According to Burlatskiy and Galkin, "Today, as never before, the general tendencies of all mankind and the system of global interrelationships exercises an ever-increasing influence on the processes of internal development in all countries."[82] Tomashevskiy has written in this regard that international affairs are more critical than ever "in resolving internal problems," especially in economic affairs, thus reversing the usual Marxist subordination of the international sphere to domestic, and especially domestic-economic policy. "History has fully confirmed," Tomashevskiy writes, "Lenin's theory of socialist revolution based on complete account of the increased role of the external factor, in particular, international relations." The two spheres, domestic and foreign, should not be lightly confused, for foreign policy "is conducted in quite a different, complex, more varied and far less controllable social environment than is domestic policy." In international relations the struggle is not between exploiter and exploited, but between ruling classes. Given the absence of a monopoly on force by any one of these ruling classes, the "class nature of foreign political interests is not as acute and readily apparent as in domestic politics . . ." As the expression of the interests "of the whole society," the state must "take into consideration in one way or another the mood of other classes" as well as the power of states organized according to opposite class principles.[83] "It is precisely in the sphere of foreign policy and international relations," Tomashevskiy writes, "that the objective interests of various classes in society can partially coincide" (e.g., the anti-Nazi coalition).[84]

Given such a model of international relations, concepts based on presumptions of national autarky or self-sufficiency can no longer apply. International relations themselves have changed fundamentally in the contemporary period. Once they could be considered infinite in time. This is no longer the case in an age of thermonuclear weapons. Once, international relations could be viewed as occurring in a homogeneous socio-economic world. The Russian Revolution invalidated that assumption. Whereas once, international relations could plausibly be interpreted as functioning primarily in the political, and primarily diplomatic, field (reflecting the limited influence of the "environment"), the scientific–technical revolution has transformed the situation. And, whereas once, international relations pertained only to a handful of great powers and a few dozen small and middle-sized states, the anti-colonial revolution has ruptured once and for all this relatively contained aspect of world politics.[85] The international relations of today, on the contrary, are characterized by "a complexity . . . of structures, greater reaction [by states] to external stimuli, and also an extreme weakness in the mechanisms of self-regulation." Today, therefore, international relations, as a developing system, demands new analytic approaches.[86]

What specific kinds of analyses are suggested by Soviet theorists advancing such approaches to international relations? Shakhnazarov, in a 1977 article, outlines a method which seems consistent with many of the critiques examined in this chapter. He indicates five major factors to be considered in the analysis of any particular constellation of international relations: (1) factors actively influencing the international situation at a particular historical moment; (2) the class nature of these forces and the ways in which they act; (3) their potential, or ability to reach their final goals and to solve "intermediate" tasks; (4) the particular form of their organization (national–international, state–private, mixed); and (5) "the mechanism of their interaction." Though class analysis, based on the global struggle of the two opposed socio-economic systems retains its validity, the center of an analysis of international relations must be "political forces of an international character and the basic trends of their interaction."[87]

The most essential such political force is the state, and it is clearly the state which Shakhnazarov had in mind as the organizing "force" in international relations in his discussion of factors affecting international power configurations. The most important activity carried on by the state, from an international perspective, is its capacity to apply armed force, without effective legal sanction, in defense of its declared interests. The logic of self-help extends to all states, regardless of their socio-economic character. A definite socializing tendency seems to be at work. Thus "patriotism," Shakhnazarov writes, "will remain the major principle of Communist doctrine . . . as long as national statehood remains a political form of social development." Shakhnazarov even seems to cite Bismarck approvingly, noting that the Iron Chancellor saw military "divisions as the final product of a country's development." Indeed, precisely because military power has been the key element in international relations, world politics has always revolved around the axis of great military power.[88] This is not to deny the influence of extra-military factors in international relations. It is, however, to affirm that the state, and with it its military potential, represents the central defining category of international relations: it is necessary to distinguish the essential from that which is important but secondary from the point of view of defining a field of study.

These secondary features, which do affect the prevailing structure and currents of international relations, reflect the influence exerted by both socialism and the scientific–technical revolution after 1900. As a result, the "power concept" of international relations, which "exercised complete sway in political theory" until that time and even "corresponded largely to the objective state of affairs," no longer explains everything of significance in international relations. Yet, if one examines Shakhnazarov's list of changes in world politics since 1900, it is difficult to avoid the conclusion that his original postulation of the analytical primacy of the state and its military arm remains intact. The shift from the national to the class sphere, for example, supposedly effected by the Russian Revolution, is contradicted by his affirmation of the durability of patriotism as "the major principle of Communist doctrine" for as long as national structures persist. The supplementing of military power by political, ideological, economic, and moral factors, accentuated by the limits imposed on the use of force by "the so-called nuclear impasse," is implicitly qualified by the observation that the expanding spheres of other forms of confrontation are either organized as states, by states, with respect to states, or else exercise very little influence. It is hard to see, for example, why "the rise of all other states, especially less-developed countries," should affect his basic point on the critical position assumed by the state, its military function, and its lack of a monopoly of force, for the analysis of international relations. The same could be said about the rise of "international political movements," which operate "as national contingents within states," and "world public opinion," which is "not a permanent phenomenon." As for these international political movements, such as the world communist movement, national liberation movements, social democracy, the peace movements, churches, and "overtly reactionary forces," they exercise influence, even as nationally organized contingents, only "as far as they can."[89]

It is nevertheless clear that Shakhnazarov does not intend to depreciate these "trans-national" and extra-military elements. The fact that they are inappropriate for defining the structural qualities of international relations does not thereby preclude their usefulness in illuminating important aspects of the subject. Shakhnazarov points to the existence of "global tasks," related to the impact of the scientific–technical revolution, for the solution of which "the power concept is now inadequate." Referring to "the dogmatism" of some Marxists, who presumably have not seen the light, Shakhnazarov emphasizes "the diversification of relations between opposite class forces on the international scene."[90] Only a "systems approach" can take adequate account of the complex mixture of traditional patterns of conflict, which occupy as definitive a role in the prevailing international order as ever, and the newer imperatives of international, and even interclass, collaboration. Such an approach would have to consider, as an integrally related whole, the influence of the rise of socialism and the increase in its power, of the appearance of thermonuclear weaponry and the relation of both to the success of the anti-colonial revolution, as well as the opportunities and dangers posed by the non-military applications of the scientific–technical revolution for the international behavior of states and indeed for the very structure of international relations themselves.

## SUBSTANTIVE APPLICATIONS: THE VISION OF CONTEMPORARY INTERNATIONAL POLITICS

In the preceding section we examined the ways in which Soviet theorists of international relations discuss the methodologies appropriate to the subject. Though glimpses have been offered of the actual vision that is held of contemporary international relations, especially in the repeated emphasis on states and interstate relations as the analytical core of the discipline, much remains to be said about the substantive content of the Soviet comprehension of the state, structure, and likely evolution of world politics. Such a discussion will provide the foundation for treatment of the narrower question of systems analysis in subsequent chapters.

Much as Zimmerman observed, contemporary Soviet analysis goes considerably beyond the "two-camp" concept in identifying the basic structural elements of the international system. This is so in two respects. First, international relations are understood as containing a plurality of corporate actors, with states, as opposed to the two camps of "capitalism" and "socialism", as dominant. Second, the quality of relations between and within "camps" of states has changed significantly. Though the United States and the Soviet Union, *qua* states, occupy the central position on the world stage, each is challenged by forces emanating from other states and from the international system as a whole. These forces, often issuing from states of the same socio-economic order, result in a relative weakening of the position of both the United States and the Soviet Union within their own alliance systems. The economic recovery of Western Europe and Japan after the Second World War, together with the loosening of tensions between the Soviet and American blocs, has led to an assertion of national claims against American interests on the part of its allies. The rise of nationalism in the former colonial countries, the increased military power of the Soviet Union, and internal constraints of public opinion in the West, have served to hinder the ability of the United States to make its writ felt throughout the underdeveloped world.

Also, "difficulties" within the Soviet alliance system, traceable to the persistence of national interests and uneven levels of economic development, have diminished the coherence of the Soviet bloc and have even thrown into question some of the "achievements of socialism." This was brought out with particular, though hardly unique, clarity in the case of the Soviet-led invasion of Czechoslovakia in 1968. The "Brezhnev Doctrine," asserting that "the entire [socialist] system was responsible for the maintenance of socialism in particular countries," in effect admitted to structural deficiency in the socialist state system. This meant an enhanced appreciation of the indeterminacy of the inter-systemic (i.e., capitalism vs. socialism) and the concession that now socialism, like capitalism, relied on "subjective" forces for its survival. In this sense the Brezhnev Doctrine depicted the socialist world as a mirror image of "imperialism," with the added proviso that the center of struggle could now be located within the socialist camp.[91]

The supplanting of classes by states as the chief actors in world politics has consequently been accompanied by a serious erosion in the ability of the two most powerful states to maintain the cohesion of their alliances. The challenge to the American position does not thereby strengthen the Soviet one, at least not necessarily. Indeed, to the degree that the same processes are at work on both countries, the international standing of the Soviet Union may be considerably weaker, both absolutely and with respect to American power.[92] What is most important in the Soviet view, though, is that American power is diminished by all of the salient processes in contemporary international politics. Nationalism, the economic recovery of Europe and Japan, the recovery of the Soviet Union itself and its vastly increased military potential – all permit a Soviet analyst to observe a qualitative transformation in the international position of the United States, which is to say an important change in the international system itself. Whereas once, in the 1950s and early 1960s, the United States, employing a diplomacy predicated on the swift deployment of armed force, could be said to occupy a "hegemonic" position, this is no longer so. One Soviet historian cites the "widespread recognition" among American scholars that American "hegemony" in Western Europe, as in international relations as a whole, is a thing of the past.[93] Its defeat in Vietnam served to catalyze a number of latent tendencies in the international system which tended to constrain the application of American power. In its search for an end to the Vietnam debacle, the United States approached the Soviet Union and began a process that culminated in American recognition of Soviet strategic-nuclear parity. The concomitant political detente told America's allies that relations with the Soviet bloc could be cultivated without incurring American displeasure, while their economic recovery gave them the means to do so. Specifically national interests could be developed, thus reinforcing the loosening of imperialist alliances which to a certain extent had been both cause and consequence of detente.

The irony for the Soviets, and it seems to be well appreciated, is that in attempting to redress the balance of power in the wake of Vietnam, the United States took measures, specifically the opening to China, which had the effect of creating further and quite serious obstacles to the achievement of Soviet goals. "The very departure of such a country as the People's Republic of China," two Soviet theorists declare, "from the forces of peace to positions relying on the forces of war has damaged the international correlation of forces on issues of war and peace."[94] Furthermore, the loosening of imperialist alliances took place within definite limits, so that antagonisms between the United States and its chief allies respected the fundamental distinction between what remained of the capitalist and socialist camps. From this point of view, the United States, though no longer a hegemon, still occupied a powerful, if not quite commanding position in world politics. This was so not because the United States can determine or influence the outcome of every conflict or dispute of importance to it but rather, as Kenneth Waltz has observed, because the United States remains the only power which by itself can substantially alter the "rules" by which other states "play the game."[95]

Whence, in the Soviet view, does this special position of the United States derive? It is to be found in the fact that the United States, uniquely, stands astride the two critical axes of world politics: the strategic–military axis, composed of the United States, the Soviet Union, and China; and the political–economic axis, composed of the United States, Western Europe, and Japan.[96] In this economic–military–political constellation, the United States disposes of formidable leverage: first, in its own right, as a great power with great mobility of power; second, as the leader of a great alliance system which incidentally incorporates the two most powerful agglomerations of economic power in the world, after the United States and the Soviet Union; and third, as the privileged beneficiary of Sino-Soviet tension and the improvement of relations between itself and the People's Republic of China. Furthermore, the United States and its allies stand to profit more than the Soviet bloc from the application of the fruits of the increasingly important scientific–technical revolution.[97]

True, the course of "the national-liberation struggle" in the underdeveloped countries has registered some marked successes for progressive, and even pro-Soviet forces in recent years (e.g., Vietnam, Angola, Ethiopia). Yet the very strength of the imperialist economy worldwide provides the capitalist alliance system with "a powerful economic potential" in its policies toward the underdeveloped countries. On the whole, victories for "progressive" forces in the "Third World" have tended against imperialism rather than directly in favor of the socialist bloc.[98] Indeed, there is a real question as to the continued validity of the Soviet model for the developing countries.[99] At best, those developing countries that have started on the road of "non-capitalist development" only find the prospects for socialism opening up before them, and they represent a minority still.[100] In short, imperialism's ability to influence events in the developing world, though certainly not what it once was, remains quite considerable.[101]

The picture of the world that is presented in much of recent Soviet analysis is quite far removed from that offered by the Moscow Conferences of Communist and Workers' Parties of 1957 and 1960, which declared that the world socialist system determined the principal content, direction, and particularities in the historical evolution of human society.[102] (Consistent with the analysis given here, the 1969 Conference did not reiterate this point.) Rather, one gets the impression of a world that, while less favorable to American interests than in the past, still presents impressive obstacles to the realization of Soviet designs. It is a world in which neither the Soviet Union nor the socialist countries together determine the main tendencies. "The imperialists," as the 1969 Conference noted, "impose on the developing countries economic agreements and military–political pacts, which infringe upon their sovereignty; they exploit them through the export of capital, unequal terms of trade, manipulation of prices, exchange rates, loans and various forms of so-called aid, and pressure from international financial organizations."[103] Seventeen years later, in 1986, the new Soviet Party Program reaffirmed that multinational corporations, greatly strengthened as a result of "the capitalist concentration and internationalization of production . . . undermine the sovereignty of young states."[104] This is a world order from which the Soviet Union is essentially excluded, isolated in its own "ghetto" of satellite states. When the Soviet Union does affect this order, it is as often a disturber of it as collaborator in it, and is certainly not, despite the rhetoric, the "determining" force in international relations. The successes it has achieved are defensive ones, securing first its right to exist and then recognition as a great power. At least, this is how it claims to see itself. When it challenges the existing order it is as an outsider, as one who does not contribute markedly to defining the rules and, as we have seen, deals from a weak position in relation to the main axes of world politics. The vision that is increasingly suggested by Soviet analyses of international relations is that of a world which, from the standpoint of Soviet interests, is beginning to get somewhat out of control.[105] In an international system with Europe as the chief "arena", China as the chief threat, and the United States – occupying a favorable position in relation to both, and thus also in relation to the Soviet Union – as the chief adversary, it is apparent that the Soviet Union is faced, and perceives itself as being faced with, an international system which both defies simple class analysis and is resistant to the easy extension of Soviet influence.[106] This emerging Soviet vision of international relations is, consequently, a thoroughly political one. In itself this should hardly be surprising since "Leninism," in its internal, revolutionary aspect, represents above all a theory of political power, based on the institution of the political party. In this way Lenin went far beyond Marx's analysis of social class in his "recognition of politics as an autonomous field of activity . . ."[107] The Soviet Revolution, unlike its bourgeois counterparts, a 1980 Soviet text on international relations theory reads, *started* with the political and accorded the political sphere primacy.[108] There is, then, a sound basis in communist theory for considering the primacy of politics, and thus of subjective elements, in the analysis of international relations. Long forgotten and overlooked amidst the Marxist vocabulary of social class and the Stalinist assertion of the "two-camp doctrine," the political, Leninist critique of revolution has survived to permeate contemporary Soviet writing on international relations.

The reemergence of the political critique in international analysis has had curious results for the Soviets. Soviet foreign policy intellectuals now generally agree that the "subjective," political sphere exercises a strong influence on foreign policy, "thereby also influencing international economic and political relations." Grishin and Nikol'skiy have embraced the notion of the dominance of the political sphere so thoroughly that they speak of "the reverse impact of economic, scientific and technological problems on international politics." Such problems as the arms race and arms control "cannot be defined by purely economic factors." In a contemporary discussion of Lenin's theory of imperialism, one Soviet analyst spoke of "the priority of politics over economics," while senior IMEMO analyst Daniil Proyektor has argued in respect of military detente that, "Everything in the final analysis depends on politics."[109] The greater weight assigned to subjective factors, in both the capitalist and socialist world, introduces the element of long-range indeterminacy into Soviet thinking. (While short-range indeterminacy had never been denied, it was always viewed in the context of the ultimate, and not-too-distant triumph of socialism around the world.)

The post-1956 interpretation of the impact of thermonuclear weapons introduced the possibility of temporal finality as well. As early as 1965, one Soviet analyst noted that nuclear weapons presented "not only unlimited possibilities for offensive strikes against any target but the absolute impossibility of effective defense against such [nuclear] strikes." Other theorists, such as the son of former Politburo member Viktor Grishin, have argued that thermonuclear weapons "have introduced qualitative changes in the posing of the problem of war and peace in the contemporary world." By threatening the very existence of civilization, nuclear weapons have eliminated the choice of general war as a means of attaining political objectives. This has led, the junior Grishin wrote in 1982, to "the impossibility of preserving the institution of military victory in an unlimited, global, nuclear missile war." "The time has come," Mikhail Gorbachev said in his Political Report to the twenty-seventh Soviet Party Congress, "to realize thoroughly the harsh realities of our day: nuclear weapons harbor a hurricane which is capable of sweeping the human race from the face of the earth."[110]

Finally, there has been a very heightened appreciation by Soviet foreign policy analysts of the underlying stability of capitalism in the West. Pessimism over the revolutionary potential of the Western proletariat is in fact deeply rooted in the Bolshevik tradition. Lenin himself felt compelled to advance the thesis of "superprofits," derived from colonial exploitation and divided among a worker aristocracy, to explain the "docility" of the Western working class. Contemporary Soviet analysts admit the high level of economic growth attained in the West after the war, while others have observed that such efforts as the European Economic Community have far surpassed the limits anticipated by their initiators. "Present-day capitalism," the new party program states, "differs in many respects from what it was . . . even in the middle of the 20th century." "The natural course of events," Vadim Zagladin, chief of the Central Committee's International Department, has thus observed, "is not going to make capitalism collapse." What is more, the late Soviet leader Konstantin Chernenko declared in April 1984 that contemporary capitalism "still possesses quite substantial and far from exhausted reserves for development."[111]

These three concepts – the indeterminacy of world politics, the possibility of general annihilation through nuclear war, and the underlying stability of the West – have severed the link between world war and revolution and have effected a progressive "deutopianization" of Soviet thinking about international relations. This insight is not, of course, a new one. Very shortly after the Russian Revolution one could detect a tendency among Soviet leaders to steadily elongate their expectations about the coming of communism from a few years to several generations to half a century or more.[112] "After the mid-1920s," Goodman writes, "the game of predicting the exact date for the arrival of stateless communism appears to have gone out of fashion."[113] Today, Soviet commentators speak of "entire historical epochs," lasting centuries, as the time for the transition to communism on a global scale, in effect placing the ultimate objective at the end of time, thereby depriving it of operational significance for the conduct of Soviet foreign policy.[114]

In certain respects, then, contemporary Soviet analyses of world politics display signs of converging with influential Western theories. International relations are increasingly seen as an open-ended phenomenon, with no fixed destination; world politics are held to be dominated by states, not classes, and the constituent states may be said to constitute a system that is more than the sum of its parts; political considerations, emanating chiefly, though not exclusively,[115] from their position in the interstate system, dominate the foreign policy calculations of these states; general war, though no longer inevitable, may now be universally fatal and so must be expunged from the course of world politics; finally, revolution, at least revolution according to the Bolshevik model, is not on the agenda – first of all because of the fundamental stability of the capitalist countries and second because thermonuclear weapons cannot be employed as its handmaiden.

The legacy of Marxism–Leninism, of course, remains an important element in Soviet thinking on international politics, particularly in the moral rejection of an international order that it sees as hopelessly illegitimate (though whether it is seen so more because of the inherent nature of that order or because of its exclusion of the Soviet Union is a difficult question). Its influence may also be seen in "an unusual sensitivity to economic and social developments in states playing a major role in international relations" and a persisting attachment to the symbols and phrases of the doctrine rather than to its analytical content."[116] Yet in all major respects but one, the contemporary Soviet analysis of international politics would not seem so foreign to a Western statesman or policy analyst. That one respect is the evaluation of the Soviet Union's international position. Behind the rhetoric of "the correlation of forces changing in favor of socialism" (which means not that socialism has acquired superiority but that it is stronger, relative to capitalism, than before) emerges a Soviet analysis which stresses the degree to which the Soviet Union is excluded from the major councils of international decision-making, is at a significant disadvantage *vis-à-vis* the United States in its ability to exploit the scientific–technical revolution, and finds itself faced with the possibility of diplomatic encirclement precisely when the capitalist encirclement had been decisively, and indeed, irreversibly, broken. Mitchell notes that "some Western analysts appear to evaluate military factors in the correlation [of forces] as more favorable to the Soviets than do the Soviets themselves."[117] When non-military factors are added to the picture, the Soviet outlook becomes more cloudy still. This pervading caution of the Soviet analysis, which contrasts so starkly with the bombastic and relentlessly optimistic rhetoric of much of the more hortatory literature, is exemplified by the comprehension that the growth of obstacles to the implementation of American foreign policy objectives does not necessarily mean a commensurate increase in Soviet influence and power in the world. To the extent that both states are seen as increasingly beset by forces they cannot control, or even easily influence in desired ways (and the Soviets clearly see themselves at a disadvantage here), the world is becoming an ever more complex and dangerous place in which to conduct power politics. The most important question under such circumstances is not, how to bring about the global revolution, or even the maximum extension of Soviet influence, but rather, how to minimize the indeterminacy of the ongoing international political contest so that the avoidance of unspeakable catastrophe is consistent with the essential interests of the Soviet Union as a state – in Adam Ulam's words, "safety first."

## CONCLUSION

The preceding examination of recent Soviet approaches to the study of international relations confirms that the trend, first identified by Zimmerman, of an increasingly self-conscious methodological attitude toward the subject on the part of Soviet theorists has continued and grown beyond the ouster of Khrushchev. Equally confirmed is Zimmerman's finding that Soviet studies of international relations have been moving away from the rigid determinism of orthodox Soviet political economy, the predominant pattern before 1956, toward conceptions that accord a greater importance to such categories as politics, the state, and the very "system" of international relations. The organization of a symposium on the theory of international relations by the Institute of the World Economy and International Relations in 1969 represented a turning point in the evolution of Soviet studies on the subject. International relations as a distinct field of scholarly inquiry began to be discussed for the first time. Theorists such as Dmitri Tomashevskiy, Georgi Shakhnazarov, Nikolay Inozemtsev, Vladimir Gantman, and Dmitri Yermolenko made major contributions in this regard. The explicitness with which these analysts, as well as others, reject traditional Soviet ideas about international relations is quite often very striking indeed. Such ideas as the identification of international relations with interstate relations; the primacy of the national factor as long as a world structured along the state principle exists; the transformation of international relations into an independent force, exercising a potentially decisive influence on the internal structures and prospects of states and socio-economic systems; and the primacy of the political sphere over economic and class forces in the conduct of foreign policy – all of these ideas have found their way into the works of respected Soviet students of international relations. The thesis that, for Soviet Marxists, the international system is divided not according to criteria of power but rather according to levels of economic development, and that therefore the state is not the critical unit of analysis, is seriously challenged by the analyses examined in this chapter. Nevertheless, the Marxist disdain for the prevailing international order has not been surrendered. Greater "realism" need not imply convergence on the normative level. In fact, the argument that Soviet theorists have employed in support of their innovations, as well as their borrowings from Western scholars, has been an instrumentalist one, that fresh approaches would improve the functioning of Soviet foreign policy.

Yet, one senses political arguments encapsulated in these novel attitudes toward international relations. It is difficult to escape the conclusion that Tomashevskiy's 1971 book, as well as much of the work by Burlatskiy, contains a veiled plea for the establishment of a detente based on long-term cooperative engagements between the Soviet Union and the West in a variety of fields. In Sanakoyev's work, on the other hand, the relative deemphasis on what has changed in international relations seems to suggest the inherent limits, and perhaps even the undesirability, of any such detente.

In any event, the issues raised by the development of the Soviet study of international relations certainly complicate the task of assessing the condition and evolution of those relations at any given moment. It would hardly be surprising if Soviet analysts, in developing more complex analytical and conceptual tools, have become more unsure of themselves.[118] Such a consequence must inevitably follow the disintegration, or rather discrediting, of the concept of international relations as a closed system endowed with established laws and hence a predictable solution point for every problem. The very purpose of theory might change in the process. Instead of seeking to answer questions of a meta-historical nature, theory would be "understood as a set of interrelated questions capable of guiding research of the empirical and of the normative variety." For how could there be "a theory of undetermined behavior,"[119] a conclusion that would necessarily follow the collapse of the essentially determinist science that the Soviet study of international relations has long been.

# 4

# The systems approach and international relations

> Each state lives in a system of states, and all find themselves in a system of a certain political balance with respect to each other.
>
> Lenin*

In the previous chapter, mention was made of Soviet interest in the application of a "systems" approach to the study of international relations. In this chapter Soviet attitudes toward systems approaches will be examined in detail, along with their consequences for the study of international relations. Discussion of more specific, structural aspects of contemporary international relations, that is, of the contemporary international "system," is reserved for the chapters to follow.

It should be made clear at the outset that the present discussion concerns systems "approaches," or "perspectives," as Oran Young put it, rather than systems theory or systems analysis.[1] Such a focus, which corresponds to the intermediate, or "middle-range" analysis advocated by some Soviet authors,[2] eschews the concept of system as the basis for a general theory of international relations (in any event, "general" theory is subsumed under dialectical materialism) and accepts it as simply a tool of analysis. Thus understood, "the concept of the system opens the way to better, more comprehensive explanation of international behavior."[3] Proceeding from Young's definition of system "as a group of actors standing in characteristic relationships to each other (structure), interacting on the basis of recognizable patterns (processes), and subject to various contextual limitations,"[4] how do Soviet specialists in international relations view the prospects of applying a systems approach to their field?

* *Polnoye sobraniye sochineniy* (Collected Works) (Moscow), vol. 42, p. 59.

Secondly, how, in their eyes, are the essential variables of the international system – the actors, structure, processes, and content – constituted and what relation does each bear to the others? How are they affected by the necessary implications of adopting an approach which assumes the existence of a system, i.e., implying that (a) outcomes cannot be inferred from the attributes and behavior of the actors; (b) interconnections are present with the result that changes in some parts of the system produce changes in other parts; and (c) "the consequences of behavior are [hence] often not expected or intended by the actors"?[5] Finally, how does their choice and treatment of essential systemic (independent) variables affect their treatment of critical dependent variables, such as power and its management, stability, change, and system transformation?

## SOVIET CRITIQUES OF WESTERN SYSTEMS METHODS

It is most important at the outset to disentangle the various meanings that the term "systems approach" has had for Soviet theorists. On one level, a "systems approach" is synonymous with the traditional Soviet understanding of international relations as the sphere for the struggle of the two competing world socio-economic "systems," capitalism and socialism. Not infrequently, one finds theorists who are apprehensive about shedding traditional Soviet concepts, but anxious to appear *à la mode*, who adopt the systems terminology but little of its analysis. One also discovers, on the other hand, analysts determined to apply more properly systemic approaches protecting themselves by affirming the continuity of the new approaches with the conceptual underpinning of the global confrontation of the two socio-economic "systems." The authority of Lenin is even invoked, as we have already seen, on behalf of the systems perspective.[6] The systems approach may also be understood as a strict, comprehensive, structural–functional method, following Talcott Parsons, which nearly all Soviet analysts deprecate because of its supposed preoccupation with questions of stability. It is thus suspected of an inalienably conservative political bias. Indeed, one Soviet theorist, Nikolay Lebedev, has argued that Parson's structural–functional approach is too deterministic.[7] Whatever the justice of this claim, it is the third aspect of the term "systems approach" which is of interest to us here and which preoccupies Soviet theorists who suggest or employ a systems approach: that is, as one perspective among others on international relations that increases conceptual understanding of the subject. It concentrates on the impact of the structure of relations among units upon the units themselves, and is concerned with the irreducible fact of the inter-relatedness, even inter-dependency, of the units.[8] Thus the editors of the first comprehensive Soviet treatment of Western theories of international relations claim that their "study is built on the systems-historic principle. The systems approach is understood in this sense as a type of logical method of knowledge."[9]

The pattern of analysis adopted by Vladimir Petrovskiy, at the time head of the International Organizations Department of the Soviet Foreign Ministry and now a Deputy Foreign Minister, is an interesting, and typical one. He first sets forth the main elements of the Western theories he is considering, and not unfairly. He then attacks them, not on the basis of their empirical insufficiency, but rather because they are somehow related to the reactionary policies of imperialist countries. Finally, he concedes the validity of the given approach: it is a potentially useful one, if used for Marxist purposes. This seems to be a fairly common way of conferring legitimacy upon Western concepts in general.[10] This is especially true in Soviet treatment of Western systems approaches to the study of international relations.

Nikolay Lebedev, for example, a leading Soviet theorist on the "restructuring" of international relations, approves of those Western scholars employing a "macropolitical" approach, which in his view "considers international relations as a system." Such an approach is "realistic and reasonable."[11] Another theorist is quite convinced of "the usefulness of the systems method." Indeed, Marxist–Leninists are said to apply their own models of systems analysis to international relations.[12] This analyst seems to imply, however, that the functioning of a system cannot be examined solely from the viewpoint of its structure. The "system" of international relations is viewed as rather strictly subordinated to laws and processes that are specific to "sub-systemic" elements: socio-economic and ideological, in particular. One might question whether an entity that is dominated by its constituent elements may properly be considered a "system" at all. And indeed, advocates of this second interpretation hope to preserve intact the sub-system dominant Leninist theory of international relations.

Soviet discussion of the utility of systems theory generally proceeds along the following lines. The advantages of such a perspective are not denied. Instead, the issue revolves around the extent to which the structure, as opposed to its units (states, socio-economic systems, revolutionary or national-liberation movements) and contextual elements (the scientific–technical revolution), is to be accorded decisive weight in the shaping of international political behavior. Those emphasizing the structure, whatever qualifications they adduce with respect to other intervening variables, can be considered representative of a "systemic" approach to the study of international relations. Those emphasizing the role of the units, or of contextual elements, can be classified according to the degree to which they depart from the orthodox Leninist conception of the subject.

Andrey Kokoshin, for example, a leading Soviet analyst of American concepts of international relations, is clearly interested in the application of systems approaches in the field. In a review of Bruce Russett's *Power and Community in World Politics* (1972), Kokoshin is highly favorable toward what he regards as Russett's view of the general macro-level stability of international relations. Yet Kokoshin's actual stance in this review accords the leading role to the subsystems, i.e., to "capitalism" and "socialism" as socio-economic systems. Likewise, in a review of Joseph Frankel's *Contemporary International Theory and the Behavior of States* (1973), Kokoshin observes that the "social and economic advance of human society determines the development and the reshaping of the entire system of international links and its separate elements, that is, states. Such is the methodological requirement of a truly systems approach to the analysis of international relations." Class contradictions, then, have been displaced to the state level and even to the level of the world system and have therefore become the fundamental contradiction in international relations. Kokoshin thus criticizes Frankel's use of the systems approach for ignoring "the qualitative differences between states, [which are] determined by their social and economic systems." It is the "multiple level competition" between capitalism and socialism emerging from these differences which, according to Kokoshin, "determines both the international environment and the politics of the leading countries of the world."[13]

For Kokoshin the systems approach is characterized by the interrelatedness of the parts rather than by any definitive influence of the structure of relations upon the behavior of the units. Although the systems approach should incorporate "the complex interdependence between politics and other spheres of social life," such interdependence apparently does not extend to relations between structure and unit. Here the character of the structure, that is, of the system, is fundamentally determined by the behavior of the units, which in turn are a product of the socio-economic system peculiar to each. Still, an important contradiction remains unresolved in Kokoshin's analysis: how is the macro-level stability that he recognizes as prevailing in international relations to be reconciled with the unceasing, relentless struggle between capitalism and socialism? The question is all the more pertinent in that it involves the Soviet Union as a unique actor in world politics. For ideological reasons at least, such a tenet must be preserved in all Soviet analyses of the subject. Yet the systems approach, as Kokoshin correctly anticipates, implies a certain "convergence" of the Soviet Union toward the position of all other states implicated in the international system. It should not be surprising, then, to encounter a somewhat tortuous tendency in Soviet critiques of systems approaches. Though admitting the compelling utility of a systems-oriented methodology of international relations, Soviet theorists can never explicitly draw the necessary conclusion that this approach envisages the subordination of the Soviet state to the same laws and tendencies of the international system to which the "imperialist" states are subject. Although one encounters a good deal of properly systemic analysis, for example, on the influence of types of "polarity" or of military technology on the international behavior of states,[14] the utility of the systems approach as applied by Western scholars is usually qualified as being insufficiently class-oriented – it accords inadequate weight to the qualitative differences between types of states and the influence of these differences on international relations.

If one examines what may be considered the "official line" on Western theories of international relations, this ambivalence in Soviet attitudes toward systems approaches becomes apparent. The volume produced by the Institute of the World Economy and International Relations entitled "Contemporary Bourgeois Theories of International Relations" (1976), which is in many ways a disguised anthology of Western theories as much as a sustained critique of them, devotes an entire section to systems theory, with particular emphasis on the works of Morton Kaplan, Charles McClelland, and Stanley Hoffmann.

Kaplan, for example, is accused, in his *System and Process in International Politics*, of "methodological voluntarism" for a "purely mechanistic imposition of systemic categories, applied in cybernetics, to a complex and specific social phenomenon – the system of contemporary international relations." The conception of the international system attributed to Kaplan is opposed on a number of grounds: it is "ultra stable," and it "ignores any social content" (i.e., of the states composing the system). His methodology, it is claimed, is excessively deductive and abstract. Kaplan is accused of being "antihistorical in his choice of criteria for defining international relations." His proposed systems hence "have little to do with contemporary international realities." In sum, Kaplan does not meet a single criterion for a genuinely theoretical analysis of international relations (the criteria being, *inter alia*, reflection of actual processes and properties, identification of the decisive contradictions, generalizing on the "active structural and dynamic changes in international relations," and forecasting of the possible tendencies of world politics).

And yet, of course, there is more to Soviet evaluations of Kaplan than that, else why deal with him at all? In fact, Kaplan is acclaimed as "the founder of a new direction in the research of international relations," a development many bourgeois authors do not recognize . . ." Though Kaplan's conception of system tends toward the ultra stable, his understanding of "balance" differs from the idea of "equilibrium" attributed to the structural–functionalist school of Talcott Parsons. "Kaplan understands," it is observed, "that balance does not necessarily signify [total] stability." It is to Kaplan's credit that his rules of transformation "recognize that behavior is as much a product of intra-systemic processes as of external influences." Kaplan's analysis, implying that under specific conditions international systems can change and "cross over into one another," yields a series of "macromodels," "instruments for studying reality." Given this, for Soviet scholars, "it is not without interest to take apart each of [Kaplan's] systems, comparing it with the tendencies of international relations in our own day."[15]

Criticism of Charles McClelland's systems approach follows similar lines. On the one hand, McClelland's systems perspective is to be praised, especially since he "is far from adhering to notions about the stability of the system in the historical long run . . ." Though McClelland rightly pays attention to "the influence of domestic politics on the international system," he nevertheless overlooks "the socio-economic and political nature, character and content of this sytem," without consideration of which "an analysis of the system of international relations on the theoretical and concrete historical plane is impossible." McClelland's systemic model is characterized by an "extremely simplistic, distorted, mechanistic assumption of a structural–functional approach through the prism of behavioralism," and is therefore "formalistic." Nevertheless, the critic notes that the influence of domestic factors is especially marked in times of crisis, thereby implying strong systemic influence on states in "normal" times.[16] In short, the idea of system, applied to international relations, is quite acceptable. What is objected to is the inference of stasis, and the effort to too rigorously work out the implications of such a concept, especially when it postulates a certain homogeneity of the constituent units and the subordination of the behavior of those units to tendencies emanating from the system itself. Though accepting the concept of interrelatedness that is implied by the systems approach, such a critique radically rejects the central tenet of any truly systemic vision. It refuses the idea that the behavior of the system cannot be inferred from the character of the units.

The Soviet volume's treatment of Stanley Hoffmann's "systems" perspective is somewhat more elaborate, and nuanced, than its critique of either Kaplan or McClelland. In a seemingly perfunctory dismissal, Hoffmann's consideration of the models of "moderate" and "revolutionary" systems in *Gulliver's Troubles* (1968) "limit his contribution to the theory of international relations." Yet Hoffmann's effort to conceptualize an international system in a state of flux is to be endorsed as an objective tendency for the future.[17] Similarly Grishin and Nikol′skiy, writing in 1982, observed that, "from the structural point of view, contemporary postwar international relations have had the tendency to be transformed into a complex, multi-levelled entity (*kompleks*) – a system of political, military, economic, scientific–technical, ideological . . . and other kinds of relations." And, unlike the "Dictionary of Diplomacy", which simply enumerates these various elements and sees international relations as their sum total, Grishin and Nikol′skiy posit a much more dynamic, "looser," interrelated and indeterminate relationship among the various factors.[18]

Given such a view, the course that the future will take is increasingly unforseeable, "since so much depends on the policies of the superpowers, and especially of the United States." In this Soviet view Stanley Hoffmann, though "far from the most reactionary thinker in American political science . . . remains full of ideological and political [nothing said of intellectual] limitations." And yet, despite Hoffmann's "abstractness", his models and analysis represent "a high caliber of professionalism . . . Certain true observations and conclusions," the critics say, "are made by him."[19]

If this brief treatment of Soviet critiques of systems theories (and theorists) seems somewhat random, it is, the author is convinced, because the Soviet critique itself is hesitant and contradictory. To a certain extent this may be explained by the nature of the volume containing the critiques. The IMEMO study of Western theories of international relations, the first of its kind published in the USSR, might well have been burdened by its very visibility and quasi-official status. This visibility, together with the focus on explicitly "bourgeois" theories, might well have impeded efforts at their consistent and dispassionate portrayal. Given the Soviet rejection of systems models in which structure significantly shapes behavior, how else is one to explain such basic contradictions as: (a) the assertion that the contemporary international system is a moderate as opposed to a revolutionary one, in spite of the revolutionary goals of some of its most important units (Kokoshin thus affirms the macro-level stability of the system in spite of his later emphasis on the relentless struggle between the two socio-economic systems); and (b) the implication that internal-political factors are less influential in determining foreign policy activity in "normal" periods than in times of crisis. Such an argument seems to confirm the interpretation that, though the structure of the system rarely determines actual behavior, it does delimit the behavioral possibilities that are open to the units, at least in non-crisis periods. It is difficult to reconcile such a view with the standard Soviet denial of a structurally oriented systems approach.

In order to determine more precisely Soviet attitudes toward systems perspectives, we should have to examine what Soviet theorists say when they are not explicitly engaged in the obligatory refutation of bourgeois theorists. Elements of a systems approach that were examined in the previous chapter, in particular the theme of the increasing influence of the external international environment on the internal development of states, suggests a greater Soviet receptivity to systemic approaches than is evident in the IMEMO volume.

## THE DEVELOPMENT OF A SOVIET SYSTEMS APPROACH

Many of these issues had been touched upon at the 1969 symposium on the theory of international relations. The problem then revolved, as it would continue to, around the question of the extent to which the admittedly interesting systemic view of international relations was compatible with the traditional Soviet idea that the behavioral development of the system reflects the particular properties of its respective units rather than supra-unit influences emanating from the very structure of the system itself. At times it is difficult to discern the exact substance of a given theorist's position. "On the one hand, on the other" analysis is quite frequent, and exasperating. Attempts to confirm the value of a "systems" approach are often qualified by mention of the determining influence of the actors and, what is more, on the socio-economic composition of the various actors as a determinant of their behavior; one then encounters the additional qualification that, "after all, though", the behavior of the units cannot be considered in complete abstraction from the systems-level. The gain in complexity and sophistication of analysis is negated by the refusal to posit criteria of priority, i.e., which elements, under what circumstances, are more influential than others in affecting the behavior of states, and to what degree. Fascination with new concepts is seldom matched by rigorous attempts to explore their logical implications.

One of the most striking examples of this tendency is the analysis advanced by Vladimir Gantman in 1969. "A system of international relations exists in the world", Gantman wrote, "shaped by many objective and subjective factors and having its own laws of development. Alongside of this, two world socio-economic systems exist, struggle and interact in the contemporary world, each with its own laws, methods, and degree of influencing international relations which are specific to each stage of development." In essence, Gantman has identified a systems-level and a subsystems-level of international relations. "In my opinion," he writes:

> the relations between the two socio-economic systems in the world arena, if we may put it that way, run deeper than the system of international relations, inasmuch as the struggle between the two systems is waged not simply in the sphere of international relations *per se*. At the same time, they also represent systems of international relations, because in the latter other forces, apart from the states of the two world systems, operate.

Gantman then cautions that "one must not consider this [class] struggle as taking place in some vacuum, outside the existing system of international relations."[20]

In the symposium discussion Gantman advocated the utility of systemic approaches because of their ability to conceive of society as an "organism," or "integrated system." Such an analysis, he said, is defined by the integrity of the system with respect to its "environment" (though environment remains undefined); by the existence of elements and subsystems; and by interconnections and relations between such elements and subsystems, on the one hand, and the "totality" on the other, thus permitting one to raise the question of the structure and organization of the system. One should above all be cognizant of the importance of a "subtle, flexible, differentiated and selective application of a systems analysis to international relations."

Of course, such a critique represents a great step forward from the unifactoral (economics), deterministic, imperialism-oriented study of international relations characteristic of the pre-Khrushchev period, especially in light of Gantman's own admission at the time of "the lack of real work on the theory of international relations in the Soviet Union."[21] Yet, as we have said, this leaves unresolved the issue of the true content of a properly systemic analysis: how does the structure of the system affect the behavior of the units, and *vice versa*?

Nikolay Inozemtsev, in the same discussion, agreed with Gantman that "the place of system in the social sciences" represented "one of the central problems of the theory of international relations." Indeed, international relations themselves should be viewed as "an integral, complex, dynamic system." Thus, Soviet scholars would do well to study "the system and structure of contemporary international relations" and, correspondingly, "the concrete roles that various actors play." The interaction of the units with the system, when combined with the simultaneous interaction and mutual conditioning of the units with subsystemic influences, makes the discipline a challenging one indeed. For, as Inozemtsev observes, contemporary international relations are

> the sphere of the interaction of extremely multifaceted, complex interweaving factors, acting on different levels and with different measures of effectiveness. This demands profound knowledge of the socio-economic system of each state, and a scrupulous study of quickly changing conditions and circumstances, of the different links between economic, scientific-technical, military, social, and political life, and the interests and *demands* of different classes, social sectors, and groups.[22]

The similarity of such a conception with Stanley Hoffmann's idea of an international system with multiple hierarchies is quite striking.

The implications of this conception of system and international relations were brought out with particular clarity by S.A. and L.A. Petrovskiy, who observed that this enormous complexity of international relations, cutting across and within levels of analysis, poses serious difficulties for adequate conceptual comprehension. "The specifics of the sphere of international relations," they write,

> are enormous, and it must be taken into account that more tolerance should be displayed in relation to accuracy and rigor . . . than one might permit in mathematics, physics, and other spheres of the natural sciences . . . A hypertrophy of demands for verification, explicitness, reproducibility, accuracy and rigor inevitably lead to an inadmissable deformation of the whole structure of scientific knowledge about international relations.[23]

In this sense, the unwillingness of Soviet theorists to reconcile the systemic and reductionist aspects that they identify in the "system" of international relations may represent a genuine hesitancy and even confusion before a subject that had not hitherto been accorded such a degree of complexity.

In time, as Soviet authors have begun dealing more rigorously with systemic approaches and their implications, a grudging recognition seems to have been granted to the value of a specifically systemic level of analysis. V.A. Pechenev, in a 1971 article entitled, "Socialism in the System of International Relations," observed that international relations, as "a complex object of theoretical, sociological research . . . is a *relatively* autonomous sphere, significantly shaping domestic societies."[24] Consequently, although the (sub)system of world socialism is the most important part of international relations, and the existence of the Soviet Union has exerted a great influence on them,[25] it is necessary to consider the Soviet Union, for example, as being located "in a network of states," to view it from the point of view of its "interrelationships with the entire international political situation." There is, thus, an "objective character to international relations" so conceived, though the international, systemic level should not be considered as an autonomous sphere of social relations. Nevertheless, it is generally only the "absolute," not the relative autonomy of the international system that is denied.[26] In thus opening the analysis to the influence of such factors as science and technology, Soviet theorists preserve the analytical integrity of a systems-level approach. While an analysis of the systems level cannot account for all behavior, it can significantly improve our understanding of the kinds of behavior we can expect to encounter in international relations.

As if to legitimize his conception of the contents of a systemic approach to international relations, one analyst, somewhat defensively, affirmed that "Marxist–Leninists are well aware of the most important factors of the processes of the contemporary world as: economic development; social class; ideological struggle; scientific–technical progress; the state and the correlations of military potential; the character, systems, structure, and long-term tendencies of international relations." These categories, though, should not be taken as providing any key for the prediction of specific behavioral phenomena in the international system, for this system, as a consequence of changes either in it or in "local conditions," is distinguished by "the unrepeatability of events."[27]

Kokoshin, whose ambivalence on this score was alluded to earlier, could write by 1978 that Western systems theorists should be judged "not only from the point of view of their political applications, but also from the perspective of their methodological positions." In this regard, "the systems approach (or 'systems theory') represents, from the methodological point of view, a relative step forward in comparison, for example, with the theory of 'political realism'." It focuses attention more sharply on the dynamic factors of international relations, such as processes of interaction and system transformation. And though this does not guarantee the validity of a "bourgeois" systems approach, it is "indisputable," Kokoshin writes, that systems theorists, as representatives of the "modernist" wing of American international relations studies, pay "much sharper attention to the dynamic factors of international relations, delineating and emphasizing the concepts of the process of interaction, transformation, and so forth [than the 'traditionalist' school does]."[28]

The systemic analysis of Charles McClelland, in Kokoshin's opinion, which states "that it is precisely the structure that determines the behavior of the states represented in it," though "too general" still, "is a significant step forward from analyses . . . [depicting] international relations as merely the simple sum of the conflicting foreign policies of the separate states."[29] That is, previous Western theories are criticized by Kokoshin for their excessively reductionist orientation – an interesting criticism, to say the least, from a theorist claiming the banner of Leninism. For the Leninist critique of international relations is, as we saw earlier, a reductionist theory par excellence.

The purest Soviet statement of such a systems perspective is contained in E.A. Pozdnyakov's "The Systems Approach and International Relations", published in 1976. Pozdnyakov, citing the "unprecedented changes" in contemporary international relations, rooted in the scientific–technical revolution and the "complexity" of international processes, stresses the need for Soviet "research" into international relations. Such research, which should be concerned with "the problem of establishing international relations as a distinct discipline," is to incorporate "concepts developed in the natural sciences for research into international relations," especially systems theory and structural–functional analysis.[30] Such conceptual aids can, if properly employed, redress "the lack of a precise understanding of the scope of international relations," which has, to a considerable extent, been the consequence of "examining structures and international relations from the point of view of the elements and not of the system as a whole." Objecting to Quincy Wright's conception of a general theory of international relations and even to the preferable idea of "world politics" as "too broad," Pozdnyakov indicates that he is devoting his main attention to "relations between states as the most important part of world politics . . . [L]imitation of the sphere of research is the first necessary step on the path to a more rigorous definition of the object of theoretical analysis."[31] As if to emphasize the state-centric concern of his approach, Pozdnyakov speaks of the Soviet Union and the other socialist countries not as constituting a distinct system of relations in themselves but as "the state-organized proletariat" (*gosudarstvenno organizovannyy proletariat*).[32]

Pozdnyakov's systems method, openly applying such concepts of bourgeois origin as integrality (*tselostnost'*), structure (*strukturnost'*), and homeostasis, focuses on the principles of interaction between states and the state system, and also between the system and "outside agents" (contextual factors, in Young's terms) such as the influence of the "scientific–technical revolution" on international economic and military relations.[33] In fact, the analysis must transcend mere interaction and view international relations as a "dynamically developing system." Unfortunately, Pozdnyakov notes, there has not hitherto been any application of the systems approach to international relations in the Soviet scholarly literature.[34] This need not have been the case, because "the systems approach is an integral part of dialectical materialism." The systems approach cannot undermine dialectical materialism just as a part cannot undermine the whole. In any event, the methodologically formative state of international relations studies signifies that systems theory is just "one example of a fruitful scientific approach to international relations."[35] Nevertheless, the systems approach, though certainly possessed of limits in its application, is able to reveal aspects of international relations which previous methods overlooked.

Pozdnyakov seems especially frustrated with the classical Leninist model, which reduces the behavior of states to a derivative of their internal, socio-economic composition. He writes that "in contemporary conditions, with such a high degree of interdependence," the theorist must "necessarily consider the foreign policy of the state not only from the point of view of its internal interests, but also from the perspective of its systemic environment," i.e., its geopolitical position in the interstate system. What is required, then, is "the isolation of the system of interstate relations as a specific object of research, the revelation of its laws and functioning . . ."[36] The system of international relations, understood in essence as political relations among sovereign states, is to be treated as an independent field of research. As another Soviet scholar put it, "the totality of the interaction between subsystems and elements of the system of international relations serve as the objective basis of its [i.e., the system's] relative autonomy."[37]

Unlike most other Soviet specialists in the theory of international relations, Pozdnyakov devotes a great deal of explicit attention to developing the implications of a structural analysis of the international system. He writes that in international relations "the task of the systems approach consists not in the analysis of the foreign policies of the separate states, but in the revelation of the functioning and development of the system as a whole, of the laws of its vital activity." Such a system is very complex; it is to be analyzed with respect to its "entire character," the mode of ties of the elements of the system (structure), and the mechanisms of the functioning and development of the system in conjunction with the system's moving forces.

Unlike Soviet theorists who accord equal, if not greater weight to the character of the units, Pozdnyakov declares that "it is only within the very framework of such integrated systems that the elements entering into them can display their fundamental characteristics." It is structure, that is, "the mode of ties for elements entering into the system," which defines the behavioral possibilities of the units. Systemic analysis, in making explicit "the structure, laws, and functioning of interstate relations, reveals the mechanics of the vital activity of the system and its fundamental behavior, namely: the conditions for preserving and supporting a dynamic balance; the mechanisms of structural crises, of processes of integration and disintegration; of the alignment of forces in the system." The supplementing of systemic analysis by "genetic" (historical) and class analysis distinguishes the Marxist from the bourgeois approach.[38]

Class analysis, though, can only serve in an auxiliary capacity in the analysis of the interstate system. The most essential characteristic of this system, according to Pozdnyakov, is that "all of these ties [among states] have, without exception, a *political* character." True, interstate relations may in one sense be considered a subsystem of the "macrosystem" of international relations, in which class analysis does have a place. But "the relative independence of interstate relations," as the core of a systemic analysis of international relations, "from the world socio-economic process is a real fact . . ." "There is", Pozdnyakov asserts, "a system of states in the world; this is an objective fact. States cannot exist without interacting in one way or another with each other."[39] In order to stay within acceptable ideological boundaries, Pozdnyakov argues that the relationship of the socio-economic milieu of the "macrosystem of international relations" to interstate relations is analagous to that between base and superstructure. As Engels put it, though the base (i.e., the socio-economic milieu) is determining "in the final analysis," the superstructure (interstate relations) possesses and exercises a good deal of independence in relation to the base, even acting upon and transforming it in the process.[40]

Nevertheless, Pozdnyakov goes far beyond any preceding Soviet analysis of the "relative" independence of the international/interstate systemic level and effectively refutes the reductionist assumptions of the Leninist critique.[41] Having posited at least an "ultimately determining" role for socio-economic processes on the "macrosystemic level of international relations," Pozdnyakov observes that "the processes of the socio-economic macrosystem are processed through the policies of states," that is, through the filter of the interstate political system. There are simply too many obstacles facing the translation of economic demands into international political reality for international relations to be interpreted in reductionist economic terms. The European Economic Community, for example, should be considered "as a political undertaking among states," rather than a logical, and inevitable reflection of the internal contradictions of capitalism. It is the political sphere "that defines the historical form of the manifestation" of socio-economic laws. The radical (in Soviet terms), and undeniably anti-Leninist conclusion that Pozdnyakov draws is that the elements constituting the interstate political system "cannot be described apart from the totality" of relations which are the system. Any discussion of the elements must lead to a discussion of the structure of the system. The concept of the system, as an integrally unified organism (and not, Pozdnyakov repeats, the sum of its parts), "with its *own* structure, functioning, and development," permits us to comprehend "the activity of states as a function of interstate relations, and not *vice-versa*."[42]

Although few Soviet theorists have made such a frank case for a systems-oriented approach to the study of international relations, many of the analyses of other Soviet specialists reflect concerns similar to those expressed in the work of Pozdnyakov. We saw in the previous chapter, for example, the growing measure of methodological self-consciousness by Soviet "international-relationists" since the twentieth Party Congress in 1956. No longer, it was implied, could international relations be considered as an adjunct of classical Marxist political economy. The arena of international relations, which was increasingly depicted in terms of the clashes of states rather than of social systems, of political as opposed to economic interests, was subject to laws specific to itself. The greater influence which "external" factors were said to be exercising on the internal structure and development of states further served to distinguish international relations from other types of social relations and drew attention to the corresponding need for an equally independent study of the subject. Pozdnyakov's analysis integrates these various tendencies and brings them to their logical conclusion – that the explanation of international political behavior can only be understood with the aid of systemic analysis. The constraining influence on the behavior of states that is exercised by the structure of their interrelationships, by the international system itself, represents for Pozdnyakov the primary analytical tool for comprehending the essential characteristics of international relations as a field of study. The reductionist critique of Lenin's *Imperialism*, it is clearly implied, is seriously inadequate for such an understanding.

Other Soviet theorists, writing after Pozdnyakov, elaborated upon aspects of his analysis. We know, for example, that Pozdnyakov's book was very favorably reviewed by at least three influential journals.[43] Themes contained in, or implicit in Pozdnyakov's work, have been developed elsewhere. These include: (a) the radical distinction between internal and international politics;[44] (b) the need to analyze the character of impulses travelling from the system of international relations to the units composing it;[45] (c) the necessity of distinguishing the international system from the subsystems of competing alliances and blocs, and the utility of focusing on the interaction between subsystems, defined, perhaps, in terms of the polar structure of the system, as an indicator of the system's stability;[46] (d) the validity of understanding international relations as an integral, independent, systemic entity, a "coherent organism" of global character distinguished by a multiplicity of kinds of relations among states and, especially in the contemporary period, by a diversification of relations between opposing class forces;[47] and (e) the consequent autonomy of international relations as a field of study, to be comprehended analytically as a multi-level, integrated system open to theoretical comprehension.[48] A final theme developed by Pozdnyakov and picked up by influential political observers is the idea that the laws of this system are reflected in the structure of relations among its constituent parts,[49] and that these parts, which are the subjects of international relations, will remain the sovereign states until (some day) socialism becomes a world system.[50]

Most significantly, perhaps, is the increasing attraction of Soviet theorists to the idea that international relations exhibit a marked tendency toward equilibrium among the major powers. "Every international system," Grishin and Nikol′skiy observe, "creates its own regulatory mechanisms." "Political balance," they observe, is the basis of a correct understanding and approach to the problems of war, peace and peaceful coexistence . . ." Indeed, "political balance, including the balance in the military sphere, is the most important characteristic of international relations as a system."[51]

There is said to be even a "structural," and not simply a political balance among the various powers in international relations, suggesting a degree of system dominance that is usually skirted in Soviet discussions of the topic. Nevertheless, as we have seen earlier, balance is not to be confused with stasis. "Bourgeois" theorists are continually chastised for ignoring laws of "development" in their focus on the functioning of the system. Both, Soviet theorists argue, should be studied. As one of them has written, "A developing system functions; as it functions, it also develops." While admitting the idea of a tendency toward structural equilibrium in the international system, Soviet theorists feel that Western analysts mistake "movement" in the system for development of the system, thereby attributing exaggerated significance to secondary processes and events and misreading the actual dynamism of the system. The key question, as Soviet theorists acknowledge, is, what are the sources of change in the structure of the system?

Such analyses inherently challenge the Leninist theory of international relations which, as we have noted, "confines the international aspect of social change to a one-directional projection of the alleged internal contradictions of capitalism onto a crisis-prone, world-capitalist system."[52] The anti-reductionist current identified in this chapter seems broadly shared among Soviet specialists in international relations and would appear to represent a true intellectual watershed in Soviet thinking on the subject. The question remains – to what extent have Soviet assessments of contemporary international relations, in particular the international relations of the 1970s, incorporated the methodological assumptions that Soviet specialists in the field have maintained are so critical for their comprehension?

# 5

# The structure of the international system: the systems level

> Although the correlation of forces is constantly changing in favor of socialism, there is still no basis for speaking of its decisive superiority over imperialism.
>
> Georgi Shakhnazarov*

## CRITERIA OF EVALUATION: POWER, CORRELATION OF FORCES, AND THE BALANCE OF POWER

In the preceding two chapters we noted the greatly increased recognition accorded by Soviet theorists of international relations to the concept of system. The "system" of international relations is understood in terms of political relations among sovereign states. Various theorists, among them Kokoshin and Pozdnyakov, have drawn attention to a certain "macrolevel stability" of the international system, whatever the dynamic qualities by which the system maintains itself (such as the evolution of a multipolar system to a bipolar one). Inevitably, the assertion of systemic stability raises an issue which, because of its imputed relation to "bourgeois" efforts to maintain the international status quo, has long been anathema in Soviet analyses of international relations, i.e., the balance of power in world politics.

At the outset, one must distinguish the balance of power as analytical tool and as policy argument in Soviet treatment of the concept. Genrikh Trofimenko, for example, a leading specialist on American politico-military strategy in the Soviet Institute of the USA

* Deputy Head of the Central Committee Department overseeing relations with ruling foreign communist parties. In his *Gryadushchiy miroporyadok* (The Coming World Order) (Moscow: Izdatel'stvo Politicheskoy Literatury, 1981), p. 94.

and Canada, observed in 1976 that "the balance of power (*balans sil*) is no longer a feasible policy in contemporary conditions."[1] In fact, Soviet analysts frequently argue that it is precisely the changing character of the balance of power as an objective, systemic characteristic (*sootnosheniye sil*, or correlation of forces) that now precludes the successful implementation of a "balance of power" policy by the "imperialist" countries. In this sense, the balance of power as policy is synonymous with the "positions of [superior] strength" policy (*politika s pozitsii sil*) that is attributed to the United States during the height of the cold war.[2] At times, though, the reasons adduced by Soviet analysts for the failure of the bourgeois policy of the balance of power shed considerable light upon Soviet conceptions of the balance of power as an objective feature of the international order. When discussing the balance of power in these terms, we shall use the more literal translation of "correlation of forces" which constitutes in Soviet analyses "the basic substructure upon which the interstate system rests."[3]

How do Soviet analysts apply the concept of power itself, clearly implicit in the ideas both of the balance of power and the correlation of forces, to the study of international relations? Increasingly, Soviet political scientists have interpreted power in behavioral, or relational terms. Power is seen as a process rather than as a quantifiable substance, and is to be distinguished from sheer force, on the one hand, and influence, on the other.

Boris Bolshakov and Larisa Vdovichenko, in their discussion of the application of mathematical models to international relations, explicitly relate them to the study of world politics. Arguing that the most important aspect of any model is that it be constructed in terms of measurable magnitudes, the authors contend that "the basic magnitude, into which all other magnitudes of the model [of international relations] are translated, is power." Though considered a "measurable magnitude," power is not to be understood as some kind of fixed quantity. Rather, power should be interpreted in terms of "possibilities." The wider the margin of choice, the greater the power that is available to the actor. There are, consequently, three aspects to power that are relevant to international relations: power as "potential possibility" – one can use power; power as "real possibility" – one does use power; and power as "realized possibility" – one uses power successfully. The "efficiency" of power can be measured by the difference between "potential" and "realized" possibility, i.e., "unused possibility." All three aspects of power are to be understood as "flows – constituting a measure of social processes, be they material, energy, or informational ones."[4]

Comprehended in this way, the exercise of power is a highly indeterminate, behavioral relationship. Given the assumption that nuclear weapons, because of their universal destructiveness, cannot be employed as the criterion of the correlation of forces in the world, it is hardly surprising to encounter arguments to the effect that military strength does not necessarily equal state power.[5] "Under the conditions of the present strategic situation in the world," Vladimir Petrovskiy, a specialist on American foreign policy doctrines and now a Deputy Foreign Minister, has noted, "increased military potential by no means increases the possibility of its utilization."[6] Pozdnyakov writes that "in interstate relations, the strongest state can prove to be powerless."[7] Any Soviet analysis of the actual correlation of forces in the world must thus "bear in mind the conditional and relative nature of objective and subjective factors applied to [this] category."[8] In what terms, then, do Soviet theorists examine the correlation of forces in international relations?

Tomashevskiy defines the correlation of forces as the relations among "the totality of economic, political, legal, diplomatic and military contacts and interrelationships among peoples, among states and state systems, [and] among the main social, economic and political forces and organizations functioning in the world." These relations constitute "the objective circumstances in which both world politics as a whole and the foreign policy of individual states are developing." One Soviet critic of the French power-realist Raymond Aron notes that the "concept of the correlation of forces in the system of interstate relations, as understood in the Marxist literature, reflects the character of the interrelationships of states with different socio-economic systems and of their interests, and is primarily (*prezhde vsego*) a political concept." More precisely still, one Soviet textbook on international relations theory observes that the correlation of forces actually represents a "correlation of external potentials," focusing attention on the latitude of choice as an aspect of power, reinforcing the indeterminacy of the ensuing political contest.[9]

Different Soviet analysts emphasize different aspects of the correlation of forces. Shalva Sanakoyev, whose skepticism regarding structural and behavioral changes in the capitalist countries remained constant throughout the period under examination, underlines the primacy of the class factor in the correlation.[10] A. Sergiyev, writing shortly afterwards in the same journal, argues that "the correlation of forces is nothing but the correlation of class forces in the worldwide system of international relations." Although for Sergiyev, "the interconnection and interaction of diverse factors of international relations provide grounds for regarding them as a peculiar dynamic system characterized by a definite political 'balance' of forces at a given period," he, like Sanakoyev, clearly subordinates the analysis of international relations to the class variable, casting doubt on the extent to which he in fact views those relations as constituting "a peculiar dynamic system." Rather, their notion of international relations, as reflected in the class-oriented conception of the correlation of forces, betrays an implicit acceptance of the continuing validity of classical Soviet categories of political economy for the analysis of international relations. For Sergiyev, international relations are "the *sum total* of interrelations and interactions between countries, nations, and national contingents *of various social classes*."[11] If class, especially in terms of entire class-oriented nations, is to be adduced as the key explanatory criterion in international relations, it is difficult to see how the study of international relations can be defended as a discipline. To the extent that Soviet theorists accept the class factor as determining, we can classify them as advocates of the traditionally reductionist Soviet school of international relations, little changed from the analysis contained in Lenin's *Imperialism*.

Examination of the concept of the correlation of forces by other Soviet theorists, whose writings reflect a concern with changes both in contemporary international relations and in the behavior of imperialism, as well as with the fundamentally systemic qualities of international relations, supports this hypothesis. E.A. Pozdnyakov, whose systems approach has been examined in the previous chapter, argues that it is the political, as opposed to class aspect, that is critical in the analysis of the correlation of forces.[12] Since the distinguishing characteristic of international relations is the behavioral subordination of the respective units to the structural constraints of the international system, the class factor, in the international sphere, becomes strictly subordinate to the transforming prism of interstate political relations.

One authoritative Soviet study, analyzing the nature of the impact of the correlation of forces "of the two world systems" on the foreign policies of the capitalist states, argued that with the rise of "the socialist system of international relations" and the corresponding polarization of the structure of the international system, the proper focus for explanatory analysis lies "in the sphere of international political relations of the two systems." As for the correlation of forces, one should consider economic and military power as central elements. Yet these objective indices of power, in and of themselves, are insufficient to explain the course of world politics. As Pozdnyakov and others have observed, the merely indirect influence of class factors in international relations enhances the importance of subjective, and inherently indeterminate, factors in the formulation of state policies. In this light the same study continues, though "cardinal changes in the correlation of forces occurred in the 1950s–1960s," "in and of themselves" they explain little of significance in international relations. For this one needs to incorporate the "moral–political factor" into the analysis.[13] Although a "change in the mode of production initially produces shifts in the correlation of forces in the world . . . the notion of strength and balance of power is not simply a matter of economics." "Only the combination of material power with moral power," Tomashevskiy writes, "can make a country invincible . . ."

The levels of political consciousness and ideological conviction within countries, therefore (as in Western analyses), occupy as critical a place in the correlation of forces as the more tangible, "objective" indices of power such as levels of economic, technological, and military development. Among the objective indices themselves, the military factor, though constituting a kind of *sine qua non* of the state's existence, is very difficult to translate into political influence. "If we bear in mind," Tomashevskiy argues, "that the direct possibilities which nuclear powers have to display their military superiority in full are, practically speaking, very restricted, then the importance of economic, political and ideological factors in the overall balance of power is even more evident." The analyst of international relations should take into particular consideration "the distinction between [the] objective power of a particular country and its subjective perception, and the importance of such a subjective factor as an evaluation of the opponent's strength . . ."[14]

This discussion of Soviet approaches to the concept of the correlation of forces reveals a remarkable analytical flexibility. Indeed, one is tempted to wonder whether the suppleness of the categories is not a consequence either of a refusal to impose standards of exclusion with respect to the phenomena observed, or of a deliberate attempt to subordinate the concept to broad policy considerations. All Soviet writers on the subject, and indeed, all Soviet writers on international affairs, concur on the existence of a balance of power, as an existing *condition*, in the world, which is defined in terms of the correlation of forces. This balance, incorporating objective and subjective factors, state and non-state actors, is primarily refracted through the prism of political, that is to say, interstate, relations between and within each of the two global socio-economic systems of socialism and capitalism.

The military factor, which occupies a most important position in this balance, or correlation, of forces, is nevertheless subject to severe constraints. These stem from the possibly suicidal consequences of the multilateral deployment of vast and diversified nuclear weapons forces, which complicates the translation of raw force into meaningful political influence. The other categories of the correlation, including especially economic, scientific–technical, ideological, and political factors, assume ever greater weight in the thermonuclear age. And yet, despite the relative weakness of the Soviet-led "camp" in these latter areas, the relative strength of the Soviet Union in the supposedly less significant military sphere, and the defection of China from the socialist "community,"[15] the correlation of class and political forces in the world is said to be constantly changing in the favor of socialism.

The concept does, however, seem to be a genuine tool of analysis for a number of Soviet theorists of international relations. Its multifactoral scope squares with their efforts to develop a more independent Soviet discipline of international relations on the basis of a systems-oriented, multi-disciplinary methodology. To the extent that the concept is taken seriously, the theorist should be impressed with the enormous complexity of making judgments as to the precise distribution of power in the international system at any given time. The relationship between this power distribution and the stability of the system itself should be more complicated still. The grudging and suspicious recognition that some Soviet specialists accord to the evolving multipolarity of the international system, with its attendant opportunities and dangers for the Soviet Union, suggests a certain fealty to the concept of the correlation of forces, though not necessarily to the official line that that correlation is ever shifting in favor of socialism. So, despite Tomashevskiy's disclaimer that "increasing polycentric tendencies do not remove the basic contradiction of the contemporary world, its divisions into two systems, nor does it diminish the role of the balance of power between them," clearly such polycentrism has had some effects, as we shall presently see, on the central relationship, that between the Soviet Union and the United States.[16]

## THE NEW CORRELATION OF FORCES AND EMERGING MULTIPOLARITIES

In one sense, the Soviet conception of the structure of the international system has always been a bipolar one, and strictly so. The correlation of forces in the global arena was said to reflect the struggle between the two world socioeconomic systems, capitalism and socialism. This bipolar conception of the fundamental tensions in world politics was preserved even as the focus of analysis shifted from the struggle of class-based systems to the politics of interstate relations. Pozdnyakov notes that the old Soviet belief that the central contradiction obtained between capitalism and socialism is the equivalent of the Western construct of a "bipolar system" of international relations.[17] Though all of international relations cannot be reduced to or interpreted through the framework of systemic bipolarity, the interstate system, through which the socio-economic processes of the "macrosystem" of international relations pass for their effect on the policies of states, is bipolar. Bipolarity, reflecting the centrality of the Soviet–American relationship to the international order, indeed conveys the essence of the international system. In the 1960s, Soviet analysis of the correlation of forces, though exhibiting this concern with the duopolistic structure of the international system, and especially with the role of states in that system, nevertheless drew relatively modest conclusions about the weight of Soviet power in the world.[18] Curiously, as international relations were said by Soviet observers to be assuming an increasingly multipolar structure, Soviet power, whose relative weight in the international system would presumably decline in a more pluralistic international environment, was held to be greater than ever and was pushing the correlation of forces constantly in favor of socialism.

In fact, Soviet analysts display considerable ambiguity about the entire discussion of types of systemic polarity and their influence on interstate relations. On the one hand, the very notion of polarity, implying the existence of more than one pole of power, reflects a diminution in the power of the United States, whose early postwar foreign policy is said to have aimed at the organization of an anti-Soviet coalition on the assumption of a *pax Americana*. To the extent that American discussions of international relations admit the existence of political multipolarity and military bipolarity, the United States can no longer view the world as a *tabula rasa* for its own designs and must adapt to changing global circumstances as the correlation of forces shifts away from it. In this light the Soviet observation that the correlation of forces is shifting in favor of socialism signifies not that the Soviet Union has reached some degree of politically meaningful superiority in the balance of power, but rather that the unprecedented American hegemony of the early postwar period has been reduced to such an extent that the United States is more nearly like other great powers than like the hegemonic presence of the period between 1945 and 1962. The United States must now treat with those powers, especially with the Soviet Union, as equals, and can no longer rely simply on the political effect of its military forces for the conduct of its diplomacy. Any discussion of bi- or multi-polarity, therefore, signifies, in the Soviet mind, an historic transformation in a postwar world that had hitherto been something of an extension of American foreign policy. This, of course, is most to be welcomed.

On the other hand, one frequently detects an element of suspicion in Soviet treatments of polarity in international relations, especially when the subject is "multi-" polarity. At first glance, this may seem odd, for such a world would seem increasingly open to Soviet manipulation, playing one side off against the other, for example, and both against the middle. Yet in such a world, characterized in Soviet minds by the increasing dispersion of international power, a fundamental transformation in the global arena with the recovery and semi-autonomy of Western Europe and Japan, and the interposition of China between the Soviet Union and the United States (and clearly leaning toward the latter),[19] the necessity for the United States to treat with the Soviet Union becomes less compelling. Secondly, the proliferation of important actors increases the scope of the uncontrollable, or catalytic, element in world politics, especially in crisis situations affecting the interests of the superpowers.[20] Thirdly, the dispersion of power, both source and consequence of the relative weakening of alliance systems, cuts both ways. If multipolarity is to signify a decrease in Soviet control over its own bloc, especially in Eastern Europe, such a concept is not an attractive one.

Finally, and perhaps most importantly, the polar triangles most frequently discussed, the economic triangle of the United States, Western Europe, and Japan, and the strategic triangle of the United States, the Soviet Union, and China, always find the United States occupying the central position.[21] This epicentral location of the United States in a number of critical polar relationships signifies a degree of American power which, though far from the dominating influence of the first two postwar decades, remains a considerable, in fact, incontestably the greatest influence in international relations. The difference, in Soviet minds, between the earlier and current power position of the United States is that, whereas previously, the United States could rest confident in its ability to translate its enormous economic capacity and potential, and its favorable position in relation to a number of key currents of world politics, into political influence, the *relative* diminution of American power now makes this a far more indeterminate proposition. This is the meaning of the slogan that the correlation of forces is "shifting in favor" of socialism: though the United States remains the single most powerful state in international relations, it is qualitatively less so since the late 1960s than before that time. Nevertheless, multipolarity and the shifting correlation of forces will not, for the foreseeable future, affect the critical position of the United States in the dialectic of world politics. Hence Soviet ambivalence before polar-oriented discussions of the international system.

As we have previously suggested, Soviet analyses of the increasing multipolarity of the international system and historically significant shifts in the correlation of forces are related to critical changes in world politics which Soviet analysts identify as having their roots in the late 1960s. Given the apparent Soviet sense of a decline, or at least stagnation, in the Soviet Union's international position in the 1960s as a consequence of the deterioration of the internal coherence of the socialist bloc,[22] it should, perhaps, not be surprising to discover that the changes of the late 1960s and early 1970s, which are said to demonstrate the reality of the changing correlation of forces in favor of socialism, are by and large related to a deterioration in the integrity of the capitalist bloc. That is, the improved international position of the Soviet Union in the 1970s reflects not so much an increase in the ability of the Soviet Union to realize its will in international affairs as a decrease in the ability of "imperialism" to do so. It is unquestionably true, however, that it is both the absolute and the relative increase in the Soviet Union's military capacity which in the Soviet mind complements, and reinforces, many of the unfavorable trends for imperialism.

In Kokoshin's analysis of the changing correlation of forces in the late 1960s to early 1970s, for example, the import of the growth of the Soviet economy from 1950 to 1965 lies not in the exemplary effect of the Soviet mode and level of production on other nations, which Khrushchev had emphasized at the twenty-second Party Congress in

1961, but "first of all, in the strengthening of the foundation of the defense capacity of the country, the existence of the necessary resources for the successful development of strategic nuclear forces as well as conventional general purpose forces."[23] The "moral–political effect" of Soviet economic prowess is listed only third, and last, after the growth of the foreign economic opportunities of the Soviet state, in the enumeration of the consequences of Soviet economic capacity for international relations.

A second order of changes concerns the *relative* weakening of the economic position of the United States in relation to its chief capitalist allies, especially in Western Europe and Japan. The importance of this alteration in the economic sphere, as in the broader strategic sphere, lies not in the collapse of the American position in the international economy, or even in the establishment of equality with its allies, but "in the loss by the late 1960s of its position of absolute superiority . . ." The conjunction of this change in the relative balance among the capitalist economies with the collapse of the Bretton Woods international monetary and, by implication, economic order in 1971, led to the transformation of economic conflicts among "the leading states of the capitalist world" to the "higher level of fundamental political problems."[24] By extension, economic conflicts of interest among capitalist countries, more important than ever for individual states since 1971, and especially since 1973, could be exploited to the economic and political benefit of the Soviet Union.

A third key change in the correlation of forces relates to "the development of the national-liberation movement as reflected in the successful struggle of the Vietnamese people against American aggression." Yet the true meaning of the Vietnamese victory lay not so much in the gross weight that Vietnam could add to the socialist bloc, but in what the conduct and outcome of the war indicated about the capacity and, more importantly, the desire of the United States to maintain an actively internationalist position in world politics. In the first place, "the moral prestige of the United States, which had expended considerable material and non-material means toward creating an image of advocate of democracy and social progress, had fallen to the lowest level." The general international-political influence of the United States and its most important allies had thus been weakened. The unpopularity of the war at home and the inability of the United States to achieve victory, were simultaneously cause and evidence "of the weakening of the possibilities of the United States to subordinate other capitalist states to its concrete foreign policy demands." The economic strain of conducting the war, as reflected in a bloated federal budget and increased tax burdens, led even "big business" to begin, by the late 1960s, "to oppose not merely the war in Vietnam but the entire foreign policy course that had resulted in American participation in that war."[25]

The most important effect of the American defeat in the war in Vietnam, though, indeed, "one of the most significant changes in the entire postwar period, occurred in the internal-political situation in the US." The anti-war movement was

> steadily transformed, assuming at times quite sharp forms, into a real political force, which directly, and through Congress, began to exert significant pressure on the president and the entire administrative system of executive power. This led [Kokoshin concludes], to a definite limitation on the aggressive direction of the foreign policy practice of the United States of America, with respect both to the national liberation movement and to many other international-political problems.[26]

The critical change in the correlation of forces, then, occurred in the intangible, subjective sphere of American political morale. The entire structure of the postwar international order, which in Soviet minds is quintessentially an American-shaped order, was thereby put into question. The position of the United States as linchpin of that order, and this, it seems, is the most important consequence of the shifting correlation of forces, is more *uncertain* than ever. Indeed, the very possibility of discussing the American role in world politics in terms of uncertainty itself represents a turning point in the evolution of the postwar world.

Yet, as Soviet analysts reluctantly but inevitably concede, the favorable shift in the balance of power toward socialism, though indisputable, is not a relentlessly smooth transition toward the establishment of socialism as a world system. Indeed, if the chief consequence of the shifting balance is the heightened uncertainty of the capitalist states, and most of all of the United States, about their world position, the Soviet Union itself was increasingly insecure about the main directions of international political processes. This is, in the first instance, a reciprocal consequence of American uncertainty and, in a sense, is directly related to the Soviet Union's improved power status by the mid-1970s. That is, the structural changes in the international system, combined with the Soviet Union's improved military posture, induces uncertainty in *everyone's* calculations as to the expected range of behavior in international politics. If, as Kokoshin notes elsewhere, the structure of the system defines its basic processes and phenomena,[27] the transition to political multipolarity (and even military bipolarity?), by inducing general uncertainty about expected behavior in particular situations, renders the positions of all actors, including the Soviet Union (which otherwise seems to benefit from these changes), more insecure because more uncertain. This is the gist of the analysis by Zhurkin and Primakov to the effect that increased multipolarity in the capitalist world enhances the significance of the "uncontrollable" factor in world politics, especially in crisis situations.

Secondly, and undoubtedly of greater urgency for the Soviet Union, has been the evolution of the People's Republic of China from ally to ideological, political, and, ultimately, security threat "to the general growth of the might and influence of the socialist community."[28] Indeed, as Wessell notes, "Soviet denunciations of the Chinese tend to reinforce the impression that the global evolution expected by Nixon and Kissinger [toward a stable multipolar balance of power] is taking place."[29] A comparison of Soviet writings on the subject from as late as 1970 with those of 1980 reveals Soviet concern with China's abandonment of a "'left', extremist, pseudo-revolutionary posture" and adoption of a policy of "outright military–political alignment with world imperialism." Soviet denials that China can be considered a superpower, that the global military balance remains essentially a bipolar Soviet–American one, though plausible, hardly conceal Soviet anxiety about the prospect of Sino-American politico-strategic collaboration.[30]

Ironically, from a dialectical perspective the incontestably worrisome Sino-American relationship can be interpreted as the Chinese and American responses to the uncertainties induced by the changes in the correlation of forces in favor of "socialism," i.e., the Soviet Union. The question remains whether the uncertainties created for the United States by the establishment of more nearly equal politico-economic relations between the state of the capitalist world, i.e., the United States–Western Europe–Japan triangle, compensate for the kinds of uncertainties created for the Soviet Union by the establishment of the Sino–Soviet–American strategic triangle.

The central position of the United States in both relationships, the relative superiority of the United States in the economic triangle, and the undoubtedly greater saliency of the Chinese problem for the Soviet Union (in the sense that the United States and the Soviet Union are "adversaries" to each other, while China is seen to represent a "threat" to the Soviet Union) than any other problem facing the United States all raise questions about the degree to which changes in the overall balance of power have actually favored the Soviet Union and, secondly, about the durability of the favorable shifts that have occurred. For the Soviets display little optimism about the stabilizing effect of a tripolar strategic world on the conduct of international relations. In terms of the Nixon–Kissinger conception,

> China is not viewed as one of the five major powers conducting a 'rational' and essentially constructive foreign policy. Instead, China is seen as a threat to international stability, driven to dominate the smaller nations on its periphery, intent on becoming a nuclear superpower, and unalterably opposed to the Soviet Union.[31]

Indeed, the possibility of war between socialist powers, i.e., between the Soviet Union and China, has been entertained by reading China's foreign policy (though not its domestic structure) entirely at odds with the interests of socialism. "In special, exceptional cases," Zhurkin and Primakov wrote in 1972, "the ground for interstate clashes can be created by the divisive, chauvinist forces which have succeeded in coming to power in a state building socialism, as has happened in the Peoples Republic of China."[32] Soviet commentators claim to perceive a Chinese desire to construct a "Sinocentric system of international relations," based upon the probability of a Soviet–American war whose aftermath would witness a world ruled by Peking. This is said to reflect the supersession of "class criteria" by China in favor of "nationalistic and geopolitical criteria."[33] This represents no momentary aberration in Chinese policy, according to Soviet analysts, in view of its continuation after Mao's death, but one which is based "on a definite strategic plan and is intended for a relatively long period of time." Global hegemony is to be achieved through regional domination, which signifies the neutralization of Soviet power, at least in Asia.[34] If the consequence of increased polarity in world politics is the constant possibility of Sino-American collaboration against the Soviet Union, clearly the Soviets can draw pessimistic as well as optimistic conclusions from recent changes in the structure of the international system. Bulkin thus concludes that, although Peking's "shift to the support of imperialism . . . has in no way altered the basic trends of world development, [it] has doubtlessly exerted a noticeable influence on the world military–political situation."[35]

Our point is not that the concept of the correlation of forces, in particular their putatively constant shift in favor of "socialism," is devoid of substantive content for Soviet theorists of international relations. It has been, and remains, an important one. The concept is not, however, to be interpreted as meaning that the Soviet Union has achieved politically meaningful military superiority, or even that it has, in its own eyes, attained the status of global equal with the United States. To the contrary; as Vernon Aspaturian has noted, Soviet leaders are "exceedingly conscious" that through the process of detente initiated in 1972 the United States was prepared to grant strategic but not global equality to the Soviet Union. In addition, and this accords with Kokoshin's analysis on the importance of a shift in a subjective, hence indeterminate variable affecting the capacity of the United States to influence the paths of global development:

> Soviet leaders are painfully aware that the favorable military equation which they have achieved largely by default, because of the continuing state of the internal situation in the United States in the wake of Vietnam and Watergate, is the critical factor in what they perceive as a favorable 'correlation of forces' and may prove temporary, should Washington decide upon new objectives and capabilities.[36]

The actual significance of the changed correlation of forces, then, is to be understood not so much in the absolute and relative increase in objective Soviet capabilities, though the achievement of strategic parity with the United States is recognized as an essential precondition for Soviet–American detente, as in the constraints placed upon the United States, both by objective factors such as Soviet military and West European and Japanese economic might, and subjective factors such as internal political constraints on the use of force, in realizing its political will in international relations.

Soviet attitudes toward the increasing economic and political multipolarity that their own analyses identify are, then, rather ambivalent. Though such trends are welcomed to the extent that they place constraints on the capacity of the United States for unilateral politico-strategic action in world politics, still, the possibility that this plurality of power centers strengthens the unpredictable and uncontrollable aspects of international relations is deeply worrisome. Soviet analysts trace a direct link between the greater diversity of power centers in the international system and the chance of catalytic war, or escalation of local political or military conflict to the superpower level, i.e., to the level of Soviet–American interstate relations. This concern is magnified by the conviction that, in spite of its reduced weight in the postwar world, the United States remains inarguably the greatest global, if not also strategic, power. It stands astride too many critical interdependencies and holds a key (though no longer *the* key) to too many important regional problems for the Soviets to take easy comfort in the greater uncertainty and insecurity the United States is said to feel in face of the changing correlation of forces.

To the degree that the United States has attempted to compensate for these deficiencies through politico-strategic collaboration with important regional actors, such as the Shah's Iran and in particular the People's Republic of China, thereby reversing, at least partially, the negative effect of the changed balance of power, Soviet analysts must be conscious of a certain dialectical quality to that balance, or correlation, that renders uniformly optimistic conclusions from its "basic" trends highly uncertain. This uncertainty behind the rhetoric is heightened by sensitivity to the crucial role of such subjective elements as changes in national psychology, or mood, in rendering the United States relatively less potent as the Soviet Union's chief adversary (if not necessarily threat) in international politics. Such developments are inherently indeterminate, hence fragile, and a change in the opposite direction, which the Soviets evidently came to fear had been effected in the United States Presidential election of 1980, might enable the United States to more effectively exploit the immensely greater choices in world politics that it is understood to possess.

Finally, if the consequence of this political multipolarity is to render the Soviet Union a less compelling problem for American foreign policy, it is to be viewed with great suspicion. Soviet theorists have reacted with subdued alarm at attempts by American theorists, and statesmen, to fashion the conceptual outline of a multipolar balance of power or a trilateral alliance of the industrially developed, capitalist countries. The suspicion lingers among Soviet theorists that these represent efforts by a United States "conscious of its deteriorating world position" to structure an international order in which Soviet consent constitutes a fundamental irrelevancy. Should this effort prove successful, then the most important consequence of the changed correlation of forces (reflected precisely in this greater plurality of decision-making centers, or poles), which was to bring the United States to the negotiating table, would then have been negated.

## THE PLACE OF SOVIET–AMERICAN RELATIONS IN THE INTERNATIONAL SYSTEM

The qualified optimism of Soviet analyses of the increasingly multipolar international political order descends into deep anxiety before Western, and especially American, theoretical elaborations on variants and implications of this new order, such as the "trilateral community" or the "pentagonal balance of power." All such efforts represent, for Soviet theorists, attempts by the United States to deprive the Soviet Union of the status and influence that should accrue to it by virtue of its attainment of strategic parity with the United States, through the construction of an international order either hostile, or, perhaps more alarming still to Soviet sensibilities, indifferent to the concerns of the Soviet Union. For Soviet analysts and political leaders it is the bipolar relationship between the two world socio-economic systems, as refracted through the bilateral relationship between the United States and the Soviet Union, that constitutes the irreducible core of the international political system. The concepts of "great power relations," though decidedly devoid of class content, may have considerable utility for the resolution of issues in which only the superpowers are involved.[37] Those concepts which, in Soviet minds, implicitly reduce the importance of the Soviet Union either for the United States or in the international system, are to be vigorously opposed. A chief criticism levelled against American "lateralist" and "polar" theorists is precisely the accusation that they are attempting to avoid the issue of the development of relations between the two socio-economic systems, i.e., the essentially bipolar politico-strategic structure of postwar international relations.[38]

Soviet theorists of international relations go to some lengths to emphasize, then, that the indisputably multipolar tendencies of the structure of the international political system in no way imply a diminution in the critical role played by the struggle of the two state-organized, socio-economic systems of capitalism and socialism. This is so because the existence of multipolarity does not necessarily signify that all poles possess equivalent weight. Various poles exercise varying degrees of influence in and on the system of which they are a part. In regard to the essential issue of international relations, the security of nations in the thermonuclear age, it is the two most powerful states, the United States and the Soviet Union, each representing one socio-economic system, whose relations are determining.[39] The analytical primacy of superpower relations can be subordinated neither to relations with, or among, other important but lesser powers or to other noteworthy but secondary phenomena of international relations, such as problems tied to economic relations between the industrially advanced countries and developing nations.[40] The Soviet perspective on the structure of the interstate system in this way transcends the state-centric tendencies previously identified and becomes in fact a "great power" or, in contemporary conditions, a "superpower" conception of international relations.[41] One may even speak of a state-centric bipolarity when considering the special responsibility of the Soviet Union and the United States for peace, for their mutual relations "are the essential core of international relations."[42] "The very possibility of preventing war," the Kremlin's most important Americanist wrote in 1973, "of preserving and strengthening peace on our planet, problems that affect the interests of all nations, depended in large measure on how relations would develop between the two leading powers of the socialist and capitalist systems."[43]

Such ideas correspond with Pozdnyakov's argument that the "great" powers play the key role in preserving the stability of the international system. This is to be understood both in the objective sense that the character of international relations inevitably reflects the tenor of relations among the great powers, and in the subjective sense that the stability of the system, and by extension the survival of the socio-economic systems represented by those powers, depends on the formulation of "correct" policies by each of the superpowers. Yet in this latter, subjective, sense, the "stability of the system" is by no means assured. Consequently, the inevitable victory of socialism is by no means certain, even in the elongated time span of the contemporary Soviet leadership. The entire process is immensely complicated by the fact that, although Soviet–American relations constitute the fulcrum of world politics, exerting tremendous influence on the entire international system, this central relationship itself is significantly affected by the broader system of which it is part.[44] And, since this broader system contains increasingly diverse and powerful actors and tendencies, the indeterminism characterizing the basically political nature of superpower relations is magnified.

The implications of this analysis of the role of Soviet–American relations in the international system have been trenchantly summarized by Georgi Shakhnazarov who, in the course of criticizing the "great powers" approach to international relations, presented a persuasive case for its validity in the analysis and explanation of interstate political relations. Arguing that theoretical elaborations on biplarity and multipolarity are simply variants of the great powers approach, Shakhnazarov sets out to explicate, in abstract form, the characteristics of a great-powers approach to world politics. To the extent that such a perspective is valid, international relations would contain, according to him, the following elements: (1) the world community would be viewed as the sum of states, whose foreign policies are unrelated to their social structures; (2) international relations would be based upon relations of domination and submission, according to the principle that might equals right; (3) the emergence of two or more power centers which divide the world into spheres of influence; and (4) rivalry among the superpowers is subject to only one restrictive rule, i.e., no thermonuclear war.[45]

Having set forth this scheme of a great-powers critique of international relations, Shakhnazarov asks, what is its utility? Noting that the propaganda function of this method "is to inculcate the idea that socialism has brought nothing new to international relations," Shakhnazarov nevertheless concedes that it could be of some use in resolving "partial" issues, in which, for example, only the interaction of the superpowers is involved.[46] This is tantamount to admitting the validity of the "power realist" theory of international relations, for such "partial" interactions among the superpowers have been identified time and again by Soviet theorists as the analytical core of international relations as a discipline. If this assessment of the Soviet perspective on the role of great-power relations in the international system is accurate, then a certain analytical "deideologization" of Soviet thinking on international relations has definitely taken place and, indeed, proceeded rather far.

In effect, Shakhnazarov has laid the basis for the rationalization, at least as far as short-term Soviet perspectives are concerned, of a manner of thinking about international relations that many observers have long ascribed to the Soviet leadership. This *realpolitik* vision of international politics, concerned above all with the activity of the most powerful states in determining the possibilities and directions of the international system, is not, however, to be interpreted as excluding the influence of other, less state-centric models from Soviet efforts to evaluate international relations. Indeed, Soviet moral rejection of the existing international order persists to this day. It is simply to say that, with respect to the critical, defining characteristics of the international system and the most pressing problems facing Soviet foreign policy, Soviet perspectives on world politics differ remarkably little in the weight they assign to the most powerful states, above all the United States and the Soviet Union, and the determining influence they ascribe to their mutual relations, from the analysis of the "power realist" school of international relations.

To be sure, the Soviet vision of international relations as a whole cannot be reduced to the bipolarity of the state system. Nevertheless, the admittedly growing polycentrism of the international system does not contradict the essential tension between the two world socio-economic systems as reflected in Soviet–American relations. "It is this contest," Nikolay Lebedev, Soviet theorist on the "restructuring of international relations," writes, "that determines the rock bottom [meaning here "bedrock"] and objective basis for the alignment of forces in all the fluctuations of international development." By extension, any attempt to restructure international relations on principles that take insufficient account of the centrality of Soviet–American relations, is doomed to failure.[47] To the degree that this belief is genuinely held by Soviet theorists and leaders, priority must be accorded to a Soviet–American as opposed to, say, a Soviet–West European detente for the West Europeans, though they can provide positive benefits for the Soviet Union, are far indeed from possessing the capacity to frustrate Soviet policies that the United States does.[48] And yet, at the same time, Soviet–American relations cannot easily be insulated from the broader currents of international relations. As Arbatov noted, the development of the international system is not a simple derivative of the state of Soviet–American relations. To a considerable degree they are reciprocally dependent on each other, though for analytical purposes one must accord priority to the superpower relationship.

How are the superpowers affected by other, subsystemic elements of the international system, including those of which they themselves are part? In particular, where do the alliance systems headed by the superpowers fit in the structure and functioning of world politics? These questions take us to an examination of the Soviet conception of "inter-imperialist" relations and contradictions, on the one hand, and intersocialist relations, or "international relations of a new type," on the other.

# 6

# Critical subsystems

> [T]he existing complex of economic, politico-military and other common interests of the three centers of power [i.e., US, Western Europe, and Japan] can hardly be expected to break up . . . But within the framework of this complex, Washington should not expect unquestioning obedience . . .
>
> Mikhail Gorbachev*

## INTER-IMPERIALIST RELATIONS

Perhaps the most significant development in the entire Soviet study of international relations is the shift in the place assigned to relations among states with capitalistic economic systems in the international system. Whereas once, the nature of international behavior could be understood, and the future of international relations predicted, on the basis of an understanding of the dynamics of "inter-imperialist contradictions," this is no longer the case. Increasingly, and indeed, one may now say decisively, inter-imperialist contradictions have been relegated by Soviet analysts to second-order phenomena of a sub-systemic character. No longer capable of shaping the basic paths of the international system, though it may have considerable impact on particular aspects of that system, the conduct of relations among "imperialist" countries is analytically subordinate, for the comprehension of that system, to relations among *different* socio-economic systems. That is to say that there is "a profound qualitative [*printsipal'noye*] difference between the existence of three centers of capitalism and the division [*raskol*, lit. "schism"] of the world into two opposing socio-economic systems."[1]

* From Mikhail Gorbachev's Political Report to the 27th Soviet Party Congress, 25 February 1986.

If this statement is interpreted in light of our previous analysis of the subordination, on the international level, of socio-economic processes to the level of relatively autonomous interstate political relations, it is evident that the main currents of international relations cannot be explained as the simple extension of the economically determined contradictions of the international capitalist system. Rather, one must examine that system in terms of relations among the greatest powers of the two global socio-economic systems, the Soviet Union and the United States. Thus the location of the influence of such a subsystem as inter-imperialist relations follows the identified tendency toward an increased Soviet concern with systemic explanations of international relations. For no subsystem, especially one whose international behavioral dynamics have been traditionally subordinated, as in the Leninist critique, to internally generated economic processes, can dominate a system. This seems to have been grasped by Soviet theorists. The rise of the Soviet Union after 1917, but especially since 1945, as the representative of an alternative socio-economic system, but also, not incidentally, as the second global power, has compelled a realignment of international political relations from an inter-capitalist to a socialist–capitalist, i.e., Soviet–American, axis.

If the influence of inter-imperialist relations on the international system has changed with the ascent of the Soviet Union, so have the nature of those relations themselves. Whereas formerly, the imminent possibility, and in fact ultimate inevitability, of war between imperialist states was deduced from the nature of the capitalist economic "foundation," the possibility of military conflict between the leading capitalist powers has now been effectively excluded from Soviet analyses of inter-imperialist relations. The dramatic extent of this change in Soviet perceptions is to be judged in light of the longstanding Soviet conviction that it was contradictions among capitalist states, rooted in economic causes to be sure, with the consequent imminent possibility of war, that would and did provide the infant Soviet Republic with the time needed to survive and consolidate its position. It was this very analysis, in fact, which supplied the justification for the policy and doctrine of socialism-in-one-country. Indeed, having emerged from the Second World War with an unprecedentedly (and unimaginably?) powerful international position, Soviet leaders must have felt vindicated in their analysis. The tenacity of the belief is revealed in Stalin's 1952 *Economic Problems of Socialism in the USSR*, in which he maintains the thesis of the inevitability of war between capitalist states against "some comrades" who apparently felt otherwise.

The death of Stalin, however, freed these other "comrades" from the political and ideological constraints of the dictator and permitted the emergence of a new analysis more in accordance with the fundamentally bipolar Soviet–American (socialist–capitalist) international politico-strategic order. One specialist, in a 1959 analysis of "the character of contemporary contradictions among capitalist countries," noted that such contradictions were simply a consequence "of the action of the law of [the] inequality [of development] in contemporary conditions" rather than of the unremittingly bellicose nature of capitalist, i.e., inter-capitalist, development.[2] Above all, Soviet students of international relations "should not simplify the situation"; specialists in the area should concentrate "not on the fanning of differences and conflicts among capitalist countries, but on an 'all-sided' scientific analysis of contemporary capitalism" that takes into consideration the primacy of politics over economics.[3] Such an analysis transforms the very idea of "contradictions" among capitalist states from one of mortal struggle, with direct implications for the structure and survival both of the individual capitalist states and of the broader interstate system, to one of significant though decidedly lesser tensions reflecting differences in levels and rates of economic adjustment. We shall see that these concepts, which trace their roots, according to Stalin himself, at least as far back as the late Stalin period, have assumed mature form in contemporary Soviet analyses of inter-"imperialist" contradictions.

It is true that one still encounters analyses in Soviet journals to the effect that inter-imperialist relations, as reflected above all in alliance policy and politics, are encompassed by the class character of capitalism and that such organizations as the North Atlantic Treaty Organization represent "association[s] of capitalist states aiming to keep capitalism going . . ."[4] Yet the prevailing tendency of contemporary Soviet analysis is to treat alliance phenomena in geopolitical terms rather than through the orthodox categories of Soviet political economy. Seen from this vantage point, "the creation of a system of inter-imperialist alliances and blocs, headed by NATO, [and] the development of processes of economic, political and military integration of a whole group (*ryada*) of capitalist states" reflects the rise of Soviet power at least as much as threats to the capitalist order within those countries.[5] Indeed, given the general Soviet consensus on the stability of the advanced capitalist countries, it must be the weight of the "state-organized proletariat," the Soviet Union and its allies, which has impelled the imperialist powers to try and compose their differences and present a united front to the socialist countries, especially in Europe, the cynosure of both class and great power interests.[6] This coincidence of the class rift (the state-organized proletariat vs. the state-organized bourgeoisie) with great international power (the United States vs. the Soviet Union) and a common stake (Europe) has transformed the pivot of the international system from inter-imperialist relations to capitalist–socialist, in the first instance, Soviet–American, relations. This means that, where international issues affecting key Soviet interests are concerned, those interests must now be taken into account. There can no longer be a Munich Conference (1938), where issues central to the international balance of power were taken in the absence of Soviet participation. In this sense, inter-imperialist relations possess now a subsystemic character, subordinate to the contradictions governing relations between the United States, as leader of the capitalist alliance, and the Soviet Union, as champion of the socialist bloc.

In this strictly bipolar view, the merging of class antagonism with state power under conditions of high international tension compels the capitalists states to act on the basis of their common interests as members of the "monopoly bourgeoisie." This is now said to constitute an "objective factor" of contemporary international relations.[7] To the extent that this is true, a strictly bipolar order, though according a leading position to the Soviet Union, limits Soviet choices by concentrating attention on the mutual irreconcilability of ultimate class interests. As tensions between the two blocs become less strained, though, alliance structures become less stable. Relaxation of tensions between the two blocs, both partial cause and consequence of an increasingly plural international order, highlights extra-class aspects of the foreign policy interests of states. Common interests between socialist and capitalist states begin to emerge, while greater attention to national interests complicates alliance management. This applies to Eastern as well as to Western Europe, though naturally Soviet analysts are more reticent about the former than the latter (see the next section for Soviet views on inter-socialist relations).

A policy of detente, by projecting a less threatening Soviet profile, takes advantage of this nascent multipolarity and encourages the maturation of latent tensions within the imperialist camp. Writing in

1982, Grishin notes a European–American argument over the very meaning and desirability of detente, with the United States concerned about the projection of Soviet influence globally, while the West Europeans are first of all motivated to preserve detente in Europe through the cultivation of direct relations with the Soviet Union.[8] This juxtaposition of American "globalism" with "Euro-centrism" pervades, in greater and lesser degree, the entire European–American relationship, and is best exploited in conditions of detente, when the image of a common threat becomes less plausible.[9] This is the case even in security policy. While the United States, it is observed, tries to "optimalize" the quantitative and qualitative levels, as well as the mobility, of its armaments, the West Europeans *and* the Japanese are concerned with strengthening the American nuclear umbrella and at the same time keeping as far removed from international conflicts as possible.[10] Proyektor writes that detente, in opening up new choices for capitalist states, helps those states "to limit the influence of their allies . . .; to equalize . . . mutual relations among the Western partners . . .; to increase . . . their foreign policy status . . .; to exercise pressure on a partner, *etc.*"[11] Elsewhere, Proyektor warns against "absolutizing the importance of Soviet–American relations for Europe" as well as underestimating the independence of the West European countries in their "partnership" with the United States. West European efforts to supplement "Atlanticism" with regional and national forms for providing for their security "create additional possibilities for the development of relations between the two parts of Europe . . ." The "profound changes" occurring in the world, reflected in the policy of detente, encourage a variety of views within NATO, with many trying to relate Atlanticism to peace with the Soviet Union. Lebedev observes that the Soviet Union is ready to cooperate with anybody in order to save and broaden detente, thereby implying both the hope and expectation that detente assists the Soviet Union in responding to strains within NATO.[12]

As the international order moves away from a strict bipolarity toward some new configuration which will preserve the two superpowers as central actors but be increasingly receptive to impulses from other sources, the force of the class factor is less directly felt. "The contradictions of the contemporary world," Doronina writes, "are not, of course, concentrated only around the main axis – the opposition of the two socio-economic systems."[13] Greater multipolarity enhances class-neutral elements such as geopolitical position and national interest and, in the critical European theater at least, affords the Soviet Union a greater space to compete for influence than would be the case in a strictly bipolar international order.

These conclusions are confirmed as Soviet theorists turn their attention from the general implications of a more plural international order to the specifics of "inter-imperialist relations." Categories of orthodox political economy are steadily being replaced by a more nuanced, politically oriented analysis. A comparison of the 1970 and 1975 editions of "The Political Economy of Contemporary Monopoly Capitalism," published by the Institute of the World Economy and International Relations, is particularly instructive in this regard and provides a good starting point.

The 1970 edition, though qualifying the role of the economic factor in "imperialist" foreign policy in its discussion of the role of the state in regulating national economies, does place primary emphasis on economics in the explanation of the foreign policy behavior of the capitalist states. The 1975 edition, by contrast, held, in drawing attention to the interdependence of economic and political factors in capitalist foreign policies, that particularly "with the deepening of the general crisis of capitalism, the influence of the [political] superstructure becomes increasingly multifaceted, extending into the broader sphere of economic relations." Centrifugal tendencies among capitalist states, though hardly denied, are accorded a qualitatively different significance from differences between the two major alliance systems, NATO and the Warsaw Treaty Organization. For the change in the correlation of forces in favor of socialism portends "the less probable utilization of such a traditional instrument as war among themselves" (i.e., among the capitalist states).[14] Thus NATO is conceded to have been formed and maintained above all by Soviet political pressure.[15] With the rise of the Soviet-led socialist bloc, international relations, as we have already noted, cease to be a reflection of inter-imperialist contradictions and instead are primarily concerned with the divisions between the two global socio-economic systems. This has a definite influence on the intensity of inter-imperialist contradictions, tending both to eliminate the possibility of war among major capitalist states and to encourage the unification of imperialism according to its class interests.[16] Such coordination of policy may extend to the economic as well as the political sphere of inter-capitalist relations, with respect to both long-term and short-term cooperation.[17] Indeed, the "relative," and at times "exceptional" success of capitalism as an economic system in the postwar period is due precisely to such collaborative measures.[18]

Under political pressure from the Soviet Union, then, the major capitalist states have coordinated their policies and prospered. The necessity of taking Soviet power into account has meant that, although the nature of imperialism has not changed throughout the postwar period, its behavior certainly has. Some Soviet analyses of changes in capitalist behavior are bold enough to suggest that a real change in kind is envisaged. Inozemtsev wrote in 1976 that, though capitalism remains capitalism, "the conditions of its existence, its place and role in history, the mark of its impact on the path of world events – all are changing, and in a radical way."[19] That is, fundamental changes have occurred not only in the way that capitalist states relate to each other, but in their attitudes and policies with respect to the socialist and developing countries as well. According to Fedor Burlatskiy, for example, the contention that just the shift in the correlation of forces in favor of socialism has induced a real change in the behavior of the capitalist states is untenable. He refers to "*a certain modification of the traditional political systems in the economically developed countries of the West.*"[20] An examination of "political factors operating within the framework of the Atlantic Alliance," Burlatskiy holds, would reveal that the domestic structures of those countries "virtually precludes the possibility of aggressive politicians taking decisions to unleash preventive or offensive nuclear war."[21] In effect, though he does not elaborate on the point, Burlatskiy is arguing that the nature of capitalism, in contemporary conditions, *has* changed, an argument that seems implicitly contained in other Soviet analyses of the behavioral modifications in the foreign policies of the capitalist states. This transformation, whether of nature or just behavior, is reflected not only in the revised definition of contradictions among capitalist countries and the greater macro-level unity of these countries, but also in their attitudes toward the class adversary whose very presence has, at the least, objectively assisted the birth of such changes.

Contradictions among capitalist states, though relegated to a second order of concern in relation to the explanation of international political phenomena, and far less intense than they once were, nevertheless persist. This, according to Soviet theorists, is a simple reflection of the law of uneven development among capitalist economies.[22] Having stabilized their politico-strategic relations in face of the challenge posed by the Soviet Union and world socialism, capitalist states have become increasingly preoccupied with the political management of inter-capitalist economic relations, especially after the postwar recovery of Western Europe and Japan. The United States, though still unquestionably occupying the dominant position in the capitalist world, finds it increasingly difficult to realize its will in intra-alliance relations, in particular when the focus of concern shifts from the military–political field, where the United States retains its preponderance, to economic and technical fields, where the outcome of disputes is far more uncertain.[23] These are, to be sure, contradictions within limits. Though Soviet theorists do not employ this kind of language in discussing capitalist states, the general thrust of much analysis seems compatible with the Soviet concept of "non-antagonistic contradictions." Tomashevskiy, for example, urges "the separation [of] the main, long-term contradictions from the secondary, temporary contradictions." Attempts to exploit contradictions between imperialist states should not lose sight of the "'unifying' trends within the imperialist camp, the changed limits today not only of alliance and cooperation, but also of the contradictions and struggle among imperialist states . . ."[24] A basic commonality of interests is thus seen to bind the capitalist countries together.

At times, increased polycentrism within the West only accentuates the superior position of the United States, as, for example, during the "energy crisis."[25] Yet these tensions are persistent enough to attract the attention of various Soviet observers who suspect that they might redound to the benefit of the Soviet Union. It is argued that the uneven pace of economic development among capitalist countries has a spillover effect in the political field, with the United States often acting in isolation from its allies.[26] This potential for serious rift among capitalist states is no mere subjective phenomenon, reflecting, for example, the personalities or policies of particular national leaders. To an important degree it corresponds to the inherent tension between the global interests of the United States and the Eurocentrism of the West Europeans, the latter of which is said to be a stable, long-term tendency.[27] The divergent perspectives which both sides bring to the Soviet Union and the very meaning of detente, reflecting, and complemented by, differing economic interests, suggests that significant degrees of potential difference exist and that they are best encouraged by a policy that reduces the projection of threat from the Soviet side. For it was such a threatening posture, some Soviet analysts are beginning to concede, which led to the forging of inter-imperialist unity in the first place.[28]

Polycentrism, then, affecting Eastern and Western Europe, makes it unlikely, in Soviet minds, that Western Europe could ever fulfill the role of a separate pole of international power.[29] A policy of detente, by reinforcing strains between Western Europe and the United States without prompting West European unity, is hence quite acceptable for the Soviet Union, especially given the apparent conviction of some leading Soviet theorists on international relations that the capitalist states are economically viable for the foreseeable future, have an ultimate common interest in resisting the advance of Soviet influence and power throughout the world, and are constitutionally incapable of launching either preventive or offensive war against the Soviet Union and the socialist camp.[30]

## INTER-SOCIALIST RELATIONS

It is relatively difficult to find Soviet work of an analytical or theoretical, as opposed to a hortatory, character on the subject of relations among socialist states. More than any other area of international relations, this subject goes to the heart both of pressing Soviet security concerns and the ideological legitimacy of the Soviet state. The preemption of much of the discussion by such notions as "international relations of a new type," distinguished by "friendship and cooperation," makes sober analysis a delicate task indeed for Soviet specialists in international relations. The official imprint of the "Brezhnev Doctrine" since 1968 simply magnifies the problem.

Soviet scholars have not, however, been insensitive to the substantive insufficiencies engendered by the constraints of the topic itself. A. Narochnitskiy, Chairman of the Scientific Council on the History of Soviet Foreign Policy and International Relations, noted in 1975 that the theoretical study of international relations among socialist countries was a key problem demanding "further" study by Soviet academics.[31] Other specialists have chafed against the muffling of serious discourse imposed by the concept of "socialist internationalism," which is said to represent the application of the principle of "proletarian internationalism" – which characterizes relations among nations and nationalities in the Soviet Union – to international relations.[32] Yelena Modrzhinskaya, for example, argued in a 1972 discussion of the "national question and the contemporary ideological struggle" that the concept of proletarian internationalism should be understood as a policy prescription and not as a methodological tool of analysis.[33] And indeed, it is possible to discern an approach among Soviet scholars which suggests that inter-socialist relations are not as qualitatively distinct as the official rhetoric maintains. This discussion revolves chiefly around the question of the application of the concepts of "contradiction" and "nation" to relations between socialist countries.

The very idea of "international relations among Communists," as Robert H. McNeal put it, is a fairly new one, stemming only from the establishment of Soviet hegemony in East Central Europe in the wake of the Second World War. There was, of course, the Communist International during the interwar period, and in a sense it "provided a more definite framework for international relations than anything the Communists have had since . . ." But the Comintern dealt exclusively with relations among communist parties, only one of which, the Soviet party, constituted the ruling power of an established state. Its form was parliamentary and thus unsuitable as a model for relations between communist states, itself one probable reason for its dissolution by Stalin in the spring of 1943. The postwar ruling communist parties, despite their claims and intention to conduct a special type of international relations, have failed to develop a satisfactory system of worldwide interparty relations. If this development, or lack thereof, is considered in light of the fact that "no serious interparty quarrel has failed to affect interstate relations" among communist countries, the question must be raised as to the extent that bilateral relations between communist *countries* differ from diplomatic relations between capitalist countries, or between capitalist and socialist countries.[34] Are the sources and nature of tension and conflict between communist countries, as identified in Soviet analyses, sufficiently distinct from those prevailing in the broader international system to warrant the Soviet claim to having founded an "international relations of a new type"?

Soviet analyses of increasing polycentric tendencies in world politics, as qualifiedly optimistic as they are concerning such developments among capitalist countries, are quite categorical when applied to relations among socialist states (the present discussion focuses only on the subsystem of intersocialist relations in East Central Europe). "Polycentrism," it is contended, applies only to the capitalist world.[35] The broader system of international relations is based upon relations between the two contending socio-economic systems, with a polarization of forces around the Soviet Union and the United States. There was considerable Soviet irritation with East European suggestions about diverging trends within the Soviet alliance system, in particular Czech analyses of the late 1960s.[36] Vladimir Gantman wrote in September 1969, after the crushing of the "Prague Spring" by the armies of the Warsaw Pact:

> Some students of international relations in the socialist countries have succumbed to the influence of bourgeois schemes of a "new polycentric world" supposedly standing above the struggle of the two world systems, and have begun to talk about the advantages of a "neutralist," "extra-bloc" policy. They fail to consider the point [he concluded], that this policy has been made possible only by the existence of the world socialist system.[37]

This denial of significiant diversity, even of degree, in inter-socialist relations is reinforced by Soviet analyses claiming that the national factor, for example, does not play a critical role in both the social life of individual states and in international relations, and that hence nationalism is not a determining factor in international politics. "Marxism," as one Soviet reviewer of Hinsley's *Nationalism and the International System* put it, "cannot be reconciled with nationalism."[38] A Soviet version of the "domino theory," which underscores the danger of "the weak link of socialism" being indirectly undermined by imperialism,[39] tends to restrict analytical discussion of the actual dynamics of inter-socialist relations and their main lines of tension. Nevertheless, an examination of the way the subject is treated by Soviet specialists in international relations, especially in discussions among themselves or in material intended for domestic circulation, reveals a considerably more nuanced approach than that revealed in the official rhetoric about "socialist internationalism."

Soviet denials of the national content of inter-socialist relations face the rather self-imposed constraint that these relations are based on the principle and juridical fact of state sovereignty. Although it is held that sovereignty is not inherent in every nation, that national sovereignty should not be confused with state sovereignty, and that both national and state sovereignty find their highest expression only in socialist internationalism, it is nevertheless true that recognition of state sovereignty is the very basis of relations between communist countries.[40] "Respect of state sovereignty," the Soviet legalist V.S. Shevtsov writes, "of all sovereign rights of the socialist state, is assumed as the very content of the principle of socialist internationalism."[41] The difficulties presented for Soviet theorists by the formal existence of state sovereignty as the basis of these international relations "of a new type" are reflected in a tortured presentation on the issue of national self-determination by Shevtsov. "The Party," he writes, "cannot support self-determination when it conflicts with the interests of the revolutionary movement and socialism. However, this does not mean that the right to self-determination is conditional . . ."[42]

In effect, the importance of the national element as a source of tension, or contradiction, between socialist countries, has to be admitted into the discussion. Shevtsov concedes as much in observing that, "Although they have the same vital class interests, they [the socialist countries] do not always have the same national interests. One important cause is the difference in levels of economic and socio-political development and national and historical features."[43] That is, the law of uneven development, so critical to the fostering and maintenance of contradictions in relations among capitalist states, applies to inter-socialist relations as well. Soviet opposition to the idea of "national communism" in no way negates the inevitability of "the natural diversity of [socialism's] concrete forms."[44]

"[R]elations between nationalities" thus "play an important part . . . [i]n relations between the socialist countries as countries whose class interests coincide . . ."[45] Increasing attention has been devoted by Soviet theorists to the role of "national interests," not just in inter-socialist relations but in the international system as a whole. A 1969 "International Meeting" held by the editorial board of the Soviet monthly *International Affairs* on the issue of "the class nature of present-day international relations" devoted itself largely to this topic. Though the issue "was seen from different angles by many participants . . ., a fact which attests to its political urgency . . .," a general consensus seems to have been reached on the importance of national factors in international relations. Gantman, who wrote up the published report of the meeting, concluded that, though "class factors are taken as a basis for analysis . . ., national interests [are] essential elements, in their importance and efficacy, both in the foreign policy of individual powers and international relations in their entirety." No passing, subjective phenomenon, "national interests have an objective content . . ."[46]

Though such national interests are always refracted through the prism of the ruling classes, precise calculation of the correlation of class forces in a given country is extremely difficult, given the dynamism of the class struggle. In effect, then, "*in relations between states there is an interaction of class interests which bears an imprint of nationally specific features. It is impossible to eliminate or ignore class factors and national elements in foreign policy, whatever the type of international relations.*"[47] Treatment of the dynamics of inter-socialist relations, then, must consider "the importance of the question of state–national and international interests, their correlation and the degree to which they mutually condition each other."[48]

The analyst must therefore distinguish the laws of the socialist socio-economic system from those of the socialist world, or international, system. The international relations of socialism are not to be considered as "a specific projection of the socio-economic laws" of socialism, according to Konstantin Zaradov, former editor in chief of the *World Marxist Review.* This "reductionist" approach is no less limited in its application to the study of inter-socialist relations as many Soviet theorists have concluded with respect to international relations as a whole. The alternative, and, it would seem, increasingly "systemic" approach to the subject would examine "the regularities governing the development of socialism as a world system or, in other words, into the objective laws of the international relations of the new type."[49] Such an approach is demanded because the "socialist character of international relations in the sphere of the world system of socialism does not arise automatically together with a socialist social structure in every specific country."[50]

O.T. Bogomolov, director of the Institute of the Economy of the World Socialist System, agreed at the round table discussion presided over by Zaradov that "[n]ot all the common regularities of building socialism . . . operate in the development of socialism as a world system." "The sphere of operation of the laws of socialist social development," he argued, "has expanded to embrace the entire world system. But inasmuch as sovereign states and their ruling Communist and Workers' parties are the main participants in international relations, their operation is definitely specific . . . [I]t is not always easy to spot this. Hence the dissonance in our scientific literature." Georgi Shakhnazarov, at the same conference, urged that attention be paid to the more classical elements of relations between socialist states. In this sense, it is the distinguishing characteristics of the object – "relations among states" – that predetermines the comprehensive nature of "laws and regularities" of the world socialist system. One of the main laws of that system, according to Shakhnazarov, is the necessity for it "to exist in the present stage as a community of socialist national societies . . ."[51]

The widespread but incorrect view that "the laws of socialism both as a social structure and as a world system, are identical," then, ignores the "interaction of the general and the specific laws in the sphere of the world socialist system" and the distinction between which kinds of laws are dominant for such a specific socio-economic and political formation as the world socialist system. According to I.V. Dudinskiy, "The [general] laws of the development of the socialist system are not merging with the laws of particular countries . . ." Instead, these national-specific laws, applicable even in inter-socialist relations, are preserved for an extended period and possess a clearly defined, autonomous significance. The reality of inter-socialist relations among nationally based sovereign states, combined with unequal levels and rates of economic development *and* "the influence of history," seems, in the minds of a number of Soviet analysts, to impose strict limitations on the extent to which inter-socialist relations can be considered qualitatively distinct from the international relations of the past.[52] Inter-socialist relations cannot be subordinated to the dynamics of socialism as a socio-economic system. In spite of the general community of class interests (as with the imperialist states – see preceding section), national divisions based on a sovereign juridical status significantly inform the content of those relations (also as with inter-imperialist relations). The "contradictions" between socialist states, or within the socialist system, that are thereby engendered suggest that relations among socialist states, even in terms of the categories employed by Soviet specialists, should be viewed rather as a particular subsystem of international relations than as a unique system of its own.

Despite the relentless barrage of official, and even academically oriented publications about the historically unique degree and kind of harmony and cooperation among socialist countries, many influential Soviet scholars maintain that "it is wrong, and what is more, misleading to deny the existence of contradictions in socialism." Such denials "divert attention from methods of solving the many complex problems" facing socialism.[53] Just as one must analytically distinguish the laws of socialism as a socio-economic system from the laws of socialism as a system of international relations, so should one separate the broad problems of the contradictions of socialism as a whole (settled by the Soviet Union in the late 1930s) from the contradictions of the world socialist system (which by implication remain to be resolved).[54] These contradictions, which by extension stem primarily from the structure of relations between the sovereign states wherein socialism is being developed, should not, however, be identified with "antagonisms." That is, the very real tensions afflicting inter-socialist relations constitute "nonantagonistic contradictions," assuming the form of "within-system" debates over the choice of means rather than profound disagreements over desired ends. As late as 1975, tensions with the Chinese Communist Party could be described as non-antagonistic though "very sharp contradictions . . ."[55] Such a relatively elastic conception of the "intra-systemic" suggests the broad latitude of tensions and conflict that the "international relations of a new type" has to contend with.

The sources of these contradictions that are adduced by Soviet theorists indicate that they are not considered to be peripheral or temporary in character, and that they are seen as constituting a critical part of inter-socialist relations. To be certain, some factors of a decidedly temporal nature, such as the relative immaturity of political and economic development of part of the socialist community, domestic remnants of capitalism, and "the distortion of Leninist norms and principles" as a consequence of the "cult of personality," i.e., of Stalin's "excesses", have contributed to the difficulties besetting the system of world socialism. The hostility of foreign reaction, which tries to exploit internal forces hostile to socialism, aggravates inter-socialist relations as well. Yet neither the simple passage of time, nor the final elimination of hostile class forces will, in this Soviet view, do away with inter-socialist contradictions. For "not all such contradictions can be attributed to foreign reaction and petit-bourgeois influences."[56] Indeed, the impact of the "subjective factor," which seems to be a euphemism in this case for nationalism, appears fundamental as both source and reflection of "inconsistencies between the direction of [internal] social development and the objective tendencies of the progress of socialism."[57]

F.T. Konstantinov's observation on the contradiction between the "melding," or integration of the socialist states and the simultaneous (consequent?) development and strengthening of their sovereignty and national independence, seems very much to the point here. P.N. Fedoseyev's assertion of "the growing role of the subjective factor in the development of socialist society in generating contradictions" can be viewed as evidence that it is politically oriented nationalism which underlies, as Politburo member Mikhail Suslov declared in 1967, the "permanence" of contradictions in socialism as a system of international relations. These contradictions, though not "antagonisms," are neither to be construed as just "differences." They are objective, real, but not necessary consequences of socialism as a socio-economic system, as R.G. Vartanov noted. Their comprehension, therefore, requires analysis that transcends the political economy of socialism and tackles "the important question of state–national and international interests, their correlation and the extent to which they mutually condition each other." In more "concrete" terms, the sources of inter-socialist contradictions are to be located in (a) differing levels of socio-economic development; (b) differing historical–cultural and political conditions; (c) remnants of the influence of "national hatred"; and (d) differing geographic positions with corresponding implications for material resources and foreign policy. The conjunction of these specific national characteristics, each of which, by itself, is insufficient to explain the distinctive quality of contradictions between sovereign socialist states (after all, each condition also obtains within the Soviet Union, itself a federal republic), explains why the "socialist character of international relations in the sphere of the world system of socialism does not arise automatically together with a socialist social structure in every specific country."[58]

Only by considering the elements of the national structure of relations among socialist states, then, can the phenomenon of inter-socialist relations be fully comprehended. This "system" of relations cannot be understood through simple knowledge of the nature of its socio-economic base, that is, of socialism as a nationally contained socio-economic system shared by a number of states. The reductionist, or classically Leninist approach of inferring the behavior of the whole from the nature of its constituent parts is clearly insufficient, according to a number of Soviet analysts, in the analysis and explanation of relations among socialist states. The very real and lasting contradictions between these states are not reducible to causes properly associated with the domestic functioning of socio-economic systems, where the issue of relations among sovereign entities does not arise. If this line of reasoning is valid, it raises the question of the extent to which Soviet analysts are persuaded by assertions of the distinctive quality of such relations in the international system. At the very least, one can identify a strong tension between the ultimate hope of a complete unity of human society, or in this case of socialist countries (*sblizheniye i sliyaniye*), and an intermediate goal, corresponding to the idea of both international and inter-socialist relations as a "transitional" stage of social relations, but occasionally turning into an ideal in itself, of "postulating nonantagonistic diversity along national lines."[59]

Indeed, one can go back to Stalin's criticism of Karl Kautsky at the sixteenth Party Day in 1930, wherein Stalin dealt with Kautsky's theory "that socialism would lead to the amalgamation of nations."[60] Stalin, to the contrary, maintained that "the differences between peoples and lands would exist for a long, long time even after the realization of the dictatorship of the proletariat on a worldwide scale." More recently the Soviet social scientist *cum* administrator A.M. Rumyantsev observed in Prague in 1964 that:

> the existence of many independent collective owners of the modern means of production in the person of individual socialist countries is a feature and basic condition of international socialist production relations . . . [S]ince there [is] no single public ownership in the economic relations between the socialist countries, there [can] be no single collective owner, despite the fact that the type of ownership [is] the same for every country.

In effect Rumyantsev is conceding the existence of essentially capitalistic relations as the rule among socialist states, each of which is the private property of its respective nation. For even an economically integrated world, as Berki points out, which still consists "of separate nations is, whatever the internal structure of these nations, a capitalist world." Sovereign "nations cannot help but be self-regarding, as long as their position is that of owners of property in a wider community characterized by economic interdependence."[61]

The increasing recognition that is being accorded, by Soviet spokesmen and theorists, to the idea that "national differences are more enduring than class distinctions" therefore reflects Soviet reconciliation to the indefinite horizontal division of the international system into states, even if every country in that system should adopt socialism. Interstate relations in those circumstances would reflect the logic of the national structure of the international system far more closely than the "laws" of socialism as a socio-economic formation common to all. It is precisely this attitude among an increasing number of Soviet analysts of international affairs which leads us to identify a progressively systemic trend in the Soviet evaluation of inter-socialist relations and a consequent Soviet skepticism toward claims of the historical distinctiveness of these "international relations of a new type."

## INTERNATIONAL ORGANIZATION

The relative paucity of Soviet theoretical and analytical work on international organization as an aspect of the system of international relations reflects the measure to which the subject is viewed by Soviet specialists as a peripheral adjunct of the broader currents of world politics. During the early postwar years, of course, the permanent minority for the Soviet view in the United Nations bodies led to Soviet reluctance to countenance any measures that might possibly result in a meaningful measure of independence for such organizations. Universal membership international organizations were accepted to the extent that they served the interests of the Soviet state and corresponded "to the actual relationship of forces that constitute their base."[62] Proceeding from the assumption that the United Nations and related international political organizations were "capitalist institutions," the Soviets conveniently mixed policy preferences and political analysis in reaching the conclusion "that neither the United Nations nor its Charter affects, in any basic fashion, the character of the contemporary international situation or the relations between states."[63] Had not Khrushchev himself observed in 1962 that "the UN, in point of fact, is a branch of the US State Department."[64] The overwhelming political approach of the Soviet Union toward the United Nations, long reflecting a sense of besieged isolation, has excluded either optimism or intellectual receptivity to such ideas as "functionalism" or "welfare internationalism" through international organizations.[65] This Soviet conviction, and preference, that universal membership international organizations are "incapable of affecting the alignment of international power, combined with a sense of isolation and of outright hostility toward any competitor institution which might lay claim to the allegiance of the Soviet people," has meant that the Soviet academic community "has failed to be attracted to international organization as a field for investigation." In fact, as Alvin Rubinstein noted in 1964 in an observation that remains true today, "the study of international organizations remains the stepchild of Soviet scholarship."[66]

Without doubt, the scholar who has done the most to advance the study of international organizations in the Soviet Union in the time since Rubinstein wrote his book in 1964 is Grigory I. Morozov, researcher at the Institute of the World Economy and International Relations. The two editions of his "International Organizations: Some Questions of Theory", appearing in 1969 and 1974, constitute the only integrated theoretical statement on the subject by a Soviet author. Although quite a number of books have been published since 1964 on various aspects of international organization, Morozov is the only

Soviet scholar to engage in a systematic effort at the classification and theoretical elaboration of the subject.[67] To a large extent, though, Morozov's work is simply a sophisticated justification of long held Soviet attitudes on the subject.

To be sure, Soviet analysis has come a long way from the days when the United Nations was considered an arm of the United States State Department. It is now recognized that international organizations "are an important element of international relations," that many of them "actively function in the fields of politics, economics, science, culture, law, and religion."[68] Such organizations can even play "a useful supplementary role" in resolving problems in (though not, one suspects, of) international relations. Even international non-governmental organizations can "exercise an influence on the international climate," for the most important activity of international organizations is associated with the consequences of the "scientific–technical revolution" and the rise of such global problems as nuclear world war, food, the environment, space, energy resources, etc., that is, precisely those areas where humanity, in spite of class and ideological conflicts, has a common stake.[69]

It is clear, however, as Morozov points out, that international relations generally reflect the condition of the broader international system, the primary elements of which are sovereign states. Such organizations belong to a lower order of significance in the international system and so cannot transcend the interstate system. Brezhnev himself had observed, Morozov notes, that the United Nations, for example, is not a "self-sufficient" (*samodovleyushchiy*) organization.[70] Given the analytical subordination of international organizations to the interstate system, the most important question in the study of any international organization concerns "its political nature and character."[71] The dynamics of international organizations can only be understood in relation to changes in the world correlation of forces and the decisive struggle between the world socialist system and the world capitalist system, headed by the Soviet Union and the United States, respectively.[72] Thus, the move toward detente by these two powers in the early 1970s broadened the possible applications of international organization by increasing the scope and stability of relations among the central state powers of the international system and, by extension, of the United Nations itself.[73] The reverse process, whereby great-power relations can be affected by the relatively autonomous workings of international organizations, such as is envisaged in the theories of functionalism and neofunctionalism, is deemed impossible by Soviet theorists. The theoretical elaboration of such ideas is denounced as an effort by reactionary forces to subvert the Soviet Union through the establishment of "world government," based on the elimination of national sovereignty. "A universal form of power," Shakhnazarov contends, "can be established only upon a uniform social foundation, and not simply on any such foundation but [only] on a socialist one . . ."[74] Until such an eventuality occurs, it is the structure of the contemporary international system, based primarily on relations between sovereign states, with inter-governmental organizations as "secondary links," which limits the possibilities for the autonomous growth and activity of such organizations.[75]

The subordination of international organizations to the "correlation of forces in the world," as expressed in the struggle of socialism and capitalism, does, however, provide the occasion for their influence in solving problems of limited scope, especially when the focus of the organization is "intra-systemic." The validity of functionalist theory is conceded when applied, for example, to Western Europe, that is, among like socio-political orders.[76] As for its application among radically opposed orders the theory, which envisages the subordination of politics to the "spillover" effect of mutually beneficial technical cooperation, does not operate. But, as we have seen in the discussion on inter-imperialist contradictions, the very logic of the balance of power, "shifting in favor" of socialism, increases both the efficacy and the need for cooperative intergovernmental efforts within the capitalist camp. So, in spite of the definite effect that processes of international economic integration have had on the activity of international organizations, such processes cannot be abstracted from the broader interstate balance of power and, indeed, are to be primarily viewed as a function of it.[77] As Vladimir Petrovskiy wrote in July 1980, the activities of the United Nations, for example, "are merely the reflection of a definite correlation of forces between states in the world . . ."[78]

Soviet critiques of the American school of "transnational relations," which examines the international influence of non-state bodies, bring this fundamental skepticism toward the autonomous potential of international organizations into sharper focus. The authors of the 1976 critique of "bourgeois" theories of international relations held that "the primitive scheme of political realism, which ignored the interconnection between the internal political situation and the foreign policy of states," was responsible for the rise of the transnational school. The excessive abstraction of the "power-realist" approach engendered an equally abstract response which, in the form of the transnational interpretation, holds that any unit, even a person, can be a subject of international relations. "[T]his approach," the Soviet critics say, "does not take into account the complex character of the system of international relations . . . The entire spectrum of international society," they observe, "is but a component part, a function (*proizvodnami*) of the system of interstate relations . . . It is intergovernmental relations that are the heart of international relations, defining its condition and development."[79] One sympathetic critic of the work of Robert Keohane and Joseph Nye argued that their writings on the influence of transnational factors in world politics is valid to the degree that the authors have chosen to concentrate mainly on capitalist countries and have not attempted to "show that the state is an anachronism."[80] "Inter-systemic" relations between capitalist and socialist countries cannot be subsumed under a transnational heading. Here it is relations of power, mediated by the state, which determine the course of the struggle of the two systems and thereby of world politics.

International organization, then, of both governmental and non-governmental kinds, is to be understood as a distinctively inferior subsystem of international relations in comparison to other subsystems composed of sovereign states of like socio-political orders. The efficacy of universal membership organizations is limited by the contractual nature of that membership, while the worth of more specific, "regional–class" organizations is directly dependent on the logic of the global correlation of forces between capitalism and socialism, as represented by the United States and the Soviet Union. It does not seem implausible to argue that the Soviet conception of international organization excludes such organizations from the international system altogether. Rather than being part *of* this system, international organizations are purely affected *by* the system. The Soviet proclivity for a state-centric model of international relations revolving around the relations of the great powers displays itself once again.

## SUMMARY

This discussion of Soviet analyses of the structure of the international system reveals, above all, a discernible degree of uncertainty and even anxiety by Soviet theorists on the implications of that structure for the international position of the Soviet Union. The basic criterion of evaluation, the "correlation of forces," predisposes Soviet analysts to caution in the estimation of the international status of the Soviet Union. For the "correlation," while according a central place to the military element that has become the Soviet forte, measures an entire series of economic, political, ideological, and even cultural factors which sensitize Soviet observers to their relative weakness in these areas. Many of these non-military, and often "transnational" economic, technical, and political processes, it is often remarked, tend to favor the United States, which is far better placed than the Soviet Union to take advantage of them. In addition, one of the effects of "the changing correlation of forces in favor of socialism" is seen to be the unleashing, in dialectical fashion, of a reaction, a kind of antithesis by the forces of capitalism and led by the United States. Interimperialist contradictions, for example, have assumed a qualitatively different character from the time when the expectation of war between capitalist countries fueled the hopes first of the survival of socialism in one country and then of its victory around the world. Tensions among capitalist countries are to be interpreted within the limits of a broad class unity. The power of socialism, as represented in the first instance by the Soviet Union, has made the common political interests of the capitalist countries explicit to themselves and has thereby reinforced the bipolar structure of the interstate system that is suggested by the global opposition of the two world socio-economic systems of capitalism and socialism.

This bipolar system of interstate political relations, which revolves around the United States and the Soviet Union, is the core of the broader system of international relations. Yet processes at work in the postwar world, notably the economic recoveries of Western Europe and Japan and the emergence of China as a security threat to the Soviet Union, have eroded the relative dominance of the two superpowers and increased the uncertainty of the calculations each has to make in order to advance and defend its international interests. Developments within the Soviet Union's own security zone in Eastern Europe magnify the greater unpredictability which Soviet analysts discern, and fear, in the international system. For it is, properly speaking, a system and thus not within the control of the Soviet Union. The Soviet Union, not to mention the other socialist states, is implicated in this system at various levels and must reconcile the uneasy tension between its complicity in the system and its concomitant desire to remain aloof in order to preserve maximum freedom of choice. It is this broad latitude of freedom, Soviet analysts feel, that has been reduced by the increasingly pluralistic tendencies of interstate politics. The Soviet recognition that even inter-socialist relations cannot be explained in relation to the common socio-economic base of the constituent countries is clear evidence both of Soviet preference for a state-centric, politically oriented model of international relations, focused on the superpowers, and of Soviet unease at the relative, though perceptible erosion of this model before the polycentric economic and political forces of the "post-cold war" world. The disdain with which international organizations are regarded in Soviet analyses of the international system, its treatment, indeed, as a mere appendage and function of great power relations, further testifies to the analytical conviction in and political preference for a "power realist" conception of international relations.

# 7

# The scientific–technical revolution and the changing face of international relations

> The question as to which purposes the fruits of the scientific and technical revolution will be used for has become one of the chief questions in the contemporary socio-political struggle.*

The mid–1970s witnessed a new tack in both Soviet assessments of the objective evolution of international relations and in Soviet declarations about the desired outcome of that evolution. International relations were said to be undergoing a fundamental "restructuring," breaking from the structural and behavioral patterns characterizing world politics from roughly 1945 to 1972, to "new" principles more in accordance with Soviet interests and, indeed, the interests of mankind. The concept of the "general restructuring of international relations," as R. Judson Mitchell notes, "emphasizes growing Soviet power in the world, changes in the relationships between competing systems, and internal structural transformations within those systems." Nevertheless, "the doctrine reflects in many respects a basic continuity in the Soviet approach to world politics."[1] To a large extent the concept is a corollary to the Soviet doctrine of peaceful coexistence which, when established as an operative principle of international relations, functions as the objective precondition for the restructuring of those relations. The very idea of "detente," which in the Soviet lexicon is the process whereby the capitalist world is compelled to accept the principle of peaceful coexistence, is critical for the achievement of the desired restructuring. Detente, which *is* the establishment of peaceful coexistence, as the Soviets define it, as a norm of international conduct, "is to insure that the inevitable collision of capitalist and socialist interests provoked by . . . [international] change . . . does not approach the line beyond which 'non-existence' begins."[2] It comprises the objective conjuncture and subjective integration (for policy

* From the new Program of the Soviet Communist Party, adopted March 1986.

purposes) of the implications of thermonuclear weapons, the changing structure of internal and international economic relations, the evolving character of the international system itself for interstate political relations, and the socio-economic systems which those states represent.

In concrete terms, detente is reflected in the compartmentalization of the various conflictual and collaborative aspects of Soviet relations with the capitalist world, both within each sphere (the relation of various collaborative elements to each other, for example) and between them (the relation of conflictual to collaborative elements). Essentially, the environment in which those relations are to be conducted in such circumstances is to be a discrete one. This does not preclude a mutually reinforcing relationship from setting in among the political, military, economic, and technical aspects of relations between states of different socio-economic systems. Success or progress in any one area, though, is not to be dependent upon progress in the others. Explicit "linkage," then, is excluded. Efforts to advance the cause of socialism worldwide, in terms of or in response to developments of a local, or regional character, are not to conflict with the maintenance of normal and even mutually profitable relations between capitalist and socialist states. Interstate relations of peaceful coexistence themselves reflect and further the progressive development of social forces throughout the world. The loss of American nuclear superiority, and so of the American nuclear "umbrella" in areas of less than vital import for the United States, is seen to inhibit the use of force by them against "progressive" forces worldwide while also protecting the state interest of the Soviet Union in the survival and development of the Soviet homeland.[3] The proliferation of economic contacts across socio-economic systems on the basis of "the international division of labor" (a euphemism for "comparative advantage"), while advancing the cause of socialist construction within socialist countries, increases the incentives and commitment of the capitalist world to the maintenance of peaceable relations with the socialist community. These economic contacts, which reinforce the intercapitalist contradictions discussed in Chapter 6, also help to institutionalize peaceful coexistence. Nurtured over time on a variety of levels – military, political, economic, and cultural – peaceful coexistence can become deeply rooted in the international system. It would then assume a permanent, or "irreversible" character, as Soviet analysts put it. Such an eventuality would constitute the restructuring of international relations of which Soviet specialists on international relations and policy-makers have so often spoken since the mid-1970s. What are the "objective factors" said to be underlying this uncertain, though evolving restructuring of the international political order?

### A NEW FACTOR IN INTERNATIONAL RELATIONS: THE SCIENTIFIC–TECHNICAL REVOLUTION

The Soviet concept of the "scientific–technical revolution" (STR) as applied to international relations seeks to account for the increasing complexity of the subject without challenging some fundamental Leninist tenets about world politics. Having acquired semi-doctrinal status with respect to internal Soviet affairs, the concept, in recognizing the conversion of science into a "direct productive force," facilitates the incorporation of changes in the conduct and structure of international relations without attributing these changes to basic alterations in the nature of "imperialist" or "socialist" states.[4] In fact, the preservation of ideological orthodoxy in the face of behavioral complexity and indeterminacy would seem to have been made easier by the introduction of the concept of the STR. Now all of the truly radical, and unforeseen changes in world politics can be explained, once again, in terms of productive forces, i.e., science and its applied issue, technology. The absence of an official theory of the STR encourages a certain latitude in the discussion of its application to international relations, depending upon the author and the point that he wishes to make, irrespective of the conceptual requirements of the idea itself.

The most dramatic effect of the STR on international relations has been the severing of the necessary bond between war and revolution through the medium of nuclear weapons. The consequences of the military application of the STR have induced "qualitative changes in the formulation of the problem of war and peace in our age." Nuclear war can no longer be a goal for achieving traditional political ends. This applies to both socialism and capitalism.[5] After military relations it is to the sphere of international economic relations that Soviet theorists most often turn in their efforts to delineate the distinctions between "traditional" and the to-be "restructured" international relations and their connection to the STR. By enhancing the benefits, and indeed in a competitive world underlining the necessity, of efficient intensive production, the STR multiplies the advantages of international trade on the basis of, in effect, comparative advantage, both within and among different socio-economic systems.[6] In this way the "socialist" economies, by exploiting the possibilities of increased international trade for the purpose of socialist construction at home, complicate the freedom of political maneuver of the "capitalist" states by creating incentives, on the state-to-state level, for good relations. Increasing economic interpenetration among states thus exerts a concomitantly greater influence on interstate political relations.[7] The tighter connections between economics and politics, science and politics, and technology and politics that is a consequence of the STR has created a new series of economic and political contradictions.[8]

A word of caution should be added at this point, for Soviet discussions on the existence and implications of economic "interdependence" emphatically reject the concept as it has been developed in the West. On the one hand, Soviet analysts assert that, by denying the class essence of international relations, theorists of interdependence serve to justify, wittingly or not, the "hegemonic pretensions" of United States foreign policy.[9] It is feared that the STR, which highlights precisely those aspects of international power in which the Soviet Union is relatively deficient, will induce the United States, which is seen to be in an excellent position to exploit it, to organize new aspects of the international order either against Soviet interests or as if Soviet interests were simply not relevant.[10]

The actual analysis of the international political economy that is offered by Soviet specialists, though, yields an interpretation which is substantially the same as that of the theorists of "interdependence." Instead of referring to "interdependence" based on the principle of comparative economic advantage, Soviet theorists allude to "the international division of labor" as an objective factor of contemporary international relations. (From one point of view this is a rather curious notion, since Marxian thought envisages the eventual abolition of the division of labor with the creation of a species of "humanist-generalists." This is, perhaps, yet another indication of a progressive movement away from utopian-like categories of thought among Soviet theorists.) "This is a question," A.S. Bogdanov writes, "of utilizing objective economic laws, ignorance of which means that one is consciously damaging oneself."[11] The Soviet Union and the socialist states, then, can no longer consider themselves a system unto themselves. They are necessarily implicated in a global system of international economic relations – partly induced and largely impelled by the "active force" of the STR – which is said to be exercising an increasing influence on the policies of all states, capitalist and socialist alike.[12] As one Soviet critic put it, in refuting Sanakoyev and Kapchenko's assertion that the uniqueness of the Soviet Union permitted it to follow different rules from other states, the foreign policy of socialism is a function of the entire interstate system.[13] In short, the STR has significantly reduced the range of choice facing the Soviet Union. It can no longer stand apart from the international economic order, which is recognized to be organized according to hostile class principles, as a fundamentally autarchic (and so autonomous) actor. The real question becomes, how will the Soviet Union engage that order, and what are the political implications therein contained?

The character of the Soviet commitment to the international economic order, which is generally interpreted as a consequence of the logic of the STR, is mainly dependent upon the corresponding Soviet interpretation of the impact of the STR on the capitalist countries who, after all, determine the structure and basic procedures of the international economy. In sum, the STR is seen to have a contradictory effect on the capitalist economies. On the one hand, it affords them the means whereby their basic economic soundness is assured for the foreseeable future. The continuation and acceleration of scientific and technological progress, Inozemtsev wrote in 1971, insures that the capitalist economies, which have already achieved a remarkable degree of prosperity, will not suffer a major setback in the next few decades.[14] In spite of its inherent defects, capitalism can exploit the benefits of the STR to its own considerable advantage.[15] Stabilizing processes at work in the capitalist economies since 1933, such as the increased intervention of the state in the economy,[16] have been reinforced by the STR. "The state-monopoly nature of contemporary capitalism," Y. Borisov wrote in 1969, has consequently "been accentuated in recent years."[17] The conjunction of state regulation of the economy with the STR has engendered a greater concentration of production and capital; the financing of scientific and technological progress; the widespread use of programming and the projection of production (i.e., planning); and the further evolution of economic integration among capitalist countries.

The consequence of these efforts, though they "have neither eliminated nor mitigated a single one of imperialism's main contradictions,"[18] is a certain underlying stability, and even dynamism, to the capitalist political economy. Inozemtsev noted in the late 1970s, in a discussion of the stimulative effect of the STR on capitalist economic growth: "It would be wrong to underestimate the vast opportunities available to modern capitalism." The STR, which may even accelerate in coming decades, is expected to effect progress in the development of computers, biology, chemistry, the oceans, and energy, all of which tend to reinforce the structural stability of the capitalist system in the advanced countries. According to an IMEMO projection of capitalist economic growth for the years 1980–2000, "the capitalist economy will grow at an appreciably lower, but nevertheless substantial, rate than in the 1950s and 1960s." The gross national product of the advanced capitalist countries for that period is expected to increase by 100 to 130 percent while industrial output is expected to grow by approximately 150 percent. Most strikingly, General Secretary Mikhail Gorbachev integrated these perspectives into the analysis of capitalism presented in his Political Report to the twenty-seventh Party Congress in February 1986. Gorbachev declared that "the present stage of the general crisis [of capitalism] does not rule out possible growth of its economy and the mastery of new scientific and technical trends." In fact, according to Gorbachev, capitalism's capacity to assimilate the effects of the scientific–technical revolution permit it "to sustain concrete economic, military, political, and other positions and in some cases even for possible social revenge, the regaining of what had been lost before."[19]

Varga's thesis regarding the relatively long-term stability of capitalism seems, finally, to have been accorded the status of received dogma by contemporary Soviet specialists on international relations, as well as by the political leadership itself. The advent of the concept of the STR, which affects both capitalism and socialism and is interpreted in class-neutral terms, has certainly eased the acceptance of this once controversial idea. Yet the underlying systemic stability of capitalism that is said to have been effected by the STR does not preclude the existence of serious problems for the capitalist economies and societies. Capitalist societies will be increasingly plagued by the social costs of ever-accelerating adjustment to the requirements of the STR. They will also be subject to mounting competition with each other, as each nation attempts to maximize the benefits from the STR and the related prospects of economic liaison with the socialist countries, and shift the burden of adjustment onto each other. These tendencies are further magnified by the STR's influence in reducing the economic gap between Western Europe and Japan, on the one hand, and the

United States on the other: this "levelling" effect tends to intensify competition among them.[20]

These tensions, though hardly of a mortal character, do serve, by heightening inter-imperialist contradictions, to restore to the socialist countries a certain freedom of maneuver they seemed to have lost with the advent of the STR. Faced in the late 1960s with the problem of converting from extensive to intensive production the socialist countries, and above all the Soviet Union, appeared unable to avoid its traditional remove from the international economy. The socially disruptive effects of the STR on the Western economies, by encouraging, within limits, inter-imperialist economic contradictions, afford the socialist countries the opportunity of choosing more freely the kinds of terms on which they will participate in the international economy. The ability of a state-organized foreign trade monopoly to play off not just Western capitalists but entire countries against each other in the search for more favorable terms of trade or less threatening, "turnkey" arrangements,[21] such as the Italian-built Fiat plant in Togliatti, south central Russia, places the Soviet Union in a more favorable negotiating position than it would be in conditions of detailed Western unity, economic as well as political and military.

The impact of the STR on international relations is, then, from a Soviet perspective, differentiated and ambivalent. Curiously, the STR is said to bring into prominence processes which have always lain at the very heart of Marxist–Leninist theory: the politicization of international economic relations and the interrelationship between foreign policy and domestic politics.[22] The opportunities and challenges offered by this fundamental change in the foreign policy processes of contemporary international relations reflect a qualitatively new level of international interdependence. This interdependence is a consequence both of the growing physical interdependence of states stimulated by the STR (and based on the "international division of labor"), and the erosion of the post-1945 political order under the pressure of Soviet power and the changes in the correlation of forces within the capitalist world itself. It is reinforced by the emergence of truly global problems, such as ecological and resources issues, whose effective resolution is said to require collaborative efforts across national and class boundaries.[23]

To the extent that the STR facilitates the consolidation of the capitalist economies, *and* the position of imperialism in the world, its effects are a cause of consternation for Soviet theorists and leaders. In its "theses" for 1979, for example, the Institute of the World Economy and International Relations observed that the STR, while capable of helping the "developing" countries, tended to bind them all the more securely to the international capitalist system.[24] In this regard the STR represents just one more force postponing any remaining Soviet hopes for the global realization of socialism in the near future. On the other hand, some ramifications of the STR, while reinforcing the "de-utopianization" of Soviet thinking on world politics, help to open new prospects for the projection of Soviet influence and the advancement of progressive social change throughout the international order. The STR, as a universal phenomena, is hence capable of being exploited by the socialist countries for the benefit of socialist construction at home.[25] Its military application by the Soviet Union has already resulted in the checking of the strategic power of the United States as an instrument of international counterrevolution. Though it strengthens the processes of concentration, specialization, and cooperation in production between capitalist countries, Soviet observers hold that the sheer pace of change induced by the STR tends to exacerbate social antagonisms within these countries. Through the instabilities it effects in all areas of social life the STR deepens the political, spiritual, and ideological crisis of bourgeois society.[26] (The STR's effects on the socialist societies in these areas are less extensively treated.) It is, consequently, increasingly difficult for the advanced capitalist countries to subordinate their foreign policies to their objective, class-rooted hostility to socialism. A variety of factors – the military power of the Soviet Union (together with its willingness to engage in constructive economic enterprises with the various countries of the capitalist world); the more equal economic relationship and so intensified competition between the three pillars of the capitalist world; and the increasing social demands placed on capitalist states by their citizenry – all combine to complicate, and at times to frustrate, the real potential that "imperialism" possesses to exploit the STR to the detriment of the Soviet Union and world socialism. For the STR raises the real possibility of "internal conflicts and contradictions arising over a great many specific problems" both within and among capitalist countries.[27]

The international–political implications of the STR, then, "call for a more differentiated approach to analyzing international socio-economic-political phenomena . . ."[28] The "dialectical interconnection and interaction between the present-day scientific and technological revolution and world politics"[29] has engendered a number of objective transformations in international relations which sharply distinguish the international relations of the era of the STR from that of the preceding period (i.e., before the 1970s). In increasing measure international relations should be viewed not as a single strategic chessboard but as a system with multiple planes, each of which functions according to its own specific logic and hierarchies. Power in one sphere, for example the military one, does not necessarily translate in such conditions into power in other spheres. It is "increasingly difficult," Kokoshin notes, "to say who depends on whom."[30] Shakhnazarov observes in reference to the correlation of forces that, while for the "long-term" one should evaluate the "general" correlation of forces in the world, the "short-term," policy-relevant future requires the assessment of the correlation of forces in accordance with the specifics of each particular field in question – the economic, the military, or the political.[31] There is an increasingly fragmented quality to international relations, a quality which is all the harder to grasp inasmuch as general systemic influences have accompanied and have even helped to induce this progressive fragmentation of the international environment.

"The STR," Kokoshin writes, is "changing the ideas about international relations which have [been] formed over the years, including the idea of the relative power of the state." By heightening both the costs of conflict through the threat of nuclear annihilation, and the rewards of collaboration through the benefits of economic interdependence, the STR persuades the capitalist world of the need to separate the various spheres of conflict and collaboration from each other, thereby "objectively creating additional conditions for the reorganization of international relations on the principles of peaceful coexistence." The "nature and scale of the utilization of these conditions," Kokoshin concludes, "depend on the progress in specific areas of international political relations."[32] The globalization of international relations in the atomic age, ironically, coincides with, if it does not actually effect, a definite erosion of the "global" character of the Soviet critique of international relations.

# Conclusion

This examination of the Soviet study of international relations largely confirms the working hypothesis that, under the shadow of nuclear weapons, Soviet analyses of world politics have evolved markedly from the model offered by Lenin. The movement, first noted by Zimmerman, toward increasing methodological self-consciousness, has been continued and consolidated in recent years. There is a broad recognition among Soviet foreign policy intellectuals of the need to go beyond traditional Soviet categories of political economy in dealing with international relations. Soviet studies of the subject are increasingly characterized by the great importance attached to (a) politics, which is conceded to be substantially independent of its economic "base"; (b) the state, and even the nation-state, as opposed to classes; and (c) the "system" of international relations.

The original Leninist deduction of international–political behavior from the class character of specific states, projecting, as Liska has noted, "the alleged internal contradictions of capitalism onto the international arena," has been qualified in so many ways that its operational significance for Soviet theorists may be questioned. Certainly the bitter dispute with communist Yugoslavia after 1948, and especially the Sino-Soviet schism, are inexplicable by a theory which ascribes the wellspring of all "antagonistic" contradictions to inter-class struggle. Contemporary Soviet analysts seem to have grasped the implications of this theoretical impasse. They responded to the confrontation with communist China not by denying the class essence of the People's Republic, but by claiming that a gang of renegades had acquired control of the state apparatus and was executing a reactionary, pro-imperialist foreign policy.

The series of challenges posed by the Chinese communists to the

Soviet Union ever since the late 1950s would appear to have moved Soviet analysts to clarify their own thinking about the moving forces in world politics in a number of fundamental ways. In the first place, Chinese insistence in the 1950s that the Soviet Union place its nuclear force at the disposal of Chinese foreign policy – in particular in its dispute with the United States over the offshore islands of Quemoy and Matsu – led the Soviet Union to distinguish sharply between the national interests of the Soviet Union and China and their nominal class solidarity. In support of their position, the Soviet leaders advanced the thesis that the catastrophic consequences of nuclear war nullified any gains to be won by the annihilation of capitalism. Furthermore, responding to Chinese taunts for a more aggressive Soviet global posture, Khrushchev argued that international conditions had changed so much that global war was no longer an inevitability. Over time, as the ideological dispute between the Soviet and Chinese communist parties grew into a political and then military confrontation between the two states, Soviet theorists were led to admit explicitly the possibility of war between communist countries. The Soviet response to the split with China alone, then, brought into question and dealt a decisive blow to such critical Leninist tenets as the predominance of class, as opposed to national factors in explaining international behavior; the inevitability of war in an international environment riven by class schism; and the impossibility of war between communist states. The fact that the schism with China largely parallels the development of international studies in the Soviet Union, and especially the progressive divergence from essential Leninist formulations on world politics, is surely a telling one. For although many of the tendencies we have examined have their roots independent of the Sino-Soviet split, the split has certainly encouraged Soviet theorists to develop the implications of their "heresies" to a far fuller extent than would otherwise have been the case.

Soviet treatment of the dispute with China suggests two further observations as far as international theory is concerned. First, Soviet theorists have conceded the independence of the political sphere from the economic base. Such a conclusion necessarily follows the admission that a socialist state can pursue a reactionary foreign policy. As a relatively autonomous sphere of social activity, politics can now exercise a decisive influence on the life of society. Second, foreign policy now can only be comprehended if factors other than class are brought into the analysis and, indeed, assigned considerable weight.

In the case of China, nationalism, stigmatized as "great-Han chauvinism,"[1] is identified as the moving force behind Chinese foreign policy. In their discussions of inter-socialist relations in Eastern Europe, "national peculiarities" are said to represent an important obstacle to perfect harmony in the "international relations of a new type." To the extent that nationalism is accorded such explanatory significance, knowledge of the socio-economic character of a state is insufficient to grasp its international conduct. Similarly, such knowledge of the ensemble of states does not enable one to understand international political relationships.

These observations on aspects of world politics are also reflected in Soviet discussions of methodology. A number of Soviet theorists are in fundamental agreement on the following points:

international relations are to be understood as essentially interstate relations;

a qualitative distinction prevails between internal and international politics, with the arena of international relations being relatively autonomous *vis-à-vis* the internal structure of states;

the international environment exercises an important, and potentially decisive influence on the domestic affairs of individual states;

consequently, one may speak of international relations as an independent field of study;

the national factor is a critical explanatory element in international relations as long as they are structured according to the principle of state-sovereignty;

international relations constitute an effective system, so that international behavior is to be understood, at least in part, as reflecting the structure of relations among the system's constituent parts;

the international system, taken as a whole, should be distinguished from its subsystems; the system's structure, expressed, for example, in terms of various "polar" configurations of international power, exercises an important influence on the behavior of states;

although contemporary international relations are to be understood as a coherent system of global scale, they are distinguished by a multiplicity of kinds of relations, and hierarchies, among states, encompassing relations between opposing class-national forces;

Although most Soviet analysts do not say so explicitly (E.A. Pozdnyakov is one exception), these points, taken together, bring Soviet theorists face to face with the implications of the systems approach as it has been developed in the West. The systems perspective yields the following key insights, which Soviet theorists, in spite of their reserve, have been led to entertain: outcomes cannot be inferred from the attributes and behavior of the actors; interconnections are present with the result that changes in some parts of the system produce changes in other parts; therefore, the consequences of behavior are often neither expected nor intended by the actors. In this view the Leninist critique is practically discarded, although some of its language and much of its hostility to the non-Soviet world is retained. From this perspective Pozdnyakov's "macrosystemic level of international relations," where socio-economic processes are "ultimately determining," is filtered through the policies, and politics, of states. This is so because, following Varga, it is the political sphere, capable of reflecting general national interests as well as narrow class ones, that defines the historical manifestation of socio-economic laws. The activity of states is to be comprehended in terms of interstate relations, and not *vice versa*. The tendency of the international political order to strive toward equilibrium, through a kind of "dynamic balance," explains the general stability of the international system (understood as a system of sovereign states rather than any particular configuration of them) in spite of the diversity, instability, and mutual hostility of many of its constituent parts.

Soviet analysts reveal a certain amount of anxiety and uncertainty in dealing with the implication of the system's structure for the Soviet Union, Soviet rhetoric about "the changing correlation of forces in favor of socialism" notwithstanding. The basic standard of evaluation, the correlation of forces, would in any event predispose Soviet analysts to prudence. While according a central place to the military factor, a Soviet strongpoint, the "correlation" includes an entire series of economic, scientific–technical, political, ideological, and even cultural factors which sensitize Soviet observers to relative Soviet weaknesses in these other fields. The United States, it is often observed, is better placed to exploit these elements of power than is the Soviet Union. In addition, the changes in the correlation in favor of "socialism," which have reflected strategic–military rather than global socio-economic processes, have generated, in dialectical fashion, a reaction by the advanced capitalist countries. Inter-"imperialist" relations are now to be interpreted within the framework of a broad class unity, a result, ironically, of the might of the Soviet Union. This has, in turn, reinforced the bipolar international political structure, itself a reflection of the bipolar international class structure, though as we have noted, China represents a considerable complicating factor for Soviet analysts here. It is this bipolar political structure, centered on

Soviet–American state-to-state relations, that constitutes the core of post-1945 international relations.

At the same time, pluralistic tendencies are seen to have made themselves felt. Their main significance has been the modification of the absolute preponderance of the United States in the postwar world in the direction of a more qualified one. The Soviet Union, though, is by no means unaffected by these developments, in particular in Eastern Europe, where deeply rooted national "contradictions" persist, and in its relations with China, which is perceived, in a way the United States is not, as a security threat to the Soviet Union. This decided Soviet preference for a state-centric, politically focused model of international relations revolving about the superpowers is also evidenced in Soviet disdain for the role of international organization, which is regarded as a mere appendage and function of great-power relations.

The question remains: how much ground has really been travelled by Soviet students of international relations? Behind the rhetoric and the propagandistic bombast, which all too often substitutes itself for genuine analysis, lie some genuine modifications of the Leninist vision of international relations. Of particular interest is the fact that all of the analyses we have identified are considered to be consistent with Marxist–Leninist ideology. Though apparently a minority viewpoint among contemporary Soviet observers of international affairs, these analyses are available to defenders of the Soviet interest, despite the implicit rebuff to the Leninist critique. "Is it consistent with the world as it is?" and "Is it useful?" seem more pressing questions asked of Soviet theorists than whether it is rigorously consistent with Leninist *dicta* on the subject. Yet the true test of theory, as of all scholarship, was posed by Burlatskiy in the 1965 debate on Soviet political science: does it pose questions whose answers are not known beforehand? On this score, it is instructive to turn to some of the views put forth elsewhere in communist Europe. Though a detailed analysis of East European viewpoints on international theory lies beyond the scope of this book (future research could profitably explore this area), the perspectives of a number of East European theorists serve to sharpen the contours of many of the Soviet views we have been examining.

The most thoroughgoing criticism of Soviet approaches comes from Yugoslav scholars. Too often, Radovan Vukadinovic notes, Soviet treatment of international relations stops at viewing the subject as anything more than the mere extension of general (and thus hard to apply) laws of social development.[2] Approaches which take international relations as the "sum total" of relations of various kinds – economic, political, military, etc. – ignore, in their effort to account for a variety of influences, that which is specific to international, as opposed to domestic-political relations.[3] Milan Sahovic argues that any treatment of international relations must emphasize "the independence of international relations as a specific sphere of the superstructure over socio-economic relations."[4] That is, class differences lose much of their resonance when translated into international relations. We have seen that a number of Soviet theorists have raised similar points in their attempt to broaden the scope of research in this field, though few will explicitly denigrate the class factor the way Sahovic has. "This is one of the main characteristics of contemporary international relations," he goes on. "Putting aside the question of differences in the worth of their goals, all states act in the international arena under the influence of more or less identical factors and perform identical functions."[5] No Soviet author would go as far as this, and indeed, were he to encounter such a viewpoint would doubtless attack it as smacking of "convergence theory" and insufficient "class consciousness." Soviet theorists either cannot, or cannot afford to, challenge prevailing dogma so directly.

The Romanian Marxist theorist Silviu Brucan, whose work has been cited elsewhere in this book, asserts that international relations cannot be understood without according central significance to the national factor. "[I]n society, class struggle is the overriding factor of politics; in the international environment, it is not."[6] For Brucan, Hobbes' "distinction between internal and international politics" constitutes a starting assumption in the analysis of international relations, and of course explicitly contradicts Marx and Lenin, who "did not articulate a well-rounded theory of international relations," on a fundamental point.[7] We "live in a world," Brucan writes, "in which the socialist nations must adapt themselves to the patterns of behavior prevailing in the international system."[8] "Socialist international relations" have not altered "the laws and behavior of the international system."[9] These laws are "objective" in character and exist quite apart from the intentions or qualities of specific states. Instead, "[t]hey lie in the inner dynamics of the international system, and not in Moscow, Peking, Belgrade, or Bucharest. Functioning as a pattern of relations between its basic units – the nation states – the international system is the final upshot of the forces operating both across and within those units according to the structure, capabilities, and power relations prevailing in the system."[10] The study of international relations thus requires what has always been absent in the history of Marxism: "a well-rounded Marxist theory on *nation* and *nationalism*."[11] As long as Soviet analysis contents itself with such pieties as "persistent national peculiarities" and refuses to take nationalism seriously, it must be considered fundamentally flawed.

Jerzy J. Wiatr, former head of the Institute of Marxism–Leninism in Warsaw, takes up many of the themes pursued by the most sophisticated Soviet theorists and either talks about them more candidly or brings out their implications more fully. Wiatr, whose work has been translated into Russian in an edition introduced by Burlatskiy,[12] writes that international relations are in fact interstate relations. "Domestic conditions are only one source for foreign policy formulation and execution: external constraints, perceptions [which are barely touched on by Soviet theorists], the foreign policies of other nations – each of these factors itself carries equal weight in Wiatr's scheme to internal conditions. International relations, therefore, cannot be comprehended on the basis of the external projection of internal contradictions. Marx, Engels, and Lenin, authors of this reductionist approach to the subject, committed a crucial error. And even where true, the Marxist–Leninist hypothesis on international relations is too general to be of much use.[13]

There are four areas where, according to Wiatr, the Marxist view of international relations stands in need of serious modification: (a) in its understanding of the extent to which socio-economic factors are determining – the pursuit of private profit, he argues, is no longer an important explanatory variable of international political relations; (b) in its appreciation of "the lasting features of national life," such as national character; (c) the value of organizational theory in explaining political behavior – political reality often defies *a priori* assumptions of rationality; and (d) attention to ideological and psychological conditions, both in relation to socio-economic conditions and as autonomous forces in international relations.[14] In all of these areas, the traditional Marxist approach is deficient. In particular, it has failed to come to grips with the fact that "there is no inevitable link between domestic socio-economic order and foreign policy orientation."[15] Were observations of this kind to become as candidly stated in the Soviet literature (Wiatr's statements to this effect were not included in the Soviet volume), a clear break with the Leninist ideological inheritance in the analysis of international relations would have been made.

Even so, the Soviet analysis that has been identified in these pages is a far cry from the crude, reductionist critique of Lenin's *Imperialism*. It is much less determinist, more sophisticated in its political analysis, and less inclined to impose preconceived ideological schemes upon the resistant "civil society" of international relations. It is also far less apocalyptic in its expectations than Lenin's critique.

Curiously, contemporary Soviet observers are in many ways poorer theorists than Lenin, who might be considered a model in this respect: clear assumptions, explicit links between variables, and bold predictive sweep characterize his approach. Lenin may have been completely wrong, but that is beside the point. Many contemporary Soviet foreign policy analysts appear to feel constrained by a number of key Leninist assumptions, and as they grasp about for explanations of contemporary world politics, their analyses lose much of their theoretical elegance. What is lost in analytical rigor, though, is often made up by a keener sense of the actual moving forces of international relations.

Does movement away from aspects of Leninism, though, imply convergence toward non-Leninist, or even anti-Leninist conceptions? Certainly not in the normative sense. The contemporary Soviet analysis of international relations retains all of the bitter moral rejection of the international order, regarding it as fundamentally illegitimate. Though condemned to participate in it, Soviet man is not barred from exploring ways of bringing about its demise, so long as this does not threaten the hard won achievements of socialism. Indeed, the core of the Marxist–Leninist paradigm, which continues to present itself as a plausible explanation of world politics, reinforces this intention while continuing to refit the world in its image. Therein lies its great tenacity, its staying power. Yet also, the basic Marxist–Leninist message does retain the ring of truth, at least as much as many Western, especially Anglo-Saxon assumptions, which see peace as normal and progress as an essentially technical, or technological problem. As Brucan observed, "The relevance of Marxism stems from its basic message – that the world in which we live is not one of harmonies of interest, tendencies to stability, and gradual change, but rather [is] dominated by conflicts of interest, tendencies to instability, and recurring breaks in the continuity of development."[16] It is this central theme, the focus on and expectation of conflict and change, that unites the contemporary Soviet analysis of international relations with its Marxist and Leninist heritage. So long as the international "order" generates enough disharmony and conflict to sustain this vision, as the Soviets both expect and prefer, this link between the Leninist past and the Soviet present may be expected to persist.

# Notes

## INTRODUCTION

1 William Zimmerman, *Soviet Perspectives on International Relations, 1956–1967* (Princeton: Princeton University Press, 1971). See also the brief but interesting analysis in Klaus von Beyme, "Das Selbstverstaendnis der Sowjetunion in der Theorie der Internationalen Politik," in von Beyme, *Die Sowjetunion in der Weltpolitik* (Munich: Piper, 1985), pp. 10–21.

2 *Pravda*, April 25, 1984, p. 1. The thesis was reaffirmed in Soviet party leader Mikhail Gorbachev's speech to the twenty-seventh Congress of the Soviet Communist Party. "The present stage of the general crisis [of capitalism – A.L.] does not lead to any absolute stagnation of capitalism and does not rule out possible growth of its economy and the mastery of new scientific and technical trends. It allows for sustaining concrete economic, military, political, and other positions . . ." Text in Foreign Broadcast Information Service. *Daily Report. Soviet Union. Supplement*, 26 February 1986, p. 5 ("Gorbachev CPSU Central Committee Report"). See also *Pravda*, 26 February 1986, p. 3.

3 *Pravda*, 7 March 1986, p. 3, as translated in Foreign Broadcast Information Service, *Daily Report. Soviet Union. Supplement*, 10 March 1986, p. 1.

4 This development has been well documented in the sphere of international analysis by Franklyn Griffiths, "The Sources of American Conduct: Soviet Perspectives and Their Policy Implications," *International Security*, vol. 9, no. 2 (Fall 1984), pp. 3–50. For economic policy, see Moshe Lewin, *Political Undercurrents in Soviet Economic Debates* (Princeton: Princeton University Press, 1974).

5 Arbatov is a Central Committee Member and Director of the Institute for US and Canadian Studies; Inozemtsev was also a member of the Central Committee and Director of the Institute of World Economy and International Relations until his death in early 1982.

6 Zimmerman, *Soviet Perspectives*, pp. 288–9.

7 George Liska, *Russia and World Order* (Baltimore: Johns Hopkins University Press, 1980), p. 141.

8 Donald Zagoria, *The Sino-Soviet Conflict* (New York: Atheneum, 1966), p. 26.

9 Ronald Hill, *Soviet Politics, Political Science, and Reform* (London: Robertson/Shape, 1980), p. 5.

## 1 THE BACKGROUND: MARX, LENIN, STALIN AND THE THEORY OF INTERNATIONAL RELATIONS

1 See Miklos Molnar, *Marx et Engels et la politique international* (Paris: Gallimard, 1975), and V. Kubalkova and A.A. Cruickshank, *Marxism–Leninism and the Theory of International Relations* (London: Routledge and Kegan Paul, 1980), pp. 12–62.
2 Molnar, *Marx et Engels*, p. 335.
3 Kubalkova and Cruickshank, *Marxism–Leninism*, p. 31.
4 Marcel Merle, *Sociologie des relations internationales* (Paris: Dalloz, 1974), pp. 81–2, 84.
5 *Ibid.*, pp. 57–9. See Engels' letter in Karl Marx and Frederick Engels, *On Colonialism* (New York: International Publishers, 1972), pp. 346–7.
6 Merle, *Sociologie*, p. 85.
7 Silviu Brucan, *The Dissolution of Power. A Sociology of International Relations and Politics* (New York: Alfred A. Knopf, 1971), p. 64.
8 Marx and Engels, *On Colonialism*, pp. 36, 41.
9 Marcel Merle, ed., *L'Anticolonialisme europeen de Las Casas a Kark Marx* (Paris: Armand Colin, 1969), p. 40. Though Marx conceded this in principle, as a rule he underestimated the possibility of significant conflict between national interest and private profit, and thus of the possibility of the survival, even prospering, of the former metropoles faced with the loss of their colonies. Soviet theorists would later have to come to grips with this discomfiting development.
10 Marx and Engels, *On Colonialism*, pp. 97–8.
11 Molnar, *Marx et Engels*, p. 171. For von Ranke see Leopold von Ranke, *Die grossen Maechte*, Friedrich Meinecke, ed. (Leipzig: Insel-Verlag, 1916).
12 Molnar, *Marx et Engels*, p. 122.
13 Kubalkova and Cruickshank, *Marxism–Leninism*, p. 41.
14 Nikolai Bukharin, *Imperialism and the World Economy* (New York: Howard Fertig, 1966/1915), p. 17. Bukharin's book received an appreciative introduction by Lenin. See *ibid.*, pp. 13–14.
15 Contained in V.I. Lenin, *Imperialism and Imperialist War (1914–1917). Selected Works*, vol. 5 (New York: International Publishers, no date), p. 6.
16 *Ibid.*, p. 23. To recognize, as Lenin did, that monopolies were the exception until that time (1897–1900), raises the question of explaining the great wave of colonialist imperialism begun about 1875 and largely spent by the late 1890s. To thereby recognize that "colonial policy and imperialism existed before the contemporary phase of capitalism, and even before capitalism, is to admit at the same time that it is a consequence of the very nature of man and not of such a political order or such an economic system." Jacques Freymond, *Lenine et l'Imperialisme* (Lausanne: Payot, 1951), p. 131.
17 Lenin, *Imperialism*, pp. 74–7, 81.
18 *Ibid.*, pp. 90, 109.

19 "The United States of Europe Slogan," in *ibid.*, p. 140.
20 V.I. Lenine, "Le Socialisme et la Guerre," in Philippe Braillard, *Theories des relations internationales* (Paris: Presses Universitaires de France, 1977), p. 109.
21 Cited in Brucan, *Dissolution of Power*, p. 11.
22 "A Few Theses," in Lenin, *Imperialism*, p. 156.
23 "Soviet Economic Development and World Revolution," in Robert C. Tucker, ed., *Lenin Anthology* (New York: Norton, 1975), pp. 635–6.
24 "Inside the CPSU Central Committee," interview by Mervyn Matthews with A. Pravdin, *Survey*, Autumn 1974, p. 97.
25 See, e.g., Georgi Kh. Shakhnazarov, "Politika skvoz′ prizmu nauki" (Politics Through the Prism of Science) *Kommunist*, no. 17 (1976), where the author undertakes a discussion of "creative Leninism." Shakhnazarov is deputy chief of the Central Committee Department for liaison with foreign communist parties and head of the Soviet Political Sciences Association.
26 Frederick C. Barghoorn, *The Soviet Image of the United States: A Study in Distortion* (New York: Harcourt, Brace and Co., 1950), p. 16 and Kubalkova and Cruikshank, *Marxism–Leninism*, p. 124. Jacques Freymond also emphasizes the continuity of Soviet thinking on international politics under Lenin and Stalin, noting Stalin's continuation of Lenin's arguments on imperialism at the Seventeenth and Eighteenth Soviet Party Congresses, and Stalin's Election Speech of 9 Feb. 1946, in which Stalin foresaw the inevitability of another world war, between capitalism and socialism, in the not so distant future. Freymond, *Lenine*, pp. 63–74.
27 Kubalkova and Cruickshank, *Marxism–Leninism*, p. 124.
28 *Ibid.*, p. 143.
29 In summarizing the effects of the theory of socialism-in-one-country upon the Soviet doctrinal goal of a world state, Elliot Goodman noted that, although the theory "did not negate the goal of a world state, it implie(d) a thoroughly pragmatic approach toward this goal . . ." Elliot R. Goodman, *The Soviet Design for a World State* (New York: Columbia University Press, 1960), p. 163.
30 See Stalin's *Economic Problems of Socialism in the USSR* (Moscow: Foreign Languages Publishing House, 1952).
31 The Soviet editors of a collection of Varga's works wrote in 1974 that Varga "leads the struggle in the name of the creative spirit of Marxism–Leninism." Nikolay Inozemtsev, late director of the Institute of World Economy and International Relations, wrote in 1970 that Varga's demonstration of the role of the state in the capitalist economy refutes the "erroneous notion of the early 1950s [i.e., Stalin's thesis] on the superficiality of such a phenomenon." "Predisloviye" (Introduction), Ye. S. Varga, *Izbrannye proizvedeniya: kapitalizm posle vtoroy mirovoy voyny* (Selected Works: Capitalism After the Second World War) (Moscow: Nauka, 1974); Inozemtsev, "Tvorcheskoye naslediye Ye. S. Varga" (The Creative Heritage of Ye.S. Varga), *Mirovaya Ekonomika i Mezhdunarodnye Otnosheniya*, no. 1 (January 1970), pp. 123–4.
32 Varga makes these points repeatedly, and in direct fashion, in *Izmeneniya v*

*ekonomike kapitalizma v itoge vtoroy mirovoy voyny* (Changes in the Economy of Capitalism as a Result of the Second World War) (Moscow: Politicheskaya Literatura, 1946). The book received a printing of 25,000, rather substantial for an academically oriented work. The tantalizing question is why such an unorthodox thesis was given such official sanction. Perhaps in the early postwar atmosphere, with its unprecedented opportunities and challenges, no firm decisions had yet been taken on these points. See Werner G. Hahn, *Postwar Soviet Politics. The Fall of Zhdanov and the Defeat of Moderation 1946–1953* (Ithaca: Cornell University Press, 1982).

33 Varga, *Izmeneniya*, pp. 9–13, 18–32, 51, 252–305 and *passim*.

34 This explicitly contradicted Stalin's view that war was among the most important objective conditions for revolution. See Historicus, "Stalin on Revolution," *Foreign Affairs*, vol. 27, no. 2 (January 1949), esp. p. 191.

35 Varga, *Izmeneniya*, p. 318.

36 *Ibid.*, p. 319.

37 Ye.S. Varga, *Kapitalizm dvadtsatogo veka* (Twentieth-Century Capitalism) (Moscow: Gosudarstvennoye Izdatel'stvo Politicheskoy Literatury, 1961). The book was issued in 50,000 copies.

38 *Ibid.*, p. 91.

39 *Ibid.*, pp. 144, 147.

40 See Ye.S. Varga, *Ocherki po problemam politekonomiki kapitalizma* (Essays on Problems of the Political-Economy of Capitalism) (Moscow: Politicheskaya Literatura, 1965).

41 See A.A. Arzumanyan, *Novyy etap obshchego krizisa kapitalizma* (The New Stage in the General Crisis of Capitalism) (Moscow: Znaniye, 1961); Arzumanyan, *Krizis mirovogo kapitalizma na sovremennom etape* (The Crisis of World Capitalism in the Contemporary Period) (Moscow: Izdatel'stvo Akademiya Nauk SSSR, 1962); and Arzumanyan, *Bor'ba dvukh sistem i mirovoye razvitiye* (The Struggle of the Two Systems and World Development) (Moscow: Nauka, 1964).

42 Jerry F. Hough, "The Evolution in the Soviet World View," *World Politics*, vol. 32, no. 4 (July 1980), p. 129.

43 Inozemtsev, "Tvorcheskoye naslediye," p. 127 (see note 31).

44 Zimmerman, *Soviet Perspectives*.

## 2 THE DEVELOPMENT OF SOVIET POLITICAL STUDIES

1 Ye.S. Varga, *Ocherki po problemam politekonomiki kapitalizma*, p. 3. The term "concrete" in this context has become a code word among Soviet academics for greater intellectual latitude in their research.

2 *Ibid.*, p. 4.

3 *Ibid.*, pp. 5–8.

4 *Ibid.*, p. 9.

5 *Ibid.*, pp. 9–10. Varga then argues that Lenin, unlike Stalin, held a correct view of dialectical materialism.

6 *Ibid.*, pp. 11–13, 15.

7 *Ibid.*, pp. 25, 29–30. Emphasis mine.

8 *Ibid.*, p. 30.

9 Yu.A. Krasin, "Nekotorye voprosy metodologii politicheskogo myshleniya" (Some Problems of the Methodology of Political Thinking) in Sovetskaya Assosiatsiya Politicheskikh Nauk, *Mezhdunarodnye otnosheniya, politika, lichnost'* (International Relations, Politics, and Personality) (Moscow: Nauka, 1976), p. 39.

10 *Ibid.*, p. 43.

11 *Ibid.*, pp. 44–5, 47, 50.

12 Cited in Krasin, "Nekotorye voprosy," p. 51, footnote 2. Aleksandr Bovin is a senior commentator for *Izvestiya*, the newspaper of the Soviet government. Bovin's book is entitled *Lenin o politike i politicheskoy deystviy* (Lenin on Politics and Political Activity) (Moscow: Znaniye, 1971). The citation is found on p. 35.

13 Fedor Burlatskiy, *Lenin. Gosudarstvo. Politika.* (Lenin. The State. Politics) (Moscow: Nauka, 1970), pp. 50–1. See the extended analysis in Fedor Burlatskiy and A.A. Galkin, *Sovremennyi Leviafan. Ocherki politicheskoy sotsiologii kapitalizma* (The Contemporary Leviathan. Perspectives on the Political Sociology of Capitalism) (Moscow: Mysl', 1985).

14 Vladimir Tumanov, "Political Mechanism of the Power of Monopoly Capital," in Soviet Political Sciences Association, *Time, Space and Politics* (Moscow: Social Sciences Today, 1977), p. 135.

15 Fedor Burlatskiy, "Improved Tools, Research Urged for Political Science," *Current Digest of the Soviet Press*, vol. 31, no. 18 (1979), p. 15.

16 "Present-Day Problems of the Theory of Materialist Dialectics," in *Marxist Dialectics Today* (Moscow: Social Sciences Today, 1979), p. 7. First printed as an editorial in *Voprosy Filosofii*, no. 6 (June 1972).

17 A futile attempt was made in the 1960s to establish a formal discipline of political science in the Soviet Union. See L.G. Churchward, "Towards a Soviet Political Science," *Australian Journal of Political Science*, April 1966, pp. 66–75. For an intensive examination of the work of Soviet "political scientists" and their analyses of power and the political process, see Neil Malcolm, *Soviet Political Scientists and American Politics* (New York: St Martin's Press, 1984).

18 Oded Eran, *Soviet Area Studies and Foreign Policy* (Santa Barbara: General Electric-Temp Center for Advanced Studies, September 1974), p. 12.

19 International Communications Agency, Office of Research, *Soviet Research Institutes Project. Volume 1: The Policy Sciences* (Washington, DC: Kennan Institute for Advanced Russian Study, 19 February 1981), p. 372. See also Oded Eran, *The "Mezhdunarodniki": an Assessment of Professional Expertise in the Making of Soviet Foreign Policy* (Tel Aviv: Turtledove, 1979).

## 3 APPROACHES TO INTERNATIONAL RELATIONS

1 Zimmerman, *Soviet Perspectives*, p. 275 and *passim*; Dmitri Tomashevskiy, *On the Peaceful Coexistence of States* (Moscow: Novosti, 1973), p. 34.

2 Kubalkova and Cruickshank, *Marxism–Leninism*, p. 167.

3 Brucan, *Dissolution of Power*, pp. 48–9.

4 Eran, *The "Mezhdunarodniki"*, *passim*; Zimmerman, *Soviet Perspectives*, p. 275.

5 Cited in Brucan, *Dissolution of Power*, pp. 65–6.
6 Zimmerman, *Soviet Perspectives*, p. 276.
7 *Ibid.*, pp. 275–9, 282.
8 Brucan, *Dissolution of Power*, p. 65.
9 Braillard, *Theories des relations internationales*, p. 74.
10 *Ibid.*, p. 77.
11 Brucan, *Dissolution of Power*, p. 49.
12 Janusz Stefanowicz, *Stary nowy swiat. Ciaglosc i zmiana w stosunkach miedzynarodowych* (The Old New World. Continuity and Change in International Relations) (Warsaw: Instytut Wydawniczny PAX, 1978). In a bibliography of 114 works dealing with contemporary international relations, only three Soviet works are cited; 70 Western works are listed, 39 Polish books and articles, one Hungarian and one East German publication (pp. 168–72). In an article treating the "Marxist" paradigm of international relations, Braillard does not mention a single Soviet author. "The International System," *Futures*, December 1980, pp. 460, 467.
13 R.N. Berki, "On Marxian Thought and the Problem of International Relations," *World Politics*, vol. 24, no. 1 (October 1971), p. 80.
14 *Ibid.*, pp. 81–2, 86.
15 Cited in Zimmerman, *Soviet Perspectives*, p. 33.
16 L.F. Ilichov, *Ciencias sociales y communismo* (Montevideo: Ediciones Pueblos Unidos, 1965), pp. 86–7. Translation from the Russian.
17 Institut Ekonomiki Mirovoy Sistemy Sotsializma, *Sotsializm i mezhdunarodnye othnosheniya* (Socialism and International Relations) (Moscow: Nauka, 1975), p. 4. For complaints about a deficiency of primary sources, in this case memoirs, see V. Petrovskiy, "Vid s 35 etazha" (The View From the 35th Floor), *Oktyabr'*, no. 3 (1977), pp. 223–4.
18 G.A. Trofimenko, *S.Sh.A.: Politika, voyna, ideologiya* (The USA: Politics, War, Ideology) (Moscow: Mysl', 1976), pp. 4–5, 10–11. Trofimenko is careful to speak of a "metasystem" of concepts (p. 4), perhaps in order to avoid the complications associated with tackling the base-superstructure issue head-on.
19 A.A. Gromyko, I.N. Zemskov, V.M. Khvostov, eds. *Diplomaticheskiy slovar'* (Dictionary of Diplomacy). (Moscow: Politicheskaya Literatura, 1973), pp. 459–60.
20 *Ibid.*, p. 459.
21 *Ibid.*
22 See Marx's *Zur Kritik der politischen Okonomie* (Berlin: Dietz, 1976) and the discussion in Kubalkova and Cruickshank, *Marxism–Leninism*, pp. 301–19.
23 *Pravda*, 27 May 1985, p. 2.
24 Gromyko *et al.*, *Diplomaticheskiy slovar'*, pp. 459–60.
25 "Vsesoyuznyy simpozium sotsiologov" (All-Union Symposium of Sociologists), *Voprosy Filosofii*, no. 10 (October 1966), pp. 164–5. Soviet use of the term "sociology" is often broader than its American application. Soviet theorists frequently refer to the study of international relations as "the sociology of international relations."
26 See, e.g., G. Gerasimov, "Teoriya igr i mezhdunarodnye otnosheniya" (Game Theory and International Relations), *Mirovaya Ekonomika i Mezh-*

*dunarodyne Otnosheniya*, no. 7 (July 1966), pp. 101–8; G.L. Smolyan, "Printsipi issledovaniya konflikta" (Principles of Conflict Research), *Voprosy Filosofii*, no. 8 (August 1968), pp. 35–41; D. Yermolenko, "Sociology and Problems of International Conflict," *International Affairs*, no. 8 (August 1968), pp. 47–53.

27 D. Yermolenko, "Sociology and International Relations: Some Results of the 6th World Sociology Congress," *International Affairs*, no. 1 (January 1967), pp. 14–19.

28 V. Israelyan, "The Leninist Science of International Relations and Foreign Policy Reality," *International Affairs*, no. 6 (June 1967), pp. 46–52

29 Yermolenko, "Sociology and International Relations," pp. 14–15, 18.

30 Shalva Sanakoyev, "The Leninist Methodology of Studying International Relations," *International Affairs*, no. 9 (September 1969), p. 53. Those opposed to a more discriminating Soviet study of the subject tend to avoid the area of international relations as such and confine themselves to the area of "foreign policy". Sanakoyev, with his colleague N.I. Kapchenko, is a prime example of this tendency.

31 Israelyan, "The Leninist Science of International Relations," pp. 46–7.

32 *Ibid.*, p. 48.

33 N.N. Inozemtsev, V.A. Martynov, and S.M. Nikitin, eds, *Leninskaya teoriya imperializma i sovremennost′* (The Leninist Theory of Imperialism and the Contemporary World) (Moscow: Izdatel′stvo Mysl′, 1977), pp. 4, 6.

34 Yermolenko, "Sociology and Problems of International Conflict," pp. 47, 53.

35 "Problemy teorii mezhdunarodnykh otnosheniy" (Problems of the Theory of International Relations), *Mirovaya Ekonomika i Mezhdunarodnye Otnosheniya*, nos 9 and 11 (September and November 1969), pp. 88–106, 78–98, respectively.

36 *Ibid.*, no. 9 (1969), p. 88.

37 *Ibid.*, no. 11 (1969), p. 97.

38 *Ibid.*, p. 98.

39 Inozemtsev, "Aktual′nye zadachi teoreticheskogo issledovaniya" (Current Problems of Theoretical Research), *ibid.*, pp. 88–9.

40 Dmitri Tomashevskiy, *Leninskiye idei i sovremennye mezhdunarodnye otnosheniya* (Moscow: Politizdat, 1971), pp. 3, 8, 20. Translated in 1974 as *Lenin's Ideas and International Relations* (Moscow: Progress).

41 For a Soviet account of such frustrations, including Chicherin's differences with Lenin and Stalin, see E.M. Chossudovsky, *Chicherin and the Evolution of Soviet Foreign Policy and Diplomacy* (Geneva: Graduate Institute of International Studies, 1973), pp. 11–12, 17.

42 See Shalva Sanakoyev, "Foreign Policy of Socialism: Unity of Theory and Practice," in Soviet Peace Committee, *Leninist Principles of Peaceful Coexistence Today* (Moscow: Social Sciences Today, 1973), p. 104. For a citation supporting Tomashevskiy's position, see I. Linden, "Lenin's Ideas on Foreign Politics," *International Affairs*, no. 2 (February 1979), p. 131.

43 *Ibid.*, pp. 89–91.

44 Vladimir Gantman, "Mesto v sisteme obshchestvennykh nauk" (Its Place in the System of the Social Sciences), *ibid.*, pp. 97–8.

45 See his comment in *International Affairs*, no. 9 (September 1969), p. 42.
46 *Ibid.*
47 Stanley Hoffman, "An American Social Science: International Relations," *Daedalus* no. 3 (Summer 1977), p. 52.
48 R. Judson Mitchell notes that, "In specific studies of the correlation of forces, Soviet analysts appear to give practical priority to the concept of the state, whose validity they are unwilling to admit." R. Judson Mitchell, *Ideology of a Superpower: Contemporary Soviet Doctrine on International Relations* (Stanford: Hoover Institution Press, 1982), p. 11.
49 "Ob "ekt nauchnogo issledovaniya," *Mirovaya Ekonomika i Mezhdunarodnye Otnosheniya*, no. 9 (September 1969), pp. 99–102.
50 V. Pechenev, "Istoricheskiy materializm i mezhdunarodnye otnosheniya" (Historical Materialism and International Relations), *ibid*, pp. 103–5.
51 Nikonov "Mezhdunarodnye otnosheniya i politika gosudarstv," *ibid.*, no. 11 (November 1969), pp. 78–9.
52 Ye. Modrzhinskaya, "Lenin's Theory and Modern International Relations," *International Affairs*, no. 1 (January 1970), pp. 56–7. See also N.I. Lebedev, "The System of World Relations," *International Affairs*, no. 12 (December 1976), p. 81.
53 Modrzhinskaya, "Lenin's Theory," pp. 56–7.
54 *Ibid.*, pp. 58–9. See also Modrzhinskaya, "O teoreticheskikh problemakh sovremennykh mezhdunarodnykh otnosheniy" (On Theoretical Problems of Contemporary International Relations) in Modrzhinskaya, *Sotsiologicheskiye problemy mezhdunarodnykh otnosheniy* (Sociological Problems of International Relations) (Moscow: Nauka, 1970), p. 7.
55 Modrzhinskaya, "Lenin's Theory," p. 59. Decision-making theory and communications theory are cited as being particular fruitful. On the utility of the decision-making approach, see I.G. Tyulin, "Nekotorye voprosy teorii mezhdunarodnykh otnosheniy v rabotakh P. Renuvena i Zh.-B.Dyurozelya" (Some Problems of the Theory of International Relations in the Works of P. Renouvin and J.B. Duroselle), in *Problemy istorii mezhdunarodnykh otnosheniy i ideologicheskaya bor'ba* (Problems of the History of International Relations and the Ideological Struggle) (Moscow: Nauka, 1976), pp. 259–73.
56 Modrzhinskaya, "Lenin's Theory," pp. 60, 62.
57 V. Gantman, *Social Sciences*, vol. 10, no. 4 (1979), pp. 263–64; Gantman, "Sotsiologicheskiy analiz mezhdunarodnykh otnosheniy" (Sociological Anlaysis of International Relations), *Mirovaya Ekonomika i Mezhdunarodnye Otnosheniya*, no. 10 (October 1978), p. 130.
58 D.V. Yermolenko, "Sotsiologicheskiye issledovaniya i mezhdunarodnye otnosheniya" (Sociological Research and International Relations), *Voprosy Filosofii*, no. 1 (January 1971), p. 75.
59 A.K. Andreyev, "Sociological Study of International Affairs," *USA*, no. 4 (April 1978), p. 82 (JPRS translation). Andreyev, reviewing Yermolenko's book, also supports his implication of the lack of interdisciplinary studies in the USSR (p. 83). See also V.V. Denisov's review in *Voprosy Filosofii*, no. 8 (August 1978), p. 180.
60 Yermolenko, "Sotsiologicheskiye issledovaniya," p. 77.

61 Yermolenko, "Sotsiologicheskiye issledovaniya," pp. 75–82. For an account which accords an important role to public opinion in Western political systems, see Georgi Arbatov, *The War of Ideas in Contemporary International Relations* (Moscow: Progress, 1973).

62 Tomashevskiy, *Lenin's Ideas*, p. 35. Yermolenko, reviewing Tomashevskiy's book, approvingly cited his emphasis on international political relations. (*Social Sciences*, vol. 4, no. 3 (1973), p. 181). On the relations of objective to subjective factors, Tomashevskiy notes that, e.g., neither geography nor demography, though indeed exercising a significant influence on international relations, can explain "by themselves the essence of international relations, the shifts and leaps which occur in this area, and the deep-going differences in the part played by individual countries in the world." Tomashevskiy, *Lenin's Ideas*, p. 30.

63 N.I. Lebedev, "The System of World Relations," p. 81.

64 See also Georgi Shakhazarov, "Vliyaniye razryadki mezhdunarodnoy napryazhennosti na polozheniye lichnosti" (The Influence of the Relaxation of International Tension on Personality) in Sovetskaya Assosiatsiya Politicheskikh (Gosudarstvovedcheskikh) Nauk, *Mezhdunarodnye otnosheniya, politika, lichnost* (International Relations, Politics, and Personality) (Moscow: Nauka, 1976), p. 7. Also Dmitri Tomashevskiy, "The Influence of Soviet Foreign Policy on International Relations," *International Affairs*, no. 10 (October 1969), p. 40 and Ye. Primakov, "Opening Speech," *International Affairs*, no. 3 (March 1981), p. 4.

65 Dmitri Yermolenko, *Sotsiologiya i problemy mezhdunarodnykh otnosheniy* (Sociology and Problems of International Relations) (Moscow: Mezhdunarodnye Otnosheniya, 1977), p. 10.

66 D.V. Yermolenko, "Sotsiologicheskiye issledovaniya i mezhdunarodnye otnosheniya," *Voprosy Filosofii*, no. 1 (January 1971), pp. 78–9, 81.

67 Yermolenko, *Sotsiologiya i problemy*, pp. 11–12, 14, 16; see also Brucan, *Dissolution of Power*, pp. 54–5.

68 Yermolenko, *Sotsiologiya i problemy*, pp. 15, 17–18, 31.

69 *Ibid.*, pp. 36–8.

70 *Ibid.*, pp. 38, 47–50. Yermolenko approvingly cited Raymond Aron, Seymour Martin Lipset (!), Morton Kaplan, Karl Deutsch, Hans Morgenthau, Ole Holsti, Quincy Wright, and Herman Kahn as "bourgeois" scholars viewing international relations as an integral whole.

71 *Ibid.*, pp. 61–2. Yermolenko cites Morton Kaplan and Charles McClelland in systems method, Lincoln Bloomfield in modelling and simulation, Karl Deutsch in "the mathematics of decisions", Lewis Richardson in the mathematics of the arms race, Raymond Tanter in the mathematics of prognoses, and Harold Lasswell in social psychology (pp. 54–5).

72 *Ibid.*, pp. 63, 214.

73 See Vitaliy Zhurkin, *Kommunist*, no. 2 (1978), p. 125, for a very positive review of Yermolenko's 1977 book.

74 Gantman, "Sotsiologicheskiy analiz," p. 129.

75 *Ibid.*, p. 130.

76 Shakhnazarov, "Politika skvoz' prizmu nauki," pp. 105–6. Emphasis mine. Note that Shakhnazarov distinguishes "international relations" from

"the struggle of different political forces in the world arena." International relations as such, then, signify for Shaknazarov a relatively narrow aspect of class-political relations and forces in the world – political relations among states.

77 Burlatskiy and Galkin, *Sotsiologiya. Pokitika. Mezhdunarodnye otnosheniya* (Moscow: Mezhdunarodnye Otnosheniya, 1974), pp. 235, 237–8.

78 Shakhnazarov, "Politika skvoz′ prizmu nauki," pp. 108–9; Burlatskiy and Galkin, *Sotsiologiya. Politika.*, pp. 238–9. They cite Gabriel Almond, Hans Morgenthau, Morton Kaplan, Bernard Brodie, Alistair Buchan, Henry Kissinger, Paul Nitze, Robert Osgood, Thomas Schelling, Herman Kahn, Raymond Aron, "*et al.*", as having performed "serious practical calculations." They mention Quincy Wright as a particularly distinguished representative of a systems approach.

79 Burlatskiy and Galkin, *Sotsiologiya. Politika*, p. 241.

80 Shakhnazarov, "Politika skvoz′ prizmu nauki," p. 111.

81 Burlatskiy and Galkin write that nuclear weapons "put everyone's existence into question." *Sotsiologiya. Politika*, p. 251; also Shakhnazarov, "Politika skvoz′ prizmu nauki," p. 112.

82 Burlatskiy and Galkin, *Sotsiologiya. Politika*, pp. 247–8, 253–5, 259, 318.

83 Tomashevskiy, *Lenin's Ideas*, pp. 44–6.

84 *Ibid.*, p. 56. See also R. Kosolapov, "Obshchestvennaya priroda mezhdunarodnykh otnosheniy" (The Social Nature of International Relations), *Mirovaya Ekonomika i Mezhdunarodnye Otnosheniya*, no. 7 (July 1979), pp. 64–7; IEMSS, *Sotsializm i mezhdunarodnye otnosheniya*, pp. 6–12.

85 Burlatskiy and Galkin, *Sotsiologiya. Politika*, pp. 276–9.

86 Georgi Shakhnazarov, "Effective Factors of International Relations," *International Affairs*, no. 2 (February 1977), p. 79.

87 *Ibid.*

88 *Ibid.*, pp. 86, 80. Shakhnazarov cites the Medieval Church as the one exception.

89 *Ibid.*, pp. 80–3.

90 *Ibid.*, pp. 81–5, 86. Shakhnazarov writes that "dogmatic Western theorists" are not above "being ironical about the 'dogmatism' of Marxists" (p. 85).

91 Mitchell, *Ideology of a Superpower*, pp. 31, 33–4. See also W.(V) I. Gantman, "Typen internationaler Konflikte," in Daniel Frei, ed., *Theorien der internationalen Beziehungen* (Munich: R. Piper and Co., Verlag, 1973), pp. 87, 90–1; N.I. Lebedev, N.P. Drameva, V.B. Knyazhinskiy, eds., *Mezhdunarodnye otnosheniya i bor′ba idey* (International Relations and the Struggle of Ideas) (Moscow: Izdatel′stvo Politicheskoy Literatury, 1981), p. 235 for an indication of a Soviet sense of weakness in the international ideological sphere.

92 For an example of recent Soviet concern over the place of Poland in the Soviet alliance system, see Diplomaticheskaya Akademiya M.I.D. SSSR, *Vneshnyaya politika i diplomatiya sotsialisticheskikh stran* (Foreign Policy and the Diplomacy of the Socialist Countries) (Moscow: Mezhdunarodnye Otnosheniya, 1981), p. 93.

93 S.I. Appatov, *S.Sh.A. i Yevropa: obshchiye problemy amerikanskoy kontinental′noy*

*politiki* (The USA and Europe: General Problems of American Foreign Policy on the Continent) (Moscow: Mysl', 1979), p. 202.

94 N.M. Nikol'skiy and A.V. Grishin, *Nauchno–tekhnicheskiy progress i mezhdunarodnye otnosheniya* (Scientific–technical Progress and International Relations) (Moscow: Mezhdunarodnye Otnosheniya, 1978), p. 55. See also Andrey A. Kokoshin, *S.Sh.A.: za fasadom global'noy politiki* (The USA: Behind the Facade of Global Policy) (Moscow: Izdatel'stvo Politicheskoy Literatury, 1981), pp. 24–5.

95 Kenneth Waltz, *Theory of International Politics* (Reading, Mass.: Addison-Wesley, 1979).

96 D.M. Proyektor, *Puty Yevropy* (European Paths) (Moscow: Znaniye, 1978), pp. 126–7; N.I. Doronina, *Mezhdunarodnyy konflikt. O burzhuaznykh teoriyakh konflikta. Kriticheskiy analiz metodologii issledovaniy* (International Conflict. On Bourgeois Theories of Conflict. A Critical Analysis of Methodologies of Research) (Moscow: Mezhdunarodnye Otnosheniya, 1981), p. 10; I.G. Usachev, *Mezhdunarodnaya razryadka i S.Sh.A.* (International Detente and the USA) (Moscow: Mysl', 1980), pp. 138, 150, 167, 120.

97 Proyektor, *Puty Yevropy*, pp. 128, 159; V.I. Antyukhina-Moskovchenko, A.A. Zlobin, and M.A. Khrustalev, *Osnovy teorii mezhdunarodnykh otnosheniy. Uchebnoye posobiye* (Foundations of the Theory of International Relations. A Teaching Aid) (Moscow: Moskovskiy Gosudarstvennyy Institut Mezhdunarodnykh Otnosheniy, 1980), p. 79.

98 Inozemtsev, *et al.*, eds., *Leninskaya teoriya imperializma*, p. 212.

99 O.B. Borisov, Yu. V. Dubinin, I.N. Zemskov *et al.*, eds., *Sovremennaya diplomatiya burzhuaznykh gosudarstv* (The Contemporary Diplomacy of Bourgeois States) (Moscow: Izdatel'stvo Politcheskoy Literatury, 1981), p. 49. Dubinin is now the Soviet Ambassador to the United States.

100 Inozemtsev *et al.*, eds., *Leninskaya teoriya imperializma*, p. 215.

101 Lebedev *et al.*, eds., *Mezhdunarodnye otnosheniya*, p. 8. This observation was made by V.V. Zagladin, candidate member of the Central Committee since 1976, deputy head of the International Department of the Central Committee since 1967.

102 Cited in Brucan, *Dissolution of Power*, p. 138. For similar formulations see N.I. Lebedev, *SSSR v mirovoy politike* (The USSR in World Politics) (Moscow: Mezhdunarodnye Otnosheniya, 1980), p. 163, and A.V. Sergiyev, *Nauka i vneshnyaya politika* (Science and Foreign Policy) (Moscow: Znaniye, 1967), pp. 38, 39.

103 Cited in Brucan, *Dissolution of Power*, p. 10.

104 *Pravda*, 7 March 1986, as translated in FBIS, *Daily Report. Soviet Union. Supplement*, 10 March 1986, p. 5.

105 See V.V. Zagladin, "Predisloviye" (Introduction), in Lebedev *et al.*, *Mezhdunarodnye otnosheniya*, pp. 3–18.

106 Kokoshin, *S.Sh.A.*, pp. 20, 24–5; Appatov, *S.Sh.A. i Yevropa*, p. 5; Proyektor, *Puty Yevropy*, pp. 109–10, 112.

107 Samuel P. Huntington, *Political Order in Changing Societies* (New Haven: Yale University Press, 1968), p. 377. See Lenin's "What is to Be Done," in Tucker, ed., *Lenin Anthology*, pp. 12–114.

108 Antyukhina-Moskovchenko *et al.*, *Osnovy teorii*, p. 71.

109 Sergiyev, *Nauka i vneshnyaya politika*, p. 25; Nikol'skiy and Grishin, *Nauchno–tekhnicheskiy progress*, pp. 283, 40; Kokoshin, *S.Sh.A.*, p. 42; Inozemtsev *et al.*, *Leninskaya teoriya imperializma*, p. 331; *Problemy voyennoy razryadki* (Problems of Military Detente) (Moscow: Mezhdunarodnye Otnosheniya, 1981), p. 53.

110 V.I. Zamkovoy, *Kritika burzhuaznykh teoriy neizh bezhnosti novoy mirovoy voyny* (A Critique of Bourgeois Theories of the Inevitability of a New World War) (Moscow: Mysl', 1965), p. 39; Grishin and Nikol'skiy, *Nauchno–tekhnicheskiy progress*, pp. 42, 263, 56, 47; *Sistemnyy analiz*, p. 35; Mikhail Gorbachev, *Political Report of the CPSU Central Committee to the 27th Party Congress* (Moscow: Novosti, 1986), p. 78.

111 Lenin, *Imperialism*, p. 12; Inozemtsev *et al.*, *Leninskaya teoriya imperializma*, p. 435; Lebedev *et al.*, *Mezhdunarodnye otnosheniya*, p. 137; FBIS, *Daily Report. Soviet Union. Supplement*, 10 March 1986, p. 5; *Pravda*, 25 April 1984, p. 1.

112 Lenin said in March 1918 that the withering-away-of-the-state would have to wait until "at least two more Party Congresses" had passed. Bukharin declared in the following year that "two or three generations" might have to go by before the coming of communism. In that same year (1919) Lenin was now speaking of 30–40 years, while Stalin, in 1925, mentioned "an entire historical era" as the period necessary for the transition to communism (Goodman, *Soviet Design for a World State*, pp. 448–9).

113 Goodman, *Ibid.*, p. 449.

114 Inozemtsev, *et al.*, editors, *Leninskaya teoriya imperializma*, pp. 15, 19.

115 Kokoshin, *S.Sh.A.*, pp. 4, 5, 6–7, 8, 74–5, 338–9, 341. Usachev, *Mezhdunarodnaya razryadka*, p. 4.

116 Adam B. Ulam, *The New Face of Soviet Totalitarianism* (New York: Praeger, 1963), pp. 72, 82.

117 Mitchell, *Ideology of a Superpower*, p. 57.

118 See, e.g., one Soviet statement to the effect that an interdisciplinary approach, while enriching the study of international relations, makes the subject more diffuse (*Sovremennye burzhuaznye teorii mezhdunarodnykh otnosheniy*, p. 66).

119 Stanley Hoffman, ed., *Contemporary Theory in International Relations* (Englewood Cliffs, NJ: Prentice Hall. 1960), v; Hoffman, "An American Social Science: International Relations," *Daedalus* no. 3 (Summer 1977), p. 52.

## 4 SYSTEMS APPROACH AND INTERNATIONAL RELATIONS

1 Oran Young, *A Systemic Approach to International Politics* (Princeton: Center of International Studies, Research Monograph no. 3, June 10, 1968), pp. 3–5; Philippe Braillard, *Philosophie et relations internationales* (Geneva: Institut Universitaire de Hautes Etudes Internationales, 1974), p. 33.

2 In addition to the authors cited in Chapter Three, footnote 59, see V.F. Petrovskiy, *Vneshnyaya politika S.Sh.A.: teoreticheskiy arsenal* (US Foreign Policy: the Theoretical Arsenal) (Moscow: Znaniye, 1973), p. 21.

3 Michael Smith, "Patterns of World Order," *Harvard International Review*, vol. 3, no. 6 (March 1981), pp. 6, 23.
4 Young, *Systemic Approach*, p. 6.
5 Robert Jervis, "Systems Theory and Diplomatic History," in Paul Gordon Lauren, ed., *Diplomacy. New Approaches in History, Theory, and Policy* (New York: The Free Press, 1979), p. 212.
6 V.F. Petrovskiy, *Amerikanskaya vneshne-politicheskaya mysl'* (American Foreign Policy Thought) (Moscow: Mezhdunarodnye Otnosheniya, 1976), p. 116 and A.L. Narochnitskiy, "O teorii i metodologii istorii mezhdunarodnykh otnosheniy" (On the Theory and Methodology of the History of International Relations), *Voprosy Istorii*, no. 2 (1976), pp. 70–1.
7 V.F. Petrovskiy, "V poiskakh teoreticheskoy osnovy" (In Search of a Theoretical Foundation), in *S.Sh.A. Vneshnepoliticheskiy mekhanizm* (USA: Foreign-Policy Mechanism) (Moscow: Nauka, 1972), p. 313. He considers this approach "too static". See also Modrzhinskaya, "O teoreticheskikh problemakh," p. 9; Lebedev, "System of World Relations," p. 82.
8 See esp. E.A. Pozdnyakov, *Sistemnyy podkhod i mezhdunarodnye otnosheniya* (The Systems Approach and International Relations) (Moscow: Nauka, 1976), which will be examined later.
9 Vladimir Gantman, ed., *Sovremennye burzhuazyne teorii mezhdunarodnykh otnosheniy* (Contemporary Bourgeois Theories of International Relations) (Moscow: Nauka, 1976), Introduction.
10 Petrovskiy, *Amerikanskaya vneshne-politicheskaya mysl'*, pp. 110–17.
11 Lebedev, "System of World Relations," pp. 81–2.
12 A. Filyev, "Mathematical Constructions and Realities," *International Affairs*, no. 11 (November 1974), p. 137.
13 A.A. Kokoshin, "Looking for a New Theory of World Politics," *USA*, no. 7 (July 1975), pp. 77–80 (JPRS translation), and Kokoshin, "A Lame Attempt to Generalize," *International Affairs*, no. 11 (November 1974), p. 137.
14 See Kokoshin's own *O burzhuaznykh prognozakh razvitiya mezhdunarodnykh otnosheniy* (On Bourgeois Forecasts of the Development of International Relations) (Moscow: Mezhdunarodnye Otnosheniya, 1978), pp. 45–148, for a discussion of kinds of polar alignments in international relations (to be treated in Chapter Five).
15 Gantman, ed., *Sovremennye burzhuaznye teorii*, pp. 216–31. See also A. Sergiyev, "Bourgeois Pseudo-Science About the Future," *International Affairs*, no. 2 (February 1972), p. 82, wherein the author considers Kaplan's macropolitical approach to be "of great interest." For a Western critique of Kaplan's approach, see John J. Weltman, *Systems Theory in International Relations: A Study in Metaphoric Hypertrophy* (Lexington, Mass: Lexington Books, 1973), Chapter Two.
16 Gantman, ed., *Sovremennye burzhuaznye teorii*, pp. 238–42. For relevant parts of McClelland's work, see Charles McClelland, *Theory and the International System* (New York: Macmillan, 1966), pp. 46, 114–134.
17 Gantman, ed., *Sovremennye burzhuaznye teorii*, pp. 233–7.
18 Nikol'skiy and Grishin, *Sistemnyy analiz*, p. 8.
19 *Sovremennye burzhuazyne teorii*, pp. 237–38. For Hoffmann's own views, see his

*Gulliver's Troubles. On the Setting of American Foreign Policy* (New York: McGraw Hill, 1968), xvi, pp. 10–26, 356–63.

20 Vladimir Gantman, "The Class Nature of Present Day International Relations," *International Affairs*, no. 9 (September 1969), p. 56.

21 Vladimir Gantman, "Mesto v sisteme obshchestvennykh nauk" ([Its] Place in the System of Social Sciences), *Mirovaya Ekonomika i Mezhdunarodnye Otnosheniya*, no. 9 (September 1969), pp. 97–99.

22 N. Inozemtsev, "Aktual'nye zadachi teoreticheskogo issledovaniya" (Current Tasks of Theoretical Research), *ibid.*, pp. 89–90.

23 S.A. Petrovskiy and L.A. Petrovskaya, "'Modernizm' protiv 'traditsionalizma' v burzhuaznykh issledovaniyakh mezhdunarodnykh otnosheniy" ("Modernism" versus "Traditionalism" in Bourgeois Research on International Relations), *Voprosy Istorii*, no. 2 (February 1974), p. 49.

24 V.A. Pechenev, "Sotsializm v sisteme mezhdunarodnykh otnosheniy," *Voprosy Filosofii*, no. 9 (September 1971), p. 15. Emphasis mine.

25 V. Gavrilov, "Sovetskiy Soyuz i sistema mezhdunarodnykh otnosheniy" (The Soviet Union and the System of International Relations), *Mirovaya Ekonomika i Mezhdunarodnye Otnosheniya*, no. 12 (December 1972), p. 19.

26 *Ibid.*, p. 19.

27 *Ibid.*, p. 26.

28 Kokoshin, *O burzhuaznykh prognozakh*, p. 39.

29 *Ibid.*, p. 32.

30 Pozdnyakov, *Sistemnyy podkhod*, pp. 3–5. This theme is echoed elsewhere in a discussion of modelling in international relations research. Though there are real limits to the application of formal models, politics, it is claimed, can be comprehended in the same way that the natural world is. Nikol'skiy and Grishin, *Sistemnyy analiz*, pp. 125, 127.

31 Pozdnyakov, *Sistemnyy podkhod*, pp. 6–7, 9.

32 *Ibid.*, p. 3. See also the striking phrase "great socialist power" used, with emphasis, and repeated twice, in a lead editorial, "Svetoch i nadezhda chelovechestva" (The Torch and Hope of Mankind), *Mirovaya Ekonomika i Mezhdunarodnye Otnosheniya*, no. 2 (February 1973), pp. 7, 11.

33 Pozdnyakov, *Sistemnyy podkhod*, pp. 9–10; Burlatskiy and Galkin, *Sotsiologiya. Politika*, p. 261, and Burlatskiy and Galkin, *Sovremennyi leviafan. Ocherki politicheskoy sotsiologii kapitalizma* (The Contemporary Leviathan. Perspectives on the Political Sociology of Capitalism) (Moscow: Mysl', 1985), pp. 304–20.

34 Pozdnyakov, *Sistemnyy podkhod*, p. 11. See also the following reviews of Pozdnyakov's book: P. Cherkasov, *Novyy Mir*, no. 9 (September 1977), p. 285, notes that Pozdnyakov has "introduced many concepts for the first time into the Soviet literature"; V. Dadayan, in *Mirovaya Ekonomika i Mezhdunarodnye Otnosheniya*, no. 5 (May 1978), p. 154, writes that "this is the first time a systems approach has been employed in the Soviet Union"; L. Leon'tev, in *Voprosy Istorii*, no. 3, 1978, termed Pozdnyakov's work "pioneering." Georgi Shakhnazarov, deputy head of the Central Committee Department in charge of relations with ruling foreign communist parties, had a polite dispute with Pozdnyakov on the relative political character of international relations. See his *Gryadushchiy miroporyadok* (The Coming World Order) (Moscow: Izdatel'stvo Politicheskoy Literatury,

1981), p. 17. Elsewhere, though, Shakhnazarov concurs with a central tenet of Pozdnyakov's systemic approach, i.e., that impulses from the international system can have an impact on, and even pose obstacles to, the internal laws of socialist development. *Ibid.*, pp. 8, 135.

35 Pozdnyakov, *Sistemnyy podkhod*, p. 12. See also Kubalkova and Cruickshank, *Marxism–Leninism*, p. 304; Fedor Burlatskiy, "Political System and Political Consciousness," in SPSA, *Time, Space and Politics* (Moscow: Social Sciences Today, 1977), p. 53; Zuyeva, *Vopreki dukhu vremeni*, pp. 38–9, 43; Shakhnazarov, *Gryadushshiy miroporyadok*, pp. 17, 21–2; Burlatskiy and Galkin, *Sovremennyi leviafan*, pp. 291–304.

36 Pozdnyakov, *Sistemnyy podkhod*, pp. 7, 13, 156, 15.

37 Fedor Burlatskiy, "O sistemnom podkhode k issledovaniyu vneshney politiki" (On the Systems Approach to Researching Foreign Policy), in SAP(G)N, *Mezhdunarodnye otnosheniya, politika, i lichnost'* (International Relations, Politics, and Personality), (Moscow: Nauka, 1976), p. 28; Burlatskiy and Galkin, *Sovremennyi leviafan*, pp. 317, 333.

38 Pozdnyakov, *Sistemnyy podkhod*, pp. 17–21. Pozdnyakov cites the following American systems theorists: Morton Kaplan, Charles McClelland, Richard Rosecrance, George Modelski, Stanley Hoffmann, Karl Deutsch, J. David Singer, Kenneth Waltz, Oran Young *et al.*, as influential "bourgeois" proponents of systemic approaches to international relations.

39 *Ibid.*, pp. 33–7. As one 1980 Soviet text on international theory has argued, it is not possible for a single state to stand outside of the global system of international relations, which is dominated by "the structure of interstate relations." Antyukhina-Moskovchenko *et al.*, *Osnovy teorii*, pp. 61, 63.

40 Pozdnyakov, *Sistemnyy podkhod*, p. 39.

41 See Chapter Four, above, for other Soviet analyses stressing the independence of international relations in relation to internal socio-economic processes, and Kosolapov, "Obshchestvennaya priroda mezhdunarodnykh otnosheniy," p. 75, and Lebedev, "System of World Relations," p. 79.

42 Pozdnyakov, *Sistemnyy podkhod*, pp. 39, 42, 45–8.

43 *Mirovaya Ekonomika i Mezhdunarodnye Otnosheniya*, *Novyy Mir*, and *Voprosy Istorii*. See footnote 33 above.

44 Kosolapov, "Obschestvennaya priroda mezhdunarodnykh otnosheniy," p. 71; Zuyeva, *Vopreki dukhu vremeni*, pp. 36, 56.

45 Burlatskiy and Galkin, *Sotsiologiya. Politika.* pp. 262–4.

46 *Ibid.*, pp. 265, 272, 276; Antyukhina-Moskovchenko, *et al.*, *Osnovy teorii*, pp. 62–7.

47 Boris Bolshakov and Larisa Vdovichenko, "Problems of Modelling International Relations (in Terms of Physically Measurable Magnitudes)," in SPSA, *Political Theory and Political Practice* (Moscow: Social Sciences Today, 1979), p. 160; Lebedev, "System of World Relations," pp. 79, 80; Georgi Shakhnazarov, "Political Science and New Factors in International Relations," in SPSA, *Time, Space and Politics* (Moscow: Social Sciences Today, 1979), p. 23.

48 Andrei Melvil, "The Leninist Concept of Foreign Policy in Our Time," *Social Sciences* vol. 12, no. 2 (1981), pp. 158, 161.

49 Burlatskiy, "O sistemnom podkhode k issledovaniyu vneshney politiki," p.

24; Bolshakov and Vdovichenko, "Problems of Modelling International Relations," p. 168; Nikol′skiy and Grishin, *Sistemnyy analiz*, p. 128.

50 Kosolapov, "Obshchestvennaya priroda mezhdunarodnykh otnosheniy," p. 65.

51 Grishin and Nikol′skiy, *Sistemnyy analiz*, pp. 133–6, 138; Doronina, *Mezhdunarodnyy konflikt*, pp. 50–2.

52 Liska, *Russia and World Order*, p. 141.

## 5 THE STRUCTURE OF THE INTERNATIONAL SYSTEM: THE SYSTEMS LEVEL

1 G.A. Trofimenko, "Skvoz′ prizmu balansa sil′: kritika sovetologicheskikh kontseptsii sovetsko-amerikanskikh otnosheniy" (Through the Prism of the "Balance of Power": A Critique of Sovietological Conceptions of Soviet–American Relations), in Institut Vseobshchey Istorii, *Problemy istorii mezhdunarodnykh otnosheniy i ideologicheskaya bor′ba* (Problems of the History of International Relations and the Ideological Struggle) (Moscow: Nauka, 1976), p. 67.

2 See William B. Husband, "Soviet Perceptions of US 'Positions of Strength' Diplomacy in the 1970s," *World Politics* vol. 31, no. 4 (July 1979), p. 499; Tomashevskiy, *Lenin's Ideas*, p. 65.

3 Vernon V. Aspaturian, "Soviet Global Power and the Correlation of Forces," *Problems of Communism*, May–June 1980, p. 11.

4 Bolshakov and Vdovichenko, "Problems of Modelling International Relations," pp. 161–5. For an intensive examination of Soviet treatment of the question of power in political relations, see Neil Malcolm, *Soviet Political Scientists and American Politics* (New York: St Martin's Press, 1984), pp. 46–116.

5 Burlatskiy and Galkin, *Sotsiologiya. Politika.*, pp. 284–5; Burlatskiy, "O sistemnom podkhode," p. 28; Trofimenko, "Skvoz′ prizmu 'balansa sil′,'" p. 68; V.F. Petrovskiy, "The Power Factor in US Strategy," *USA*, no. 5 (May 1979), p. 20 (JPRS translation).

6 *Ibid.*, p. 30.

7 Pozdnyakov, *Sistemnyy podkhod*, p. 98.

8 Tomashevskiy, *Lenin's Ideas*, p. 65.

9 *Ibid.*, pp. 64–5; Zuyeva, *Vopreki dukhu vremeni*, p. 48; Antyukhina-Moskovchenko *et al.*, *Osnovy teorii*, p. 81.

10 Shalva Sanakoyev, "The World Today: Problem of the Correlation of Forces," *International Affairs*, no. 11 (November 1974), pp. 40–50.

11 A. Sergiyev, "Lenin on the Correlation of Forces as a Factor of International Relations," *International Affairs*, no. 5 (May 1975), pp. 101–2.

12 Pozdnyakov, *Sistemnyy podkhod*, pp. 98, 101.

13 IMEMO, *Politicheskaya ekonomika sovremennogo monopolisticheskogo kapitalizma* (The Political Economy of Contemporary Monopoly Capitalism) (Moscow: Mysl′, 1970), pp. 185–7.

14 Tomashevskiy, *Lenin's Ideas*, pp. 70–83.

15 Though conceded to remain a socialist country, China is no longer recognized as having a socialist foreign policy. Internal constitution no longer implies external conduct.

16 Tomashevskiy, *Lenin's Ideas*, p. 101.
17 Pozdnyakov, *Sistemnyy podkhod*, pp. 39–40.
18 Zimmerman, *Soviet Perspectives*, pp. 158–210; Mitchell, *Ideology of a Superpower*, p. 20.
19 Nils H. Wessell, "Soviet Views of Multipolarity and the Emerging Balance of Power," *Orbis*, vol. 22, no. 4 (Winter 1979), p. 788.
20 V.V. Zhurkin and E.M. Primakov, eds., *Mezhdunarodnye konflikty* (International Conflicts) (Moscow: Mezhdunarodnye Otnosheniya, 1972), p. 21.
21 Petrovskiy, *Vneshnyaya politika S.Sh.A.: teoreticheskiy arsenal*, p. 28.
22 Wessell, "Soviet Views on Multipolarity," p. 795. According to Wessell, a dissident Soviet historian (Medvedev?) produced a confidential analysis in 1970 suggesting that chronically optimistic claims about the world "correlation of forces" "might not represent the collective perception" of the Soviet leadership. The report is said to have noted that the USSR's world position had weakened in the 1960s due to (a) Soviet economic and political stagnation, leading to a rejection by European and Third World leftists of the USSR as a model of development, and even more so as a central political authority; (b) Soviet lag in converting to intensive production; (c) the disintegration of the socialist camp (China, Yugoslavia, Romania, Albania). See also Mitchell, *Ideology of a Superpower*, pp. 56, 20; Zimmerman, *Soviet Perspectives*, pp. 158–210; and Chapter Three, above.
23 Kokoshin, *O burzhuaznykh prognozakh razvitiya mezhdunarodnykh otnosheniy*, p. 45.
24 *Ibid*., p. 47.
25 *Ibid*., pp. 47–8.
26 *Ibid*., p. 49.
27 A.A. Kokoshin, "Amerikanskiye predstavleniya o mezhdunarodnykh otnosheniyakh 80–90-kh godov" (American Writings on the International Relations of the 1980s–1990s), in G.A. Trofimenko, ed., *Sovremennye vneshnepoliticheskiye kontseptsii S.Sh.A.* (Contemporary Foreign Policy Conceptions of the USA) (Moscow: Nauka, 1979), p. 13.
28 Kokoshin, *O burzhuaznykh prognozakh razvitiya mezhdunarodnykh otnosheniy*, p. 49.
29 Wessell, "Soviet Views on Multipolarity," pp. 809.
30 A. Bulkin, "Behind the Maoist 'Three-Worlds' Theory," in *Post-Mao Maoism*. Part 1 (Moscow: Social Sciences Today, 1980), p. 73. Compare with F.V. Konstantinov, *et al*., *Kritika teoreticheskikh kontseptsiy Mao Tsze-duna* (A Critique of the Theoretical Conceptions of Mao Tse-tung) (Moscow: Mysl', 1970), pp. 100–16; Petrovskiy, *Amerikanskaya vneshnepoliticheskaya mysl'*, pp. 211–12; P.T. Podlesnyy, "American Foreign Policy Conceptions in the 1970s," *USA*, no. 4 (April 1974), p. 116 (JPRS translation).
31 Wessell, "Soviet Views on Multipolarity," p. 811.
32 Zhurkin and Primakov, *Mezhdunarodnye konflikty*, pp. 15, 36.
33 Bulkin, "Behind the Maoist 'Three-Worlds' Theory," pp. 103–4, 79.
34 Vladimir Krivtsov, "The Maoists' Foreign Policy Strategy," in *Post-Mao Maoism*. Part 1, p. 122.
35 Bulkin, "Behind the Maoist 'Three-Worlds' Theory," p. 75.

36 Aspaturian, "Soviet Global Power," p. 4; Kokoshin, *O burzhuaznykh prognozakh*, p. 50.
37 Georgi Shakhnazarov, "'Great Powers' Approach to International Politics," *World Marxist Review*, vol. 15, no. 5 (May 1972), p. 117.
38 Kokoshin, "Amerikanskiye predstavleniya," p. 46.
39 Petrovskiy, *Amerikanskaya vneshnepoliticheskaya mysl'*, pp. 193–4; Gantman, ed., *Sovremennye burzhuaznye teorii*, p. 437.
40 IMEMO, *Politicheskaya ekonomika kapitalizma*, p. 190.
41 "Velikiye derzhavy" (The Great Powers), *Diplomaticheskiy slovar'*, vol. 1, p. 283; Gavrilov, "Sovetskiy Soyuz i sistema mezhdunarodnykh otnosheniy," p. 23; V.F. Petrovskiy, "Rol' i mesto sovetsko–amerikanskikh otnosheniy v sovremennom mire" (The Role and Place of Soviet–American Relations in the Contemporary World), *Voprosy Istorii*, no. 10 (October 1978), pp. 79, 82, 91.
42 Pozdnyakov, *Sistemnyy podkhod*, pp. 58, 39–40; Burlatskiy, "O sistemnom podkhode," p. 28.
43 Georgi Arbatov, "Soviet–American Relations Today," in Soviet Peace Committee, *Leninist Principles of Peaceful Coexistence in the Contemporary World* (Moscow: Social Sciences Today, 1973), p. 13.
44 Georgi Arbatov, "Soviet–American Relations in the 1970s," *USA*, no. 5 (May 1974), p. 11 (JPRS translation).
45 Shakhnazarov, "'Great Powers' Approach to International Politics," pp. 113–14.
46 *Ibid.*, pp. 114, 117–18.
47 Lebedev, "System of World Relations," p. 85.
48 Anatoly Gromyko and A. Kokoshin, "US Foreign Policy Strategy for the 1970s," *International Affairs*, no. 10 (October 1973), p. 73. The authors write: "Compared with other capitalist countries, the USA has been and will be distinguished by its ability to continue pursuing a global policy . . ." The first-cited author is son of the former Soviet Foreign Minister. See also Seweryn Bialer and Joan Afferica, "Reagan and Russia," *Foreign Affairs* vol. 61, no. 2 (Winter 1982/3), p. 256.

## 6 CRITICAL SUBSYSTEMS

1 A.S. Bogdan, *Tsentry sopernichestva: osobennosti mezh-imperialisticheskikh protivorechiy na sovremennom etape* (Centers of Competition: Characteristics of Inter-Imperialist Contradictions in the Contemporary Period) (Moscow: Mezhdunarodnye Otnosheniya, 1978), p. 4.
2 I.M. Levin, "K kharakteristike sovremennykh protivorechiy mezhdu kapitalisticheskimi stranami" (On the Character of Contemporary Contradictions Between Capitalist Countries), in A.A. Arzumanyan, ed., *Problemy sovremennogo kapitalizma; sbornik statey. K 80-letiyu akademika Ye. S. Varga* (Problems of Contemporary Capitalism; a Collection of Articles in Honor of the Eightieth Birthday of Academician Ye. S. Varga) (Moscow: Akademiya Nauk, 1959), pp. 354, 362.
3 *Ibid.*, pp. 362, 368. Tomashevskiy notes that "the thesis of the inevitability of war between capitalist countries that was advanced in the early 1950s

has not been borne out in international relations" (*Lenin's Ideas*, p. 145).

4 A. Antonov, "Small Powers and Policy of Alignment," *International Affairs*, no. 10 (October 1975), p. 120.

5 Inozemtsev, *et al.*, eds., *Leninskaya teoriya imperializma*, p. 12.

6 Usachev, *Mezhdunarodnaya razryadka*, p. 131; Zamkovoy, *Kritika burzhuaznykh kontseptsiy*, p. 30; Proyektor, *Puty Yevropy*, pp. 110, 112; Kokoshin, *S.Sh.A.*, p. 20.

7 Inozemtsev *et al.*, *Leninskaya teoriya imperializma*, p. 12.

8 Nikol'skiy and Grishin, *Sistemny analiz*, p. 22.

9 A.D. Nikonov, ed., *Problemy voyennoy razryadki* (Problems of Military Detente) (Moscow: Nauka), 1981, pp. 71, 110, 172.

10 Inozemtsev *et al.*, *Leninskaya teoriya imperializma*, p. 396.

11 Proyektor, *Puty Yevropy*, p. 120.

12 *Ibid.*, pp. 122, 130; Lebedev *et al.*, *Mezhdunarodnye otnosheniya*, pp. 158–9. See also the important analyses of Sergei Karaganov, "Amerikanskiye rakety i yevropeyskaya bezopasnost'" (The US Missiles and European Security), *S.Sh.A.*, no. 11 (November 1985), pp. 49–54, which maintains that the deployment of Pershing II and cruise missiles in Western Europe since November 1983 has not resolved the growing strains in US–West European security relations; G. Vorontsov, "S.Sh.A., NATO i yevrorakety" (The US, NATO and the Euromissiles), *Mirovaya Ekonomika i Mezhdunarodnye Otnosheniya*, no. 11 (November 1984), pp. 15–24; Daniil Proyektor, "Reconsidering Values?" *Izvestiya*, 8 April 1984, p. 5, in *FBIS. Daily Report. Soviet Union*, 11 April 1984, p. G1, and the unsigned lead article, "Yevropa v mirovoy politike 80-kh godov" (Europe in the World Politics of the 1980s), *Mirovaya Ekonomika i Mezhdunarodnye Otnosheniya*, no. 2 (February 1984), pp. 3–10.

13 Doronina, *Mezhdunarodnyy konflikt*, p. 97.

14 *Politekonomika imperializma*, vol. 2 (1970), pp. 176, 48–9, 198.

15 G. Vorontsov, "Protivorechiya 'atlanticheskoy zony'" (Contradictions of the "Atlantic zone"), *Mirovaya Ekonomika i Mezhdunarodnye Otnosheniya*, no. 2 (February 1979), p. 145; IEMSS, *Sotsializm i mezhdunarodnye otnosheniya*, p. 345.

16 *Politekonomika imperializma*, vol. 2 (1970), p. 198; Gantman, "Class Nature of International Relations," p. 56.

17 Bogdan, *Tsentry sopernichestva*, pp. 3, 22–3.

18 Nikolay Inozemtsev, "Capitalism's Current Crisis Analyzed," *Current Digest of the Soviet Press*, vol. 26, no. 33 (1974), p. 3. The article appeared in *Pravda* on 20 August 1974, pp. 4–5; Shalva Sanakoyev, "Soviet Foreign Policy and Current International Relations," *International Affairs*, no. 3 (March 1981), p. 9; Bogdan, *Tsentry sopernichestva*, pp. 22–3; and N. Volkov and N. Shmelyev, "Strukturnye sdvigi v ekonomike kapitalizma" (Structural Changes in the Economy of Capitalism), *Mirovaya Ekonomika i Mezhdunarodnye Otnosheniya*, no. 8 (August 1985), pp. 28–40.

19 Nikolay Inozemtsev, "O novom etape v razvitii mezhdunarodnykh otnosheniy" (On the New Stage in the Development of International Relations), *Kommunist*, no. 13 (1973), p. 96; Inozemtsev, "O Leninskoy metodologii analiza mirovogo obshchestvennogo razvitiya" (On the

Leninist Methodology for Analyzing World Social Development), *Kommunist*, no. 12 (1976), p. 76.

20 Fedor Burlatskiy, "Political System and Political Consciousness," in SPSA, *Time, Space and Politics* (Moscow: Social Sciences Today, 1977), p. 63.

21 Burlatskiy, "O sistemnom podkhode k issledovaniyu vneshney politiki," p. 79.

22 Inozemtsev, "O Leninskoy metodologii," p. 73; Bogdanov, *Tsentry sopernichestva*, p. 3.

23 IEMSS, *Sotsializm i mezhdunarodnye otnosheniya*, pp. 352–67; *Politekonomika kapitalizma*, vol. 2 (1970), p. 198; Vorontsov, "Protivorechiya 'atlanticheskoy zony'," p. 147; Bogdanov, *Tsentry soperhichestva*, pp. 6, 165.

24 Tomashevskiy, *Lenin's Ideas*, pp. 224–5, 209. See also the analyses of Central Committee member Georgi Arbatov, "Europe and International Security," *Review of International Affairs* (Belgrade), vol. 35, no. 831 (20 November 1984), pp. 5–8, and of now Central Party Secretary Aleksandr Yakovlev, "Voprosy teorii: Imperialism–Sopernichestvo i protivorechiya" (Problems of Theory: Imperialism–Competition and Contradictions), *Pravda*, 23 March 1984, pp. 4–5.

25 *Politekonomika kapitalizma*, vol. 2 (1975), pp. 53–54; Proyektor, *Puty Yevropy*, pp. 112, 134.

26 *Politekonomika kapitalizma*, vol. 2 (1975), p. 54.

27 O. Bykov, "Obshchaya strategiya imperializma: 'globalizm' i 'yevroptsentrizm'" (The General Strategy of Imperialism: "Globalism" and "Eurocentrism"), *Mirovaya Ekonomika i Mezhdunarodnye Otnosheniya*, no. 11 (November 1969), p. 85.

28 Bogdanov, *Tsentry sopernichestva*, pp. 167–9.

29 *Politekonomika kapitalizma* (1975), vol. 2, p. 54.

30 The study edited by Inozemtsev, in listing the goals of the "imperialist alliance," did not include the destruction of the USSR. The goals were stated to be: (a) the achievement of military–strategic superiority; (b) weakening the political positions of socialism; and (c) undermining socialism's international prestige (Inozemtsev *et al.*, eds., *Leninskaya teoriya imperializma*, p. 354). See also Burlatskiy's analysis on p. 114, above.

31 V. Milyukova, "International Relations of a New Type," *International Affairs*, no. 5 (May 1975), p. 149.

32 E. Bagramov, "World History and Problems of Internationalism," *International Affairs*, no. 2 (February 1979), p. 136; see also Teresa Rakowska-Harmstone, "Socialist Internationalism and Eastern Europe," *Survey*, Part 1 (Winter 1976), pp. 38–54, Part 2 (Spring 1976), pp. 81–6.

33 Ye.D. Modrzhinskaya, *Leninizm i sovremennaya ideologicheskaya bor'ba* (Leninism and the Contemporary Ideological Struggle) (Moscow: Mysl', 1972), Chapter Six: "National'nyy vopros i sovremennaya ideologicheskaya bor'ba" (The National Question and the Contemporary Ideological Struggle).

34 Robert MacNeal, ed., *International Relations Among Communists* (Englewood Cliffs, NJ: Prentice Hall, 1967), pp. 12, 18–20.

35 *Politekonomika kapitalizma* (1970), vol. 2, p. 193.

36 See, e.g., Vaclav Kotyk, "Problems of East–West Relations," *Journal of International Affairs*, vol. 22, no. 1 (1968), pp. 48–58.
37 Vladimir Gantman, "The Class Nature of International Relations," *International Affairs*, no. 9 (September 1969), pp. 55–7.
38 A. Dubinin, "Nationalism and Foreign Policy," *International Affairs*, no. 8 (August 1975), pp. 131, 138.
39 V.S. Shevtsov, *Natsional'nyy suverenitet* (National Sovereignty) (Moscow: Politicheskaya Literatura, 1978), p. 192.
40 *Obshchestvennye nauki SSSR*, no. 2 (1979), p. 24; Shevtsov, *Natsional'nyy suverenitet*, pp. 13, 171, 175.
41 *Ibid.*, p. 175.
42 V.S. Shevtsov, *National Sovereignty and the Socialist State* (Moscow: Progress, 1974), p. 18.
43 *Ibid.*, p. 145; Tomashevskiy, *Lenin's Ideas*, p. 274.
44 IEMSS, *Sotsializm i mezhdunarodnye otnosheniya*, pp. 31–2.
45 Tomashevskiy, *Lenin's Ideas*, p. 259.
46 Gantman, "Class Nature of International Relations," pp. 55–6; and R. Kosolapov (ex-editor of *Kommunist*), "Sotsializm i Protivorechiya" (Socialism and Contradictions), *Pravda*, 20 July 1984, pp. 2–3.
47 *Ibid.*, p. 56. Emphasis his. I would draw attention to the closing phrase: "*whatever the type of international relations.*" That is, intersocialist relations are included. See also I.V. Krivozhikha, "The Concept of 'National Interest' in American Foreign Policy," *USA*, no. 11 (November 1974), pp. 121–6 (JPRS translation).
48 IEMSS, *Sotsializm i mezhdunarodnye otnosheniya*, p. 75; Georgi Shakhnazarov, *Gryadushchiy miroporyadok* (The Coming World Order) (Moscow: Izdatel'stvo Politicheskoy Literatury, 1981), p. 84.
49 "Round Table: Laws governing the development of the socialist world system," *World Marxist Review*, no. 10 (October 1971), pp. 4–5, 42–3.
50 IEMSS, *Sotsializm i mezhdunarodnye otnosheniya*, p. 124.
51 "Round Table: Laws of the socialist world system," pp. 9, 15–16.
52 IEMSS, *Sotsializm i mezhdunarodnye otnosheniya*, pp. 46, 48, 63.
53 *Ibid.*, p. 65; Gantman, "Typen internationaler Konflikten," pp. 84, 90; Doronina, *Mezhdunarodnyy konflikt*, p. 90; IEMSS, *Sotsializm i mezhdunarodnye otnosheniya*, p. 65.
54 *Ibid.*, p. 64.
55 *Ibid.*, pp. 65–6.
56 *Ibid.*, pp. 69, 67; Gantman, "Typen internationaler Konflikten," p. 91.
57 IEMSS, *Sotsializm i mezhdunarodnye otnosheniya*, p. 67.
58 *Ibid.*, pp. 71–5, 258, 124.
59 Diplomaticheskaya Akademiya MID SSSR, *Vneshnyaya politika i diplomatiya*, p. 22; R.N. Berki, "On Marxian Thought and the Problem of International Relations," *World Politics*, vol. 24, no. 1 (October 1971), p. 86; IEMSS, *Sotsializm i mezhdunarodnye otnosheniya*, p. 34.
60 Cited in Shevtsov, *National Sovereignty*, pp. 158–9.
61 Berki, "On Marxian Thought," pp. 101, 103.
62 Alexander Dallin, *The Soviet Union at the United Nations* (New York: Praeger, 1962), pp. 11, 192.

63 Alvin S. Rubinstein, *The Soviets in International Organizations* (Princeton: Princeton University Press, 1964), pp. 290, 304.
64 Cited in *Ibid.*, p. 307.
65 Dallin, *The Soviet Union at the UN*, p. 190.
66 Rubinstein, *Soviets in International Organizations*, pp. 315, 302.
67 G.I. Morozov, *Mezhdunarodnye organizatsii: nekotorye voprosy teorii* (International Organizations: Some Questions of Theory) (Moscow: Mysl', 1969, 1974). See bibliography in 1974 edition, pp. 320–8.
68 *Ibid.*, p. 46.
69 G.I. Morozov, "Mezhdunarodnye organizatsii i podderzhaniye mira" (International Organizations and Reinforcing Peace), in SAPN, *Politika mira i razvitiye politicheskikh sistem* (The Peace Policy and the Development of Political Systems) (Moscow: Nauka, 1979), pp. 107–8.
70 *Ibid.*, pp. 108–9.
71 Morozov, *Mezhdunarodnye organizatsii*, p. 54.
72 V.M. Gevorgyan, "Mezhdunarodnye organizatsii: nekotorye voposy teorii" (International Organizations: Some Questions of Theory), *S.Sh.A.*, no. 5 (May 1975), pp. 98–9. Gevorgyan is here favorably reviewing Morozov's book.
73 Morozov, *Mezhdunarodnye organizatsii*, p. 108.
74 Georgi Shakhnazarov, "Political Science and New Factors in International Relations," in SPSA, *Time, Space and Politics* (Moscow: Social Sciences Today, 1977), p. 25.
75 Grigory Morozov, "International Organizations and World Peace," in SPSA, *Soviet Policy of Peace* (Moscow: Social Sciences Today, 1979), p. 130.
76 V. Sojak, "Western Models," *International Affairs*, no. 6 (June 1974), p. 73; Morozov, "Mezhdunarodnye organizatsii i podderzhaniye mira," p. 110.
77 Morozov, *Mezhdunarodnye organizatsii*, p. 95–6.
78 V. Petrovskiy, "The UN and World Politics," *International Affairs*, no. 7 (July 1980), p. 11.
79 *Sovremennye burzhuaznye teorii mezhdunarodnykh otnosheniy*, pp. 167, 169.
80 E. Obminskiy, "Upravlyaemy li 'nadnatsional'nye' faktory?" (Are "transnational" factors governing?), *Mirovaya Ekonomika i Mezhdunarodnye Otnosheniya*, no. 12 (December 1972), pp. 141, 145.

## 7 THE SCIENTIFIC–TECHNICAL REVOLUTION AND THE CHANGING FACE OF INTERNATIONAL RELATIONS

1 R. Judson Mitchell, "A New Brezhnev Doctrine: The Restructuring of International Relations," *World Politics*, vol. 30, no. 2 (January 1978), p. 366.
2 Aleksandr Bovin, "Lenine et la politique exterieure de l'URSS," *Sciences Sociales* (Moscow), vol. 12, no. 3 (1981), p. 185.
3 See, for example, Nikolay Inozemtsev, ed., *Mirovoy revolyutsionnyy protsess i sovremennost'* (The World Revolutionary Process and the Contemporary World) (Moscow: Nauka, 1980), pp. 111–14.
4 See the review essay by Erik P. Hoffmann, "Soviet Views of the Scientific

Technological Revolution," *World Politics*, vol. 30, no. 4 (July 1978), pp. 615–44; and B. Bessonov, "The Scientific and Technological Revolution and the Ideological Struggle," *International Affairs*, no. 2 (February 1974), p. 68.

5 Nikol'skiy and Grishin, *Nauchno–teknicheskiy progress*, p. 42; see also Nikolay Lebedev and I. Tyulin, "International Aspects of the Scientific and Technological Revolution," *International Affairs*, no. 12 (December 1979), p. 107, favorably reviewing Nikol'skiy and Grishin. For an account of the evolution of Soviet views on nuclear war, see Raymond Garthoff, *Detente and Confrontation. American–Soviet Relations From Nixon to Reagan* (Washington, DC: The Brookings Institution, 1985), pp. 768–85.

6 Bogdanov, *Tsentry Sopernichestva*, p. 166.

7 V. Gantman, ed., *Sovremennye burzhuaznye teorii mezhdunarodnykh otnosheniy*, p. 445.

8 *Politekonomika kapitalizma* (1975), vol. 2, p. 185; Georgi Shakhnazarov, *Gryadushchiy miroporyadok* (The Coming World Order) (Moscow: Izdatel'stvo Politicheskoy Literatury, 1981), pp. 14, 116.

9 V.F. Petrovskiy, *Burzhuaznye vneshnepoliticheskiye kontseptsii i ideologicheskaya bor'ba na mezhdunarodnom arene* (Bourgeois Foreign Policy Concepts and the International Ideological Struggle) (Moscow: Znaniye, 1977), p. 20. The same criticism can be made of Soviet analyses, which hold that "techniques," though not "technologies," are informed by class elements (Hoffmann, "Soviet Views on the Scientific–Technological Revolution," p. 625).

10 Anatoly Gromyko and Andrei Kokoshin, "US Foreign Policy for the 1970s," *International Affairs*, no. 10 (October 1973), p. 72; and Petrovskiy, *Burzhuaznye vneshnepoliticheskiye kontseptsii*, pp. 17–18; Vorontsov, "West in Search of a Coordinated Policy," pp. 103, 107.

11 Bogdanov, *Tsentry Sopernichestva*, p. 166; A.V. Nikiforov, "American Concepts of Interdependence," *USA*, no. 7 (July 1979), p. 17 (JPRS translation).

12 Dmitry Yermolenko, *International Relations in the Era of the Scientific–Technological Revolution* (Moscow: Novosti, 1973), pp. 11, 156; I.A. Kozikov, "Problems of the Correlation Between the Scientific and Technical and Social Revolutions," *Nauchnyi Kommunizm* (JPRS, *Translations on USSR Political and Sociological Affairs*, no. 450, 31 October, 1973, p. 34).

13 L. Nezhinskiy, "Issledovaniya osnov sotsialisticheskoy vneshney politiki" (Research on the Bases of Socialist Foreign Policy), *Mirovaya Ekonomika i Mezhdunarodnye Otnosheniya*, no. 5 (May 1978), p. 147.

14 Nikolay Inozemtsev, "Nauchno–tekhnicheskaya revolyutsiya, bor'ba dvukh sistem i protivorechiya kapitalizma" (The Scientific–Technical Revolution, the Struggle of the Two Systems and the Contradictions of Capitalism), in *Mezhdunarodnyy Yezhegodnik* (International Yearbook) (Moscow: Nauka, 1971), pp. 11–12, 23.

15 Ye.D. Modrzhinskaya, ed., *The Future of Society: A Critique of Modern Bourgeois-Philosophical and Socio-Political Conceptions* (Moscow: Progress, 1973), p. 350.

16 N. Inozemtsev, "O Leninskoy metodologii, p. 70.

17 Y. Borisov, "Some Distinctions of Present-Day International Relations," *International Affairs*, no. 9 (September 1969), p. 53.

18 *Ibid.*

19 Nikolay Inozemtsev, "The STR and the Modern World," *Social Sciences* vol. 11, no. 3 (1980), pp. 13–14; *Pravda*, 26 February 1986, p. 3.

20 Borisov, "Some Distinctions of Present-Day International Relations," p. 53; Inozemtsev, "The STR and the Modern World," p. 10; *Politekonomika kapitalizma* (1975), vol. 2, pp. 49, 50, 185, 186.

21 In which the entire plant is constructed by foreigners and is then turned over *in toto* to the Soviets to run by themselves.

22 Nikoforov, "American Concepts of Interdependence," p. 11.

23 See Yury Fyodorov, *Mezhdunarodnaya bezopasnost′ i global′nye problemy* (International Security and Global Problems) (Moscow: Nauka, 1983); Vadim Zagladin and Ivan Frolov, "Global′nye problemy i budushchee cheloveka" (Global Problems and the Future of Man), *Kommunist*, no. 7 (May 1979), pp. 92–105; Arbatov, "Detente and the Problem of Conflict," p. 39; Zagladin and Frolov, "The Global Problems of Our Times," *Social Sciences*, vol. 8, no. 4 (1977), pp. 66–79.

24 "Tezisy Instituta MEMO AN SSSR" (Theses of the Institute of the World Economy and International Relations, Academy of Sciences, USSR), *Mirovaya Ekonomika i Mezhdunarodnye Otnosheniya*, no. 6 (June 1979), p. 36; Karen Brutents, the leading Soviet expert on the "developing" countries, observed that in response to demands for a "new international economic order", the West has accelerated its efforts to integrate the developing countries with the West, especially in the economic domain, "where the West still occupies a strong position." "Questions of Theory: Imperialism and the Newly Liberated Countries," *Current Digest of the Soviet Press* vol. 30, no. 6 (1978), p. 10. The article appeared in *Pravda* on 10 February 1978, pp. 3–4.

25 One source of Soviet fascination with the STR seems to be the opportunity that is perceived to revitalize Soviet-bloc economies without entailing any of the economic reforms that might threaten the position of the Communist Party in those countries. See Robert H. Miller, "The Scientific–Technical Revolution and the Soviet Administrative Debate," in Paul Cocks, Robert V. Daniels, and Nancy Whittier Heer, eds., *The Dynamics of Soviet Politics* (Cambridge, Mass.; Harvard University Press, 1976), pp. 137–55.

26 "Tezisy Instituta IMEMO," pp. 39–40.

27 Kokoshin writes that, in spite of American technological supremacy, the STR has a constraining effect on the conduct of US foreign policy (*O burzhuaznykh prognozakh razvitiya mezhdunarodnykh otnosheniy*, pp. 165–8; "Tezisy Instituta IMEMO," p. 45; and Yermolenko, *International Relations in the Era of the STR*, p. 87.)

28 "Tezisy Instituta IMEMO," p. 62.

29 I. Shatalov, "The Scientific and Technological Revolution and International Relations," *International Affairs*, no. 8 (August 1971), p. 30.

30 Kokoshin, *O burzhuaznykh prognozakh razvitiya mezhdunarodnykh otnosheniy*, pp. 172, 200.

31 Georgi Shakhnazarov, "K probleme sootnosheniya sil v mire" (On the Problem of the Correlation of Forces in the World), *Kommunist*, no. 3 (1974), p. 86; Shakhnazarov, *Gryadushchiy miroporyadok*, pp. 22–30.
32 A.A. Kokoshin, "Foreign Policy of Democratic Presidents," *USA*, no. 8 (August 1979), p. 102 (JPRS translation).

## CONCLUSION

1 See S. Tikhvinskiy, "Apologetics of Great-Han Hegemonism in Chinese Historiography," *Social Sciences*, vol. 11, no. 1 (1980), pp. 83–100, and Shakhnazarov, *Gryadushchiy miroporyadok*, pp. 89, 102–3.
2 Radovan Vukadinovic, *Osnove teorije vanjske politike* (Foundations of the Theory of Foreign Policy) (Zagreb: Biblioteka suvremene politicke misli, 1981), p. 24.
3 *Ibid.*, p. 26.
4 Milan Sahovic, *Medunarodni odnosi i drustveni napredak* (International Relations and Social Progress) (Belgrade: Savremena Administracija, 1978), p. 6.
5 *Ibid.*, p. 178.
6 Silviu Brucan, *The Dialectic of World Politics* (New York: The Free Press, 1978), p. 24.
7 *Ibid.*, pp. 2, 9.
8 *Ibid.*, p. viii.
9 Brucan, *Dissolution of Power*, p. 8.
10 *Ibid.*
11 *Ibid.*, p. 48.
12 Yezhi Viatr (Jerzy Wiatr), *Sotsiologiya politicheskikh otnosheniy* (The Sociology of Political Relations) (Moscow: Progress, 1979).
13 Yezhi Viatr (Jerzy Wiatr), "A Sociological Perspective in the Study of International Relations," in Viatr, *Essays in Political Sociology* (Wroclaw: The Polish Academy of Sciences Press, 1978), p. 54.
14 *Ibid.*, pp. 54–5.
15 *Ibid.* See also the work by Longin Pastusiak, "International Relations: Remarks on the Subject: Methodology and Theory," in Polish Association of Political Sciences, *Polish Round Table. Yearbook 1969*. Volume 3 (Wroclaw: Wydawnictwo Polskiej Akademii Nauk, 1971), pp. 161–74; Pastusiak, "A Marxist Approach to the Study of International Relations," *East European Quarterly*, vol. 3, no. 3 (September 1969), pp. 285–93, and "International Relations Studies in Poland," *International Studies Quarterly* vol. 22, no. 2 (June 1978), pp. 299–318. The following two works have also been brought to the author's attention: P. Frid'esh, *Sotsialisticheskaya vneshnyaya politika* (Socialist Foreign Policy) (Moscow: Progress, 1978), translated from the Hungarian; and Yu. Kukulka, *Problemy teorii mezhdunarodnykh otnosheniy* (Problems of the Theory of International Relations) (Moscow: Progress, 1980), translated from the Polish.
16 Brucan, *Dissolution of Power*, p. 47.

# Select bibliography


Adomeit, Hannes. "Capitalist Contradictions and Soviet Policy," *Problems of Communism*, May–June 1984, pp. 1–18.

Afanasyev, Sergei and Melikhov, Sergei. "Model Concepts of the Foreign Policy Decision Making Process," in Soviet Political Sciences Association. *Political Theory and Political Practice*. Moscow: Social Sciences Today, 1979, pp. 172–81.

Alexandrov, V. "Fundamental Principles of Socialist Foreign Policy," *International Affairs* (Moscow), no. 5 (May 1980), pp. 13–21.

*Amerikanskaya istoriografiya vneshney politiki S.Sh.A.* (American Historiography of US Foreign Policy). Moscow: Nauka, 1972.

Andreyev, A.K. and Semeiko, L.S. "International Relations Forecasting in US Research Circles," *USA*, no. 5 (May 1974), pp. 121–7 (Joint Publications Research Service translation).

Anichkina, V.S. "Peace Research in the US," *USA*, no. 9 (September 1973), pp. 111–18 (Joint Publications Research Service translation).

Antyukhina-Moskovchenko, V.I., Zlobin, A.A., and Khrustalev, M.A. *Osnovy teorii mezhdunarodnykh otnosheniy. Uchebnoye posobiye* (Foundations of the Theory of International Relations. A Teaching Aid). Moscow: Moskovskiy Gosudarstvennyy Institut Mezhdunarodnykh Otnosheniy, 1980.

Appatov, S.I. *S.Sh.A. i Yevropa: obshchiye problemy amerikanskoy kontinental'noy politiki* (The USA and Europe: General Problems of American Policy on the Continent). Moscow: Mysl', 1979.

Arbatov, Aleksei. *Voyenno-strategicheskiy paritet i politika S.Sh.A.* (Military-Strategic Parity and US Policy). Moscow: Izdatel'stvo Politicheskoy Literatury, 1984.

Arbatov, Georgi. "Detente and the Problem of Conflict," in Soviet Political Sciences Association, *Soviet Policy of Peace*. Moscow: Social Sciences Today, 1979, pp. 28–45.

"Europe and International Security," *Review of International Affairs* (Belgrade), vol. 35, no. 831 (20 November 1984), pp. 5–8.

"Soviet–American Relations in the 1970s," *USA*, no. 5 (May 1974) (Joint Publications Research Service translation).

"Soviet–American Relations Today," in Soviet Peace Committee. *Leninist*

*Principles of Peaceful Coexistence in the Contemporary World*. Moscow: Social Sciences Today, 1973, pp. 9–36.

"US Foreign Policy at the Outset of the 1980s," in *Peace and Disarmament*. Moscow: Progress, 1980, pp. 64–80.

*The War of Ideas in Contemporary International Relations*. Moscow: Progress, 1973.

Arzumanyan, A.A. *Bor'ba dvukh sistem i mirovoye razvitiye* (The Struggle of the Two Systems and World Development). Moscow: Nauka, 1964.

*Krizis mirovogo kapitalizma na sovremennom etape* (The Crisis of World Capitalism in the Contemporary Period). Moscow: Akademiya Nauk SSSR, 1962.

*Novyy etap obshchego krizisa kapitalizma* (The New Stage in the General Crisis of Capitalism). Moscow: Znaniye, 1961.

ed. *Problemy sovremennogo kapitalizma; sbornik statey. K 80-letiyu akademika Ye. S. Varga* (Problems of Contemporary Capitalism; a Collection of Articles in Honor of the Eightieth Birthday of Academician Ye. S. Varga). Moscow: Akademiya Nauk, 1959.

Aspaturian, Vernon. *Process and Power in Soviet Foreign Policy*. Boston: Little Brown, 1971.

"Soviet Global Power and the Correlation of Forces," *Problems of Communism*, May–June 1980, pp. 1–18.

Baklanov, A.G. and Viktorov, A.V. *Yevropa i sovremennyi mir* (Europe and the Contemporary World). Moscow: Mezhdunarodnye Otnosheniya, 1982.

Barghoorn, Frederick. *The Soviet Image of the US*. New York: Harcourt, Brace and Co., 1950.

Berki, R.N. "On Marxian Thought and the Problem of International Relations," *World Politics*, vol. 24, no. 1 (October 1971), pp. 80–105.

Besançon, Alain. *Les Origines intellectuelles du Leninisme*. Paris: Calmann Levy, 1977.

von Beyme, Klaus. "Das Selbstverstaendnis der Sowjetunion in der Theorie der Internationaler Politik," in von Beyme, *Die Sowjetunion in der Weltpolitik*. Munich: Piper, 1985, pp. 10–21.

Bialer, Seweryn. "Ideology and Soviet Foreign Policy," in Schwab, George, ed., *Ideology and Foreign Policy. A Global Perspective*. New York: Cyrco Press, 1978, pp. 76–102.

Bialer, Seweryn and Afferica, Joan. "Reagan and Russia," *Foreign Affairs*, vol. 61, no. 2 (Winter 1982/3), pp. 249–71.

Blasier, Cole. "The Soviet Latin Americanists," *Latin American Research Review*, no. 1 (1981), pp. 107–23.

Bolshakov, Boris and Vdovichenko, Larisa. "Problems of Modelling International Relations," in Soviet Political Sciences Association. *Political Theory and Political Practice*. Moscow: Social Sciences Today, 1979, pp. 158–71.

Borisov, O.B., Dubinin, I.N., and Zemskov, I.N. *et al*., eds. *Sovremennaya diplomatiya burzhuaznykh gosudarstv* (The Contemporary Diplomacy of Bourgeois States). Moscow: Izdatel'stvo Politicheskoy Literatury, 1981.

Borisov, Y. "Some Distinctions of Present Day International Relations," *International Affairs*, no. 9 (September 1969), pp. 53–5.

Bovin, Aleksandr. "Lenine et la politique exterieure de l'URSS," *Sciences Sociales*, vol. 12, no. 3 (1981), pp. 173–87.

*Lenin o politike i politicheskoy deyatel'nosti* (Lenin on Politics and Political Activity). Moscow: Znaniye, 1971.

Braillard, Philippe. *Theories des relations internationales*. Paris: Presses Universitaire de France, 1977.

Braillard, Philippe and de Senarclens, Pierre. "The International System. Limits to Forecasting," *Futures*, vol. 12, no. 6 (December 1980), pp. 453–64.

Brucan, Silviu. *The Dialectic of World Politics*. New York: The Free Press, 1978.

*The Dissolution of Power. A Sociology of International Relations and Politics*. New York: Alfred A. Knopf, 1971.

Brutents, Karen. "Neocolonialism Changes its Strategy," *Current Digest of the Soviet Press*, vol. 30, no. 6 (1978), pp. 10–11.

Bukharin, Nikolai. *Imperialism and World Economy*. New York: Howard Fertig, 1966.

Bulkin, A. "Behind the Maoist 'Three Worlds' Theory," in *Post-Mao Maoism*. Part 1. Moscow: Social Sciences Today, 1980, pp. 71–114.

Burlatskiy, Fedor. "Improved Tools, Research Urged for Political Science," *Current Digest of the Soviet Press*, vol. 31, no. 8 (1979), p. 15.

*Lenin. Gosudarstvo. Politika* (Lenin. The State. Politics). Moscow: Nauka, 1970.

"Modelirovaniye mezhdunarodnykh otnosheniy: printsipi i predposylki" (International-Relations Modelling: Principles and Premises), in Soviet Political Sciences Association, *Novyi mirovoy poryadok i politicheskaya obshchnost'* (The New World Order and Political Community). Moscow: Nauka, 1983, pp. 26–34.

*The Modern State and Politics*. Moscow: Progress, 1978.

"O sistemnom podkhode k issledovaniyu vneshney politiki" (On the Systems Approach to Researching Foreign Policy), in Sovetskaya assotsiatsiya politicheskikh nauk. *Mezhdunarodnye otnosheniya, politika, i lichnost'* (International Relations, Politics, and Personality). Moscow: Nauka, 1976.

"Political System and Political Consciousness," in Soviet Political Sciences Association. *Time, Space and Politics*. Moscow: Social Sciences Today, 1977.

"Politika i Nauka" (Politics and Science), *Pravda*, 10 January 1965, p. 4.

"Preventing World War and Planning Universal Peace," in Soviet Political Sciences Association. *Soviet Policy of Peace*. Moscow: Social Sciences Today, 1979, pp. 74–85.

Burlatskiy, Fedor and Galkin, A. *Sotsiologiya. Politika. Mezhdunarodnye otnosheniya* (Sociology. Politics. International Relations). Moscow: Mezhdunarodnye Otnosheniya, 1974.

*Sovremennyi leviafan. Ocherki politicheskoy sotsiologii kapitalizma* (The Contemporary Leviathan. Perspectives on the Political Sociology of Capitalism). Moscow: Mysl', 1985.

Bykov, O. "Obshchaya strategiya imperializma, 'globalizm' i 'yevroptsentrizm'" (The General Strategy of Imperialism, "Globalism" and "Eurocentrism"), *Mirovaya Ekonomika i Mezhdunarodnye Otnosheniya*, no. 11 (November 1969), pp. 83–5.

Bykov, O. and Tomashevskiy, D. "Real'naya sila mezhdunarodnogo razvitiya" (The Real Strength of International Development), *Mirovaya Ekonomika i Mezhdunarodnye Otnosheniya*, no. 7 (July 1972), pp. 4–15.

Chirkin, Veniamin. "The Evolution of Political Consciousness in the Developing Countries," in Soviet Political Sciences Association. *Time, Space and Politics*. Moscow: Social Sciences Today, 1977, pp. 119–33.

Chossudovsky, E.M. *Chicherin and the Evolution of Soviet Foreign Policy and Diplomacy*. Geneva: Graduate Institute of International Studies, 1973.

Churchward, L.G. *The Soviet Intelligentsia*. London: Routledge and Kegan Paul, 1973.

"Towards a Soviet Political Science," *Australian Journal of Political Science*, April 1966, pp. 66–75.

Clarkson, Stephen. *The Soviet Theory of Development*. Toronto: University of Toronto Press, 1978.

"The Cold War of 1948 Compared to Detente Today," *Current Digest of the Soviet Press* vol. 30, no. 11 (1978), p. 11.

Davydov, V.F. *Nerasprostraneniye yadernogo oruzhiya i politika S.Sh.A.* (The Non-Proliferation of Nuclear Weapons and US Policy). Moscow: Nauka, 1980.

Davydov, Yuriy P. "Printsipi podkhoda S.Sh.A. k razvitym kapitalisticheskim gosudarstvam" (Principles of the US Approach to the Developed Capitalist Countries), in Institute of US and Canadian Studies, *Sovremennaya vneshnyaya politika S.Sh.A.* (Contemporary US Foreign Policy). Vol. 1. Moscow: Nauka, 1984, pp. 227–54.

Dement'yev, I.P. "The Mahan Doctrine of Sea Power," *USA*, no. 5 (May 1972), pp. 44–61 (Joint Publications Research Service translation).

"The Dialectics of Economics and Politics During the Struggle for the Revolutionary Transformation of Society," *World Marxist Review*, part 1, no. 3 (1978), pp. 70–87; part 2, no. 5 (1978), pp. 21–48.

Diplomaticheskaya Akademiya M.I.D. SSSR. *Vneshnyaya politika i diplomatiya sotsialisticheskikh stran* (Foreign Policy and Diplomacy of the Socialist Countries). Moscow: Mezhdunarodnye Otnosheniya, 1981.

Djilas, Milovan. *Consversations with Stalin*. New York: Harcourt, Brace and World, 1962.

Dmitriyev, V.D. "Conflicts in Contemporary International Relations," *USA*, no. 5 (May 1973), pp. 85–8 (Joint Publications Research Service Publication).

Doronina, N.I. *Mezhdunarodnyy konflikt. O burzhuaznykh teoriyakh konflikta. Kriticheskiy analiz metodologii issledovaniy* (International Conflict. On Bourgeois Theories of Conflict. A Critical Analysis of Methodologies of Research). Moscow: Mezhdunarodnye Otnosheniya, 1981.

Eran, Oded. *The "Mezhdunarodniki." An Assessment of Professional Expertise in the Making of Soviet Foreign Policy*. Tel Aviv: Turtledove, 1979.

*Soviet Area Studies and Foreign Policy*. Santa Barbara: General Electric-Temp Center for Advanced Studies, September 1974.

Fedoseyev, A.A. *Politka kak ob'yekt sotsiologicheskogo issledovaniya* (Politics as an

Object of Sociological Research). Leningrad: Leningradskiy Universitet, 1974.

"Fedoseyev Sets Marxist Scholars' Tasks," *Current Digest of the Soviet Press* vol. 31, no. 52 (1979), pp. 10–11, 24.

Fedotova, Evelina. "The Developing Countries and World Politics," in Soviet Political Sciences Association. *Soviet Policy of Peace*. Moscow: Social Sciences Today, 1979, pp. 161–74.

Foreign Broadcast Information Service. *Daily Report. Soviet Union. National Affairs. Supplement*. Vol. 3, no. 038, Supp. 041, 26 February 1986 (Gorbachev CPSU Central Committee Political Report).

*Daily Report. Soviet Union. Supplement*. Vol. 3, no. 046, Supp. 051, 10 March 1986 (CPSU Program – 1986).

Fox, William T.R. *The Superpowers*. New York: Harcourt, Brace and Co., 1944.

Frankel, Joseph. *Contemporary International Theory and the Behavior of States*, New York: Oxford University Press, 1973.

Frei, Daniel, ed. *Theorien der internationalen Beziehungen*. Munich: R. Piper and Co., Verlag, 1973.

Freymond, Jacques. *Lenine et l'Imperialisme*. Lausanne: Librarie Payot, 1951.

Frid'esh, P. *Sotsialisticheskaya vneshnyaya politika* (Socialist Foreign Policy). Moscow: Progress, 1978. Translated from the Hungarian.

Fyodorov, Yevgeny. "Scientific and Technical Aspects of Certain Political Decisions," in *Peace and Disarmament*. Moscow: Progress, 1980, pp. 32–48.

Fyodorov, Yury E. *Mezhdunarodnaya bezopasnost' i global'nye problemy* (International Security and Global Problems). Moscow: Nauka, 1983.

Gantman, Vladimir. "The Class Nature of Present Day International Relations," *International Affairs*, no. 9 (September 1969), pp. 55–7.

"Ekonomicheskoye razvitiye i vneshnyaya politika imperializma" (Economic Development and the Foreign Policy of Imperialism), in Inozemtsev, N.N. *et al*. *Politekonomika sovremennogo monopolisticheskogo kapitalizma* (The Political Economy of Contemporary Monopoly Capitalism). Moscow: Mysl', 1970.

"The Impact of Detente on the System of International Relations," in Soviet Political Sciences Association. *Soviet Policy of Peace*. Moscow: Social Sciences Today, 1979, pp. 115–28.

"Mesto v sisteme obshchestvennykh nauk" ([Its] Place in the System of the Social Sciences), *Mirovaya Ekonomika i Mezhaunarodnye Otnosheniya*, no. 9 (September 1969), pp. 96–9.

"Osnovnye tendentsii i problemy mezhdunarodnykh otnosheniy na rubezhe 70-kh godov" (Basic Tendencies and Problems of International Relations at the Turn of the 1970s), in *Mezhdunarodnyy yezhegodnik* (International Yearbook). Moscow: Politicheskaya Literatura, 1971, pp. 26–47.

"Sovremennyy kapitalizm i mezhdunarodnye otnosheniya" (Contemporary Capitalism and International Relations), in Inozemtsev, N.N. *et al*., eds, *Politekonomika sovremennogo monopolisticheskogo kapitalizma* (The Political Economy of Contemporary Monopoly Capitalism). Moscow: Mysl', 1975.

"Typen internationaler Konflikte," in Frei, Daniel, ed. *Theorien der internationalen Beziehungen*. Munich: R. Piper and Co., Verlag, 1973, pp. 79–87.

editor in chief. *Sovremennye burzhuaznye teorii mezhdunarodnykh otnosheniy* (Contemporary Bourgeois Theories of International Relations). Moscow: Nauka, 1976.

Garthoff, Raymond. *Detente and Confrontation. American–Soviet Relations From Nixon to Reagan*. Washington, DC: The Brookings Institution, 1985.

"Mutual Deterrence and Strategic Arms Limitation in Soviet Policy," *International Security*, vol. 3, no. 1 (Summer 1978), pp. 112–47.

Gasteyger, Curt. "Soviet Global Strategy," *Atlantic Community Quarterly*, Fall 1977, pp. 460–6.

Gati, Toby Trister. "The Soviet Union and the North-South Dialogue," *Orbis*, vol. 24, no. 2 (Summer 1980), pp. 241–70.

Gavrilov, V. "Sovetskiy Soyuz i sistema mezhdunarodnykh otnosheniy" (The Soviet Union and the System of International Relations), *Mirovaya Ekonomika i Mezhdunarodnye Otnosheniya*, no. 12 (December 1972), pp. 18–30.

George, Alexander L. "The Operational Code," *International Studies Quarterly*, June 1969, pp. 190–222.

"Georgian Sociologists Suggest New Topics for 'Sotsiologicheskoye Issledovaniye'," *Current Digest of the Soviet Press*, vol. 30, no. 34 (1978), pp. 12–13.

Gerasimov, G. "Teoriya igr i mezhdunarodnye othnosheniya" (Game Theory and International Relations), *Mirovaya Ekonomika i Mezhdunarodnye Otnosheniya*, no. 7 (July 1966), pp. 101–8.

Goodman, Elliot R. *The Soviet Design for a World State*. New York: Columbia University Press, 1960.

Gorbachev, Mikhail. *Political Report of the CPSU Central Committee to the 27th Party Congress*. Moscow: Novosti, 1986.

Grant, Steven A. "The Role of the Soviet Academy of Sciences in the Soviet Foreign Policy Process and the Impact of Institute Contacts with the US." Unpublished manuscript, January 1985.

Griffiths, Franklyn. "Limits of the Tabular View of Negotiation," *International Journal*, Winter 1979/80, pp. 33–46.

"The Sources of American Conduct: Soviet Perspectives and Their Policy Implications," *International Security*, vol. 9, no. 2 (Fall 1984), pp. 3–50.

Grishin, A.V. and Nikol′skiy, N.M. *Sistemnyy analiz i dialog s EVM v issledovanii mezhdunarodnykh otnosheniy* (Systems Analysis and Dialogue with the Computer in Researching International Relations). Moscow: Mezhdunarodnye Otnosheniya, 1982.

Gromyko, Anatoly and Kokoshin, Andrey. "US Foreign Policy Strategy for the 1970s," *International Affairs*, no. 10 (October 1973), pp. 67–73.

Gromyko, A.A., Zemskov, I.N., and Khvostov, V.M., eds. *Diplomaticheskiy slovar′* (Dictionary of Diplomacy). Moscow: Politicheskaya Literatura, 1973.

"Guidelines for Sociologists' Research," *Current Digest of the Soviet Press*, vol. 30, no. 34 (1978), p. 4.

Gvishiani, Djerman. "Global Modelling: Complex Analysis of World Development," *World Marxist Review*, no. 8 (1978), pp. 96–104.

Hahn, Werner G. *Postwar Soviet Politics. The Fall of Zhdanov and the Defeat of Moderation, 1946–1953*. Ithaca: Cornell University Press, 1982.

Henrikson, Alan K. "The Emanation of Power," *International Security*, vol. 6, no. 1 (Summer 1981), pp. 152–64.

Herod, Charles C. *The Nation in the History of Marxian Thought*. The Hague: Martinus Nijhoff, 1976.

Herrmann, Richard K. "Comparing World Views in East Europe: Contemporary Polish Perspectives," in Linden, Ronald H., ed. *The Foreign Politics of East Europe: New Approaches*. New York: Praeger, 1980, pp. 46–95.

Hill, Ronald J. "Political Sciences in Soviet Politics," *Irish Slavonic Studies*, no. 1 (1980), pp. 92–107.

*Soviet Politics, Political Science, and Reform*. England: Robertson/Sharpe, 1980.

Historicus. "Stalin on Revolution," *Foreign Affairs*, vol. 27, no. 2, January 1949, pp. 175–214.

Hoffmann, Erik P. "Soviet Views of the STR," *World Politics*, vol. 30, no. 4 (July 1978), pp. 615–44.

Hoffmann, Stanley. *Gulliver's Troubles. On the Setting of American Foreign Policy*. New York: McGraw-Hill Book Co., 1968.

Hough, Jerry F. "The Evolution in the Soviet World View," *World Politics*, vol. 32, no. 4 (July 1980), pp. 509–30.

"The Evolving Soviet Debate on Latin America," *Latin American Research Review*, no. 1 (1981), pp. 124–43.

*Soviet Leadership in Transition*. Washington, DC: Brookings Institution, 1980.

Huntington, Samuel P. *Political Order in Changing Societies*. New Haven: Yale University Press, 1968.

Husband, William B. "Soviet Perceptions of US 'Positions of Strength' Diplomacy in the 1970s," *World Politics*, vol. 31, no. 4 (July 1979), pp. 495–517.

"How About Social Science?" *Current Digest of the Soviet Press*, vol. 31, no. 39 (1979), p. 5.

Ilichov, L.F. *Ciencias sociales y communismo*. Montevideo: Ediciones Pueblos Unidos, 1965. Translation from the Russian.

Inozemtsev, N.N. "Aktual'nye zadachi teoreticheskogo issledovaniya" (Current Tasks of Theoretical Research), *Mirovaya Ekonomika i Mezhdunarodnye Otnosheniya*, no. 9 (September 1969), pp. 88–92.

ed. *Mirovoy revolyutsionnyy protsess i sovremennost'* (The World Revolutionary Process and the Contemporary World). Moscow: Nauka, 1980.

"O Leninskoy metodologii analiza mirovogo obshchestvennogo razvitiya" (On the Leninist Methodology for Analyzing World Social Development), *Kommunist*, no. 12 (1976), pp. 66–77.

"O novom etape v razvitii mezhdunarodnykh otnosheniy" (On the New Stage in the Development of International Relations), *Kommunist*, no. 13 (1973), pp. 89–103.

"Policy of Peaceful Coexistence: Underlying Principles," in Soviet Political Sciences Association. *Soviet Policy of Peace*. Moscow: Social Sciences Today, 1979, pp. 6–27.

"Questions of Theory: Capitalism in the 1970s. The Aggravation of Contradictions," *Current Digest of the Soviet Press*, vol. 26, no. 33 (1974), pp. 3–5, 13.

"The STR and the Modern World," *Social Sciences*, vol. 11, no. 3 (1980), pp. 8–17.

"Unity of Theory and Practice in the Leninist Peace Policy," *Kommunist*, no. 18 (1975), translated by Foreign Broadcast Informations Service, 9 January 1976, pp. A1–10.

Inozemtsev, N.N. *et al.*, eds. *Politicheskaya ekonomika sovremennogo monopolisticheskogo kapitalizma* (The Political Economy of Contemporary Monopoly Capitalism). Two vols. Moscow: Mysl', 1970, rev. edn 1975.

Inozemtsev, N.N., Martynov, V.A., Nikitin, S.M., eds. *Leninskaya teoriya imperializma i sovremennost'* (The Leninist Theory of Imperialism and the Contemporary World). Moscow: Mysl', 1977.

"Inside the CPSU Central Committee," *Survey*, Autumn 1974, pp. 94–104 (interview with A. Pravdin by Mervin Matthews).

Institute of the Economy of the World Socialist System. *Sotsializm i mezhdunarodnye otnosheniya* (Socialism and International Relations). Moscow: Nauka, 1975.

Institute of US and Canadian Studies. *Sovremennaya vneshnyaya politika S.Sh.A.* (Contemporary US Foreign Policy). Moscow: Nauka, 1984. Two vols.

Institute of World Economy and International Relations. *European Security and Cooperation: Premises, Problems, Prospects*. Moscow: Progress, 1978.

*Western Europe Today: Economics, Politics, The Class Struggle, International Relations*. Moscow: Progress, 1981.

*Mezhdunarodnyi Yezhegodnik* (International Yearbook). Moscow: Akademiya Nauk, 1971.

*Razryadka mezhdunarodnoy napryazhennosti i ideologicheskaya bor'ba* (Detente and the Ideological Struggle). Moscow: Nauka, 1981.

*Sovremennyi kapitalizm: politicheskiye otnosheniya i instituty vlasti* (Contemporary Capitalism: Political Relations and Institutions of Power). Moscow: Nauka, 1984.

International Communications Agency, Office of Research. *Soviet Research Institutes Project. Volume 1: The Policy Sciences*. Washington, DC: Kennan Institute for Advanced Russian Study, 1981.

Israelyan, V. "The Leninist Science of International Relations and Foreign Policy Reality," *International Affairs*, no. 6 (June 1967), pp. 46–52.

*Issledovaniye problem mira v sovetskoy i finskoy nauchnoy literature* (Peace Research in the Soviet and Finnish Scholarly Literature). Moscow: Institute of Scientific Information on the Social Sciences, 1983.

Ivanyan, I. "Burzhuaznoye obshchestvovedeniye i 'nauka o mire'" (Bourgeois Social Management and "Peace Research"), *Mirovaya Ekonomika i Mezhdunarodnye Otnosheniya*, no. 2 (February 1979), pp. 111–17.

Ivashin, I. and Yeshin, S. "O periodizatsii istorii vneshney politki SSSR" (On the Periodization of Soviet Foreign Policy), *Mezhdunarodnaya Zhizn'*, no. 7 (July 1958), pp. 80–5.

Jackson, William D. "Soviet Images of the US as Nuclear Adversary," *World Politics*, vol. 33, no. 4 (July 1981), pp. 614–38.

Jewitt, Kenneth. *Images of Detente and the Soviet Political Order*. Berkeley: Institute of International Studies, 1977.

Kalenskiy, V.G. *Gosudarstvo kak ob"yekt sotsiologicheskogo analiza* (The State as an Object of Sociological Analysis). Moscow: Yuridicheskaya Literatura, 1977.

*Politicheskaya nauka v S.Sh.A.* (Political Science in the USA). Moscow: Yuridicheskaya Literatura, 1969.

Kapchenko, N. "Marxism–Leninism: The Scientific Basis of Socialist Foreign Policy," *International Affairs*, no. 10 (October 1972), pp. 73–81.

"The Policy of Historical Optimism," *International Affairs*, no. 3 (March 1981), pp. 55–8.

"Socialist Foreign Policy and the Restructuring of International Relations," *International Affairs*, no. 4 (April 1975), pp. 3–13.

Karaganov, Sergei A. "Amerikanskiye rakety i yevropeyskaya bezopasnost'" (The US Missiles and European Security), *S.Sh.A.*, no. 11 (November 1985), pp. 49–54.

Katz, Mark N. *The Third World in Soviet Military Thought*. London: Croom Helm, 1982.

Keohane, Robert O., and Joseph S. Nye, Jr, eds., *Transnational Relations and World Politics*. Cambridge, Mass: Harvard University Press, 1972.

Kokoshin, Andrey A. "Amerikanskiye predstavleniya o mezhdunarodnykh otnosheniyakh 80–90-kh godov" (American Writings on the International Relations of the 1980s–1990s), in Trofimenko, Genrikh, ed. *Sovremennye vneshnepoliticheskiye kontseptsii S.Sh.A.* (Contemporary Foreign Policy Conceptions of the USA). Moscow: Nauka, 1979.

*O burzhuaznykh prognozakh razvitiya mezhdunarodnykh otnosheniy* (On Bourgeois Prognostications of the Development of International Relations). Moscow: Mezhdunarodnye Otnosheniya, 1978.

*Prognozirovaniye i politika* (Political Forecasting). Moscow: Mezhdunarodnye Otnosheniya, 1975.

*S.Sh.A.: za fasadom global'noy politiki* (The USA: Behind the Facade of Global Policy). Moscow: Izdatel'stvo Politicheskoy Literatury, 1981.

"Scholar Into Politician," *USA*, no. 5 (May 1974), pp. 80–90 (Joint Publications Research Service translation).

Kondykov, E. "Rol' sotsial'no-psikhologiya" (The Role of Social Psychology), *Mirovaya Ekonomika i Mezhdunarodnye Otnosheniya*, no. 11 (November 1969), pp. 81–2.

Konstantinov, F.V. *et al.* *Kritika teoreticheskikh kontseptsiy Mao Tsze-duna* (A Critique of the Theoretical Conceptions of Mao Tse-tung). Moscow: Mysl', 1970.

Kosolapov, R. "Ob"yekt nauchnogo issledovaniya" (An Object of Scholarly Research), *Mirovaya Ekonomika i Mezhdunarodnye Otnosheniya*, no. 9 (September 1969), pp. 99–102.

"Obshchestvennaya priroda mezhdunarodnykh otnosheniy" (The Social Nature of International Relations), *Mirovaya Ekonomika i Mezhdunarodnye Otnosheniya*, no. 7 (July 1979), pp. 61–80.

"Questions of Theory: Socialism and Contradictions," in *Pravda*, 20 July 1984, pp. 2–3, as translated in Foreign Broadcast Information Service. *Daily Report. Soviet Union*, 24 July 1984, pp. R1–R7.

Kotyk, Vaclav. "Problems of East–West Relations," *Journal of International Affairs*, vol. 22, no. 1 (1968), pp. 48–58.

Kozikov, I.A. "Problems of the Correlation Between the Scientific and Technical and Social Revolutions," *Nauchnyy Kommunizm* (JPRS, *Translations on USSR Political and Sociological Affairs*, no. 450, 31 October 1973).

Krasin, Yu. A. "Nekotorye voprosy metodologii politicheskogo myshleniya" (Some Problems of the Methodology of Political Thinking), in Sovetskaya Assotsiatsiya Politicheskikh Nauk. *Mezhdunarodnye otnosheniya, politika, i lichnost'* (International Relations, Politics, and Personality). Moscow: Nauka, 1976, pp. 15–23.

"Some Question of the Methodology of Political Thinking," in Soviet Political Sciences Association. *Time, Space and Politics*. Moscow: Social Sciences Today, 1977, pp. 39–52.

Kremenyuk, V.A. "Regional Salients in US Foreign Policy," *USA*, no. 5 (May 1974), pp. 45–51 (Joint Publications Research Service translation).

Krivozhika, V.I. "The Concept of 'National Interest' in American Foreign Policy," *USA*, no. 11 (November 1974), pp. 121–6 (Joint Publications Research Service translation).

Krivtsov, Vladimir. "The Maoists' Foreign Policy Strategy," in *Post-Mao Maoism*. Part 1. Moscow: Social Sciences Today, 1980, pp. 115–38.

Kubalkova, V. and Cruickshank, A.A. *Marxism–Leninism and the Theory of International Relations*. London: Routledge and Kegan Paul, 1980.

Kucera, Jaroslav. "On Problems of International Class Struggle," *International Relations* (Prague), 1975, pp. 32–44.

Kukulka, Yu. *Problemy teorii mezhdunarodnykh otnosheniy* (Problems of the Theory of International Relations). Moscow: Progress, 1980. Translated from the Polish.

Kunina, A. "A Critique of Bourgeois Theories of the Development of International Relations," *International Affairs*, no. 2 (February 1973), pp. 63–70.

Lasswell, Harold. *World Politics and Personal Insecurity*. New York: Whittlesley House, McGraw-Hill Book Co., 1935.

Lebedev, Nikolay. "The Decisive Force in the Struggle for Peace and the Security of Peoples," *International Affairs*, no. 3 (March 1981), pp. 14–19.

"The System of World Relations," *International Affairs*, no. 12 (December 1976), pp. 79–88.

*Velikiy oktyabr' i perestroyka mezhdunarodnykh otnosheniy* (Great October and the Restructuring of International Relations). Moscow: Mezhdunarodnye Otnosheniya, 1980.

*SSSR v mirovoy politike* (The USSR in World Politics). Moscow: Mezhdunarodnye Otnosheniya, 1980.

"The Vital Power of Lenin's Foreign Policy Theory," *International Affairs*, no. 12 (December 1974), pp. 88–93.

Lebedev, N.I., Drameva, N.P., Knyazhinskiy, V.B., eds. *Mezhdunarodnye otnosheniya i bor'ba idey* (International Relations and the Struggle of Ideas).

Moscow: Izdatel'stvo Politicheskoy Literatury, 1981.

Lebedev, Nikolay and Tyulin, I. "International Aspects of the STR," *International Affairs*, no. 12 (December 1979), pp. 107–8.

Leites, Nathan. *The Operational Code of the Politburo*. New York: McGraw-Hill, 1951.

Lenczowski, John. *Soviet Perceptions of US Foreign Policy*. Ithaca: Cornell University Press, 1982.

Lenin, V.I. *Imperialism and Imperialist War (1914–1917)*. *Selected Works*, vol. 5. New York: International Publishers, no date.

*What is to be Done?* New York: International Publishers, 1929.

"Le Socialisme et la Guerre," in Braillard, Philippe. *Theories des relations internationales*. Paris: Presses Universitaire de France, 1977, pp. 109–19.

*Leninskaya politika mira i bezopasnosti narodov* (The Leninist Peace Policy and International Security). Moscow: Nauka, 1982.

Levishin, L. and Oreshkin, V. "O politekonomicheskikh issledovaniyakh v sisteme akademii nauk SSSR" (On Research in Political Economy in the System of the Academy of Sciences of the USSR), *Voprosy Ekonomiki*, no. 5 (1974), pp. 12–24.

Lewytzkyj, Borys, ed. *Who's Who in the Soviet Union*. Munich: K.G. Saur, 1984.

Lewytzkyj, Borys and Stronynowski, Juliusz, eds. *Who's Who in the Socialist Countries*. Munich: K.G. Saur Publishing, Inc., 1978.

Loseva, T.D. and Ramzin, M.M., eds. *Voyennaya sila i mezhdunarodnye otnosheniya* (Military Force and International Relations). Moscow: Mezhdunarodnye Otnosheniya, 1972.

Lukashchuk, Igor. "Forecasting of International Legal Relations," in Soviet Political Sciences Association. *Soviet Policy of Peace*. Moscow: Social Sciences Today, 1979, pp. 175–86.

McClelland, Charles. *Theory and the International System*. New York: Macmillan, 1966.

MacNeal, Robert. ed. *International Relations Among Communists*. Englewood Cliffs, NJ: Prentice Hall, 1967.

Maksimov, V.V. "Frantsiya v NATO v 1966–1974" (France in NATO from 1966 to 1974), in *Mezhdunarodnye otnosheniya i klassovaya bor'ba v epokhu obschchego krizisa kapitalizma* (International Relations and the Class Struggle in the Period of the General Crisis of Capitalism). Gor'kiy, 1975, pp. 66–75.

Maksimova, M. "Vsemirnoye khosyaystvo, NTR i mezhdunarodnye otnosheniya" (The World Economy, the STR and International Relations), *Mirovaya Ekonomika i Mezhdunarodnye Otnosheniya*, no. 5 (May 1979), pp. 21–33.

Malcolm, Neil. *Soviet Political Scientists and American Politics*. New York: St Martin's Press, 1984.

Marcuse, Herbert. *Soviet Marxism*. New York: Columbia University Press, 1958.

Marx, Karl. *Zur Kritik der politischen Okonomie*. Berlin: Dietz, 1976.

Marx, Karl and Engels, Frederick. *On Colonialism*. New York: International Publishers, 1972.

*Selected Works*. New York: International Publishers, 1972.

Mel'nikov, Yu. M. *Imperskaya politika S.Sh.A.: Istoki i sovremmenost'* (The

Imperial Policy of the US: Sources and Realities). Moscow: Mezhdunarodnye Otnosheniya, 1984.

Melvil, Andrei. "The Leninist Concept of Foreign Policy in Our Time," *Social Sciences* vol. 12, no. 2 (1981), pp. 158–69.

Menzhinskiy, V. "The Moscow Meeting on the Problems of Peaceful Coexistence," *International Affairs*, no. 10 (October 1969), pp. 44–5.

Merle, Marcel. *Sociologie des relations internationales*. Paris: Dalloz, 1974.

ed. *L'Anticolonialisme europeen de Las Casas a Karl Marx*. Paris: Armand Colin, 1969.

*Mezhdunarodnye otnosheniya posle vtoroy mirovoy voyny* (International Relations after the Second World War). Moscow: Izdatel'stvo Politicheskikh Nauk, 1962.

Miletic, Andreja. *Nacionalni interes u Americkoj teoriji medunarodnih odnosa* (The National Interest in American Theory of International Relations). Belgrade: Savremena Administracija, 1978.

Miller, Robert H. "The Scientific–Technical Revolution and the Soviet Administrative Debate," in Cocks, Paul, Daniels, Robert V., and Heer, Nancy Whittier, eds. *The Dynamics of Soviet Politics*. Cambridge, Mass.: Harvard University Press, 1976, pp. 137–55.

Milshtein, Mikhail. "The Military–Political Doctrine of the US," *World Marxist Review*, no. 11 (November 1980), pp. 44–8.

Milshtein, Mikhail and Semeyko, Lev. "Problems of the Inadmissability of Nuclear Conflict," *International Studies Quarterly*, vol. 20, no. 1 (March 1976), pp. 87–104.

Milyukova, V. "International Relations of a New Type," *International Affairs*, no. 5 (May 1975), pp. 148–51.

Mitchell, R. Judson. *Ideology of a Superpower. Contemporary Soviet Doctrine on International Relations*. Stanford: Hoover Institution Press, 1982.

"A New Brezhnev Doctrine: The Restructuring of International Relations," *World Politics*, vol. 30, no. 2 (January 1978), pp. 366–90.

"The Revised 'Two Camps' Doctrine in Soviet Foreign Policy," *Orbis*, vol. 16, no. 1 (Spring 1972), pp. 21–34.

Modrzhinskaya, Yelena. "Lenin's Theory and Modern International Relations," *International Affairs*, no. 1 (January 1970), pp. 56–62.

Modrzhinskaya, Yelena, Grigoryan, V.T., Kondratkov, T.R., eds. *Problemy voyny i mira* (Problems of War and Peace). Moscow: Mysl', 1967.

Molnar, Miklos. *Marx et Engels et la politique internationale*. Paris: Gallimard, 1975.

Morozov, Grigory. "International Organizations and World Peace," in Soviet Political Sciences Association. *Soviet Policy of Peace*. Moscow: Social Sciences Today, 1979, pp. 129–37.

*Mezhdunarodnye organizatsii: nekotorye voprosy teorii* (International Organizations: Some Problems of Theory). Moscow: Mysl', 1974.

"Mezhdunarodnye organizatsii i podderzhaniye mira" (International Organizations and Reinforcing Peace), in Sovetskaya Assotsiatsiya Politicheskikh Nauk. *Politika mira i razvitiye politicheskikh sistem* (The Policy of Peace and the Development of Political Systems). Moscow: Nauka, 1979, pp. 107–14.

Morozov, Grigory *et al.*, eds. *Obshchestvennost' i problemy voyny i mira* (Public

Opinion and Problems of War and Peace). Moscow: Mezhdunarodnye Otnosheniya, 1976.

Narochnitskiy, A.L. "O teorii i metodologii istorii mezhdunarodnykh otnosheniy" (On the Theory and Methodology of the History of International Relations), *Voprosy Istorii*, no. 2 (1976), pp. 64–85.

Narochnitskiy, A.L. and Nezhinskiy, L.N. "Aktual'nye problemy istorii vneshney politiki SSSR i mezhdunarodnykh otnosheniy" (Current Problems of the History of Soviet Foreign Policy and International Relations), *Voprosy Istorii*, no. 10 (1981), pp. 12–31.

"Nauchnye osnovy politiki – v tsentre vnimaniya sovetskoy assotsiatsii politicheskikh (gosudarstvovedcheskikh) nauk" (The Scientific Bases of Politics – at the Center of Attention of the Soviet Association of Political (State) Sciences), *Sovetskoye Gosudarstvo i Pravo*, no. 7 (July 1965), pp. 148–51.

Nikiforov, A.V. "American Concepts of Interdependence," *USA*, no. 7 (July 1979), pp. 8–19 (Joint Publications Research Service translation).

Nikol'skiy, N.M. and Grishin, A.V. *Nauchno–tekhnicheskiy progress i mezhdunarodnye otnosheniya* (Scientific–technical Progress and International Relations). Moscow: Mezhdunarodnye Otnosheniya, 1978.

Nikonov, A.D. "Mezhdunarodnye otnosheniya i politika gosudarstv" (International Relations and the Policy of States), *Mirovaya Ekonomika i Mezhdunarodnye Otnosheniya*, no. 11 (November 1969), pp. 78–80.

editor in chief. *Problemy voyennoy razryadki* (Problems of Military Detente). Moscow: Nauka, 1981.

"Sovremennaya revolyutsiya vo voyennom dele i nauka o mezhdunarodnykh otnosheniyakh" (The Contemporary Revolution in Military Affairs and Science on International Relations), *Mirovaya Ekonomika i Mezhdunarodnye Otnosheniya*, no. 2 (February 1969), pp. 3–14.

"Obzor kruglogo stola o teorii mezhdunarodnykh otnosheniy" (A Review of the Round Table on the Theory of International Relations), *Mirovaya Ekonomika i Mezhdunarodnye Otnosheniya*, no. 11 (November 1969), pp. 97–8.

"O merakh po dal'neyshemu razvitiyu obshchestvennykh nauk i povysheniyu ikh role v kommunisticheskom stroitel'stve" (On Measures for the Furthest Development of the Social Sciences and Raising their Role in Communist Construction), *Kommunist*, no. 13 (1967), pp. 3–13.

"O razrabotke problem politicheskikh nauk" (On the Elaboration of Problems of Political Sciences), *Pravda*, 13 June 1965, p. 4.

Palmer, Norman D. "The Study of International Relations in the United States," *International Studies Quarterly*, vol. 24, no. 3 (September 1980), pp. 243–364.

Pastusiak, Longin. "International Relations," in Polish Association of Political Sciences. *Polish Round Table. Yearbook, 1969. III.* Wydawnictwo Polskiej Akademii Nauk: Wroclaw, 1971, pp. 161–74.

"International Relations Studies in Poland," *International Studies Quarterly*, vol. 22, no. 2 (June 1978).

"A Marxist Approach to the Study of International Relations," *East European Quarterly*, September 1969, pp. 285–93.

Pechenev, V. "Sotsializm v sisteme mezhdunarodnykh otnosheniy" (Socialism in the System of International Relations), *Voprosy Filosofii*, no. 9 (1971), pp. 15–25.

Petrov, V. "Mathematical Models in Foreign Policy Research," *International Affairs*, no. 1 (January 1981), pp. 119–20.

"Sovremennaya amerikanskaya literatura po voprosam mezhdunarodnykh otnosheniy i vneshnyaya politika S.Sh.A." (The Contemporary American Literature on Problems of International Relations and American Foreign Policy), *Voprosy Istorii*, no. 3 (1967), pp. 178–90.

Petrovskaya, L. "Teoriya igr v primenenii 'professional'nykh strategov'" (Game Theory as Applied by "The Professional Strategists"), *Mirovaya Ekonomika i Mezhdunarodnye Otnosheniya*, no. 11 (November 1969), pp. 94–7.

Petrovskiy, S.A. and Petrovskaya, L.A. "'Modernizm' protiv 'traditsionalizma' v burzhuaznykh issledovaniyakh mezhdunarodnykh otnosheniy" ("Modernism" versus "Traditionalism" in Bourgeois Research on International Relations), *Voprosy Istorii*, no. 2 (1974), pp. 39–54.

Petrovskiy, V.F. *Amerikanskaya vneshnepoliticheskaya mysl'* (American Foreign Policy Thought). Moscow: Mezhdunarodnye Otnosheniya, 1976.

*Burzhuaznye vneshnepoliticheskiye kontseptsii i ideologicheskaya bor'ba na mezhdunarodnom arene* (Bourgeois Foreign Policy Concepts and the International Ideological Struggle). Moscow: Znaniye, 1977.

"Current US Thinking on Foreign Policy," *International Affairs*, no. 11 (November 1973), pp. 74–9.

"Novye tendentsii v amerikanskikh burzhuaznykh kontseptsiyakh mezhdunarodnykh otnosheniy" (New Tendencies in American Bourgeois Research on International Relations), *Novaya i Noveyshaya Istoriya*, no. 1 (1975), pp. 67–82.

"The Power Factor in US Global Strategy," *USA*, no. 5 (May 1979), pp. 17–27 (Joint Publications Research Service translation).

"Rol' i mesto sovetsko–amerikanskikh otnosheniy v sovremennom mire" (The Role and Place of Soviet–American Relations in the Contemporary World), *Voprosy Istorii*, no. 10 (1978), pp. 79–96.

"The UN and World Politics," *International Affairs*, no. 7 (July 1980), pp. 10–20.

*Vneshnyaya politika S.Sh.A.: teoreticheskiy arsenal* (US Foreign Policy: The Theoretical Arsenal). Moscow: Znaniye, 1973.

Powell, David E. and Shoup, Paul. "The Emergence of Political Science in Communist Countries," *American Political Science Review*, June 1970, pp. 572–88.

Pozdnyakov, E.A. "Elementy metodologii prognozirovaniya" (Elements of the Methodology of Prognostication), *Mirovaya Ekonomika i Mezhdunarodyne Otnosheniya*, no. 11 (November 1969), pp. 91–3.

*Sistemnyy podkhod i mezhdunarodnye otnosheniya* (The Systems Approach and International Relations). Moscow: Nauka, 1976.

"Predotvratit' yadernyy apokalipsis" (To Prevent a Nuclear Apocalypse), *Literaturnaya Gazeta*, 29 August 1979, back page (interview with Karl Deutsch).

"Present-Day Problems of the Theory of Marxist Dialectics," in *Marxist Dialectics Today*. Moscow: Social Sciences Today, 1979, pp. 5–26.

Primakov, Yevgeny. "The Arms Race and the Local Conflicts," in *Peace and Disarmament*. Moscow: Progress, 1980, pp. 81–94.

"Opening Speech" (at conference at Moscow State Institute of International Relations), *International Affairs*, no. 3 (March 1981), pp. 4–6.

*Problems of War and Peace. A Critical Analysis of Bourgeois Theories*. Moscow: Progress, 1972.

"Problemy teorii mezhdunarodnykh otnosheniy" (Problems of the Theory of International Relations), *Mirovaya Ekonomika i Mezhdunarodnye Otnosheniya*, no. 9 (September 1969), pp. 88–106, and no. 11 (November 1969), pp. 78–98.

Proyektor, D.M. *The Foundations of Peace in Europe*. Moscow: Nauka, 1984.

"Problems and Opinions: Reconsidering Values?" in *Izvestiya*, 8 April 1984, as translated in Foreign Broadcast Information Service. *Daily Report. Soviet Union*, 11 April 1984, pp. G1–G4.

*Puty Yevropy* (European Paths). Moscow: Znaniye, 1978.

Ra′anan, Uri. "Soviet Decision-Making and International Relations," *Problems of Communism*, November–December 1980, pp. 41–7.

Rakowska-Harmstone, Theresa. "Socialist Internationalism and Eastern Europe," *Survey*, Part 1 (Winter 1976), pp. 38–54; Part 2 (Spring 1976), pp. 81–6.

Ranke, Leopold von. *Die grossen Maechte*. Friedrich Meinecke, ed. Leipzig: Insel-Verlag, 1916.

Razmerov, V. "Politicheskoye modelirovaniye v zapadnoy yevrope" (Political Modelling in Western Europe), *Mirovaya Ekonomika i Mezhdunarodnye Otnosheniya*, no. 11 (November 1969), pp. 85–8.

Remnek, Richard. *Social Scientists and Policy Making in the USSR*. New York: Praeger, 1977.

*Soviet Scholars and Foreign Policy: A Case Study in Soviet Policy Towards India*. Durham, NC: Carolina Academic Press, 1975.

"Research Needs 'Sunset Laws', Rigorous Planning, Competition," *Current Digest of the Soviet Press*, vol. 33, no. 4 (1981), pp. 17–18.

Revesz, Laszlo. "Political Science in Eastern Europe: Discussion and Initial Stages," *Studies in Soviet Thought*, September 1967, pp. 185–207.

"Revolution, Class Struggle in an Era of Detente," *Current Digest of the Soviet Press*, vol. 30, no. 38 (1978), pp. 3–43.

Roshchin, A.A. *Poslevoyennoye uregulirovaniye v Yevrope* (The Postwar Settlement in Europe). Moscow: Mysl′, 1984.

"Round Table: Laws Governing the Development of the Socialist World System," *World Marxist Review*, no. 10 (1971), pp. 3–43.

Rudenko, G. "Lenin's Theory of Imperialism: the General Crisis of Capitalism Today," *International Affairs*, no. 5 (May 1980), pp. 22–30.

Russet, Bruce. *Power and Community in World Politics*. New York: W.H. Freeman, 1972.

*S.Sh.A.: Vneshnepoliticheskiy mekhanizm* (The USA: Foreign-Policy Mechanism). Moscow: Nauka, 1972.

Sahovic, Milan. *Medunarodni odnosi i drustveni napredak* (International Relations and Social Progress). Belgrade: Radnicka Stampa, 1977.

Sanakoyev, Shalva. "Foreign Policy of Socialism: Sources of Theory," *International Affairs*, no. 5 (May 1975), pp. 108–18.
"Foreign Policy of Socialism: Unity of Theory and Practice," in Soviet Peace Committee. *Leninist Principles of Peaceful Coexistence in the World Today*. Moscow: Social Sciences Today, 1973, pp. 94–116.
"Imperialist Foreign Policy and Bourgeois Politology," *International Affairs*, no. 2 (February 1978), pp. 76–85.
"The Leninist Methodology of Studying International Relations," *International Affairs*, no. 9 (September 1969), pp. 50–3.
"The New Stage in International Relations," *International Affairs*, no. 2 (February 1972), pp. 80–5.
"Soviet Foreign Policy and Current International Relations," *International Affairs*, no. 3 (March 1981), pp. 6–14.
"The World Today: Problem of the Correlation of Forces," *International Affairs*, no. 11 (November 1974), pp. 40–50.
Sanakoyev, Shalva and Kapchenko, N.I. *O teorii vneshney politiki sotsializma* (On the Theory of the Foreign Policy of Socialism). Moscow: Mezhdunarodnye Otnosheniya, 1976.
*Socialism: Foreign Policy in Theory and Practice*. Moscow: Progress, 1976.
Schwarz, Morton. *Soviet Perceptions of the United States*. Berkeley: University of California Press, 1978.
Schwarz, Siegfried, Basler, Gerhard, and Winter, Martin. *Imperialistische Aussenpolitik am Beginn der 80er Jahre*. Berlin, DDR: IPW-Forschungshefte, vol. 16, no. 1, 1981.
Semeyko, Lev. "The Interdependence of Political and Military Detente," in Soviet Political Sciences Association. *Soviet Policy of Peace*. Moscow: Social Sciences Today, 1979, pp. 187–94.
Semyonov, Vadim. "Cumulative Growth in Political Knowledge Since 1950," in Soviet Political Sciences Association. *Political Theory and Political Practice*. Moscow: Social Sciences Today, 1979, pp. 10–21.
Sergiyev, A. "Bourgeois Pseudo-Science About the Future," *International Affairs*, no. 2 (February 1972), pp. 80–5.
*Nauka i vneshnyaya politika* (Science and Foreign Policy). Moscow: Znaniye, 1967.
"Lenin on the Correlation of Forces as a Factor of International Relations," *International Affairs*, no. 5 (May 1975), pp. 99–107.
Shakhnazarov, Georgi Kh. "Effective Factors of International Relations," *International Affairs*, no. 2 (February 1977), pp. 79–87.
Shakhazarov, Georgi Kh. "'Great Powers' Approach to International Politics," *World Marxist Review*, no. 5 (1972), pp. 110–18.
*Gryadushchiy miroporyadok* (The Coming World Order). Moscow: Izdatel'stvo Politicheskoy Literatury, 1981.
"K probleme sootnosheniya sil v mire" (On the Problem of the Correlation of Forces in the World), *Kommunist*, no. 3 (1974), pp. 77–90.
"O nekotorykh kontseptsiyakh mira i mirovogo poryadka" (On Certain Conceptions of Peace and World Order), *Mirovaya Ekonomika i Mezhdunarodnye Otnosheniya*, no. 11 (November 1980), pp. 100–12.
"Policy of Peace and Our Time," in Soviet Political Sciences Association. *Soviet Policy of Peace*. Moscow: Social Sciences Today, 1979, pp. 187–94.

"Political Science and New Factors in International Relations," in Soviet Political Sciences Association. *Time, Space and Politics*. Moscow: Social Sciences Today, 1977, pp. 8–26.

"Politika skvoz' prizmu nauki" (Politics through the Prism of Science), *Kommunist*, no. 17.

"The Problem of Peace: An Analysis of Basic Concepts," *The Soviet Review*, vol. 21, no. 3.

"Vliyaniye razryadki mezhdunarodnoy napryazhennosti na polozheniye lichnosti" (The Influence of the Relaxation of International Tension on Personality), in Sovetskaya Assotsiatsiya Politicheskikh Nauk. *Mezhdunarodnye otnosheniya, politika, i lichnost'* (International Relations, Politics, and Personality). Moscow: Nauka, 1976, pp. 7–13.

Shatalov, I. "The Scientific and Technological Revolution and International Relations," *International Affairs*, no. 8 (August 1971), pp. 30–2.

Sheydina, I.L. *Nevoyennye faktory sily vo vneshney politike S.Sh.A.* (Non-military Factors of Power in US Foreign Policy). Moscow: Nauka, 1984.

Shevtsov, V.S. *National Sovereignty and the Soviet State*. Moscow: Progress, 1974.

*National'nyy suverenitet* (National Sovereignty). Moscow: Politicheskaya Literatura, 1978.

Shimanovskiy, V.V. "Ideologicheskiye rascheti avtorov kontseptsii 'mirnogo vzaimodeystviya'" (The Ideological Calculations of the Authors of the Conception "Peaceful Interaction"), in *V nauchnom poiske* (In Scholarly Investigation). Moscow: Mezhdunarodnye Otnosheniya, 1967.

Singer, J. David. "Soviet and American Foreign Policy Attitudes, Content Analysis of Elite Articulations," *Journal of Conflict Resolution* vol. 8, no. 4 (December 1964), pp. 424–75.

"Slavnyy yubiley otechestvennoy nauki" (Glorious Jubilee of Native Science), *Narody Azii i Afriki*, no. 2 (1974), pp. 3–4.

Smolyan, G.L. "Printsipi issledovaniya konflikta" (Principles of Conflict Research), *Voprosy Filosofii*, no. 8 (August 1968), pp. 35–41.

Sobakin, V. "Constitutional Principles of Soviet Foreign Policy," in *Constitution of the USSR: Theory and Policy*. Moscow: Social Sciences Today, 1978, pp. 178–93.

"Social Sciences," in *Current Digest of the Soviet Press* vol. 31, no. 34 (1979), p. 16.

Sojak, Vladimir. "New Aspects of International Relations in the 1970s," *International Relations* (Prague), 1976, pp. 14–28.

"Western Models," *International Affairs*, no. 6 (June 1974), pp. 71–4.

Solodovnikov, V. and Gavrilov, N. "Africa: Tendencies of non-Capitalist Development," *International Affairs*, no. 3 (March 1976), pp. 31–9.

Solodovskiy, V.D., ed. *Voyennaya strategiya* (Military Strategy). Moscow: Voyennaya Literatura, 1968. Second edition.

Solomon, Peter H. review of V.G. Kalenskiy, *Politicheskaya nauka v S.Sh.A.* (Political Science in USA). *American Political Science Review*, March 1970, pp. 188–9.

*Sotsiologicheskiye problemy mezhdunarodnykh otnosheniy* (Sociological Problems of International Relations). Moscow: Nauka, 1970.

Soviet Political Sciences Association. *Novyi mirovoy poryadok i politicheskaya obshchnost'* (The New World Order and Political Community). Moscow: Nauka, 1983.

*Politicheskiye otnosheniya: prognozirovaniye i planirovaniye* (Political Relations: Prognostication and Planning). Moscow: Nauka, 1979.

"Soviet–American Relations and European Security," *USA*, no. 9 (September 1974), pp. 125–7 (Joint Publications Research Service translation).

"Specialists in International Affairs Examine Implementation of the Peace Programme," *International Affairs*, no. 3 (March 1976), pp. 145–9.

Stalin, Joseph. *Economic Problems of Socialism in the USSR*. Moscow: Foreign Language Publishing House, 1952.

Stefanowicz, Janusz. *Stary nowy swiat. Ciaglosc i zmiana w stosunkach miedzynarodowych* (The Old New World. Continuity and Change in International Relations). Warsaw: Instytut Wydawniczny PAX, 1978.

Stepanov, I.A. "Assimilyatsiya idey makiavelli i proyavleniya makiavelizma v politologii S.Sh.A." (Assimilation of the Ideas of Machiavelli and Manifestations of Machiavellianism in US Political Science), in Sovetskaya Assotsiatsiya Politicheskikh Nauk. *Politicheskiye otnosheniya* (Political Relations). Moscow: Nauka, 1979, pp. 188–98.

"Svetoch i nadezhda chelovechestva" (The Torch and Hope of Mankind), *Mirovaya Ekonomika i Mezhdunarodnye Otnosheniya*, no. 2 (February 1973), pp. 3–15.

Tadevosyan, E.V. "Diskussiya o politicheskoy nauki" (Discussion on Political Science), *Voprosy Filosofii*, no. 10 (October 1965), pp. 164–6.

"Tezisy Instituta IMEMO AN SSSR" (Theses of the Institute of the World Economy and International Relations, Academy of Sciences, USSR), *Mirovaya Ekonomika i Mezhdunarodnye Otnosheniya*, no. 6 (June 1979), pp. 27–62.

Theen, Rolf H.W. "Political Science in the USSR: 'To Be or Not to Be'," *World Politics*, vol. 23, no. 4 (July 1971), pp. 684–703.

Tikhvinskiy, S. "Apologetics of Great-Han Hegemonism in Chinese Historiography," *Social Sciences* vol. 11, no. 1 (1980), pp. 83–100.

Tomashevskiy, Dmitri. "The Influence of Soviet Foreign Policy on International Relations," *International Affairs*, no. 10 (October 1969), pp. 40–2.

*Leninskiye idei i sovremennye mezhdunarodnye otnosheniya* (Leninist Ideas and Contemporary International Relations). Moscow: Politizdat, 1971.

*Lenin's Ideas and Modern International Relations*. Moscow: Progress, 1974.

"Na puti k korennoy perestroykoy mezhdunarodnykh otnosheniy" (On the Path to a Radical Restructuring of International Relations), *Mirovaya Ekonomika i Mezhdunarodnye Otnosheniya*, no. 1 (January 1975), pp. 3–13.

*On the Peaceful Coexistence of States*. Moscow: Novosti, 1973.

"The USSR and the Capitalist World," *International Affairs*, no. 3 (March 1966), pp. 3–17.

"Zakonomernaya tendentsiya obshchestvennogo razvitiya" (The Objective Tendency of Social Development), *Mirovaya Ekonomika i Mezhdunarodnye Otnosheniya*, no. 9 (September 1969), pp. 92–5.

Trofimenko, Genrikh. "Europe for the Europeans," interview in *El Pais* (Madrid), 5 June 1984, pp. 11–12, as translated in Foreign Broadcast Information Service. *Daily Report. Soviet Union*, 18 June 1984, pp. CC12–CC15.

*S.Sh.A.: Politika, voyna, ideologiya* (The USA: Politics, War, Ideology). Moscow: Mysl', 1976.

"Skvoz' prizmu 'balansa sil'" (Through the Prism of the "Balance of Power"), in *Problemy istorii mezhdunarodnykh otnosheniy i ideologicheskaya bor'ba* (Problems of the History of International Relations and the Ideological Struggle). Moscow: Nauka, 1976, pp. 35–74.

ed. *Sovremennye vneshnepoliticheskiye kontseptsii S.Sh.A.* (Contemporary US Foreign Policy Concepts). Moscow: Nauka, 1979.

Tucker, Robert C., ed. *The Lenin Anthology*. New York: Norton, 1975.

Tumanov, Vladimir. "Political Mechanism of the Power of Monopoly Capital," in Soviet Political Sciences Association. *Time, Space and Politics*. Moscow: Social Sciences Today, 1977, pp. 134–55.

Turner, Carl B. *An Analysis of Soviet Views of Keynes*. Durham, NC: Duke University Press, 1969.

"Tvorcheskoye naslediye Ye.S. Varga" (The Creative Heritage of Ye. S. Varga), *Mirovaya Ekonomika i Mezhdunarodnye Otnosheniya*, no. 1 (January 1970), pp. 123–31.

Tyulin, I.G. "Nekotorye voprosy teorii mezhdunarodnykh otnosheniy v rabotakh P. Renuvena i Zh.-B. Dyurozelya" (Some Problems of the Theory of International Relations in the Works of P. Renouvin and J.B. Duroselle), in *Problemy istorii mezhdunarodnykh otnosheniy i ideologicheskaya bor'ba* (Problems of the History of International Relations and the Ideological Struggle). Moscow: Nauka, 1976, pp. 259–73.

Ulam, Adam B. *Expansion and Coexistence. A History of Soviet Foreign Policy, 1917–1973*. New York: Praeger, 1974. Second edn.

*The New Face of Soviet Totalitarianism*. New York: Praeger, 1963.

Ulyanovsky, R. "The Leninist Concept of Non-Capitalist Development and Our Time," *Social Sciences*, April–June 1971, pp. 91–108.

Usachev, Igor G. *Mezhdunarodnaya razryadka i S.Sh.A.* (International Detente and the USA). Moscow: Mysl', 1980.

"Vneshnepoliticheskiye faktory, vliyayushchiye na povedeniye S.Sh.A. na mirovoy arene" (Factors of the International Environment Influencing US Behavior on the World Arena), in Institute of US and Canadian Studies, *Sovremennaya vneshnyaya politika S.Sh.A.* (Contemporary US Foreign Policy), vol. 1. Moscow: Nauka, 1984, pp. 121–37.

Ustinov, N. "Mathematical Models in the Analysis of International Relations," *International Affairs*, no. 12 (December 1968), pp. 74–82.

Utkin, A.I. "Amerikano–zapadnoyevropeyskiye otnosheniya" (US–West European Relations), in Institute of US and Canadian Studies, *Sovremennaya vneshnyaya politika S.Sh.A.* (Contemporary US Foreign Policy), vol. 2. Moscow: Nauka, 1984, pp. 202–30.

"Atlanticism v. Europeism," *USA*, no. 4 (April 1974), pp. 28–38 (Joint Publications Research Service translation).

*S.Sh.A. i zapadnaya Yevropa: torgovlya oruzhiyem (mezhdonarodno–politicheskiy aspekt)* (The US and Western Europe: The Weapons Trade – International–Political Aspect). Moscow: Nauka, 1984.

"'Atlantizm' i Yaponiya" ("Atlanticism" and Japan), *Mirovaya Ekonomika i Mezhdunarodnye Onosheniya*, no. 6 (June 1976), pp. 56–63.

Varga, Yevgeny S. *Izbrannye proizvedeniya: kapitalizm posle vtoroy mirovoy voyny* (Selected Works: Capitalism after the Second World War). Moscow: Nauka, 1974.

*Izmeneniya v ekonomike kapitalizma v itoge vtoroy mirovoy voyny* (Changes in the Economy of Capitalism as a Result of the Second World War). Moscow: Politicheskaya Literatura, 1946.

*Kapitalizm dvadtsatogo veka* (Twentieth-Century Capitalism). Moscow: Politicheskaya Literatura, 1961.

*Ocherki po problemam politekonomiki kapitalizma* (Essays on Problems of the Political Economy of Capitalism). Moscow: Politicheskaya Literatura, 1965.

*Osnovnye voprosy ekonomiki i politiki imperializma (posle vtoroy mirovoy voyny)* (Fundamental Problems of the Economy and Policy of Imperialism [After the Second World War]). Moscow: Politicheskaya Literatura, 1953.

Vidyasova, L. "Crisis of Imperialism's Foreign Policy," *International Affairs*, no. 1 (January 1973), pp. 56–63.

Volkov, N. and Shmelyev, N. "Strukturnye sdvigi v ekonomike kapitalizma" (Structural Changes in the Economy of Capitalism), *Mirovaya Ekonomika i Mezhdunarodnye Otnosheniya*, no. 8 (August 1985), pp. 28–40.

*Voprosy istorii vneshney politiki SSSR i mezhdunarodnykh otnosheniy* (Problems of the History of Soviet Foreign Policy and International Relations). Moscow: Nauka, 1976.

Voronov, A. "Following Lenin's Course," *International Affairs*, no. 5 (May 1978), pp. 120–2.

Vorontsov, G.A. *Burzhuaznaya nauka na sluzhbe politiki* (Bourgeois Science in the Service of Policy). Moscow: Mezhdunarodnye Otnosheniya, 1975.

"S.Sh.A., NATO i yevrorakety" (The US, NATO and the Euromissiles), *Mirovaya Ekonomika i Mezhdunarodnye Otnosheniya*, no. 11 (November 1984), pp. 15–24.

"The West in Search of a Coordinated Policy," *International Affairs*, no. 5 (May 1977), pp. 101–10.

"Vsesoyuznyy simpozium sotsiologov" (All-Union Symposium of Sociologists), *Voprosy Filosofii*, no. 10 (October 1966), pp. 156–65.

Vukadinovic, Radovan. *Osnove teorije vanjske politike* (Foundations of the Theory of Foreign Policy). Zagreb: Biblioteka suvremene politicke misli, 1981.

Waltz, Kenneth. *Theory of International Politics*. Reading, Mass.: Addison-Wesley, 1979.

Wessell, Nils H. "Soviet Views of Multipolarity and the Emerging Balance of Power," *Orbis*, vol. 22, no. 4 (Winter 1979), pp. 785–813.

Wetter, Gustav A. *Dialectical Materialism. A Historical and Systematic Survey of Philosophy in the Soviet Union*. New York: Praeger, 1963.

Wiatr, Jerzy J. "A Sociological Perspective in the Study of International Relations," in Wiatr, *Essays in Political Sociology*. Wroclaw: The Polish Academy of Sciences Press, 1978, pp. 50–62.

*Sotsiologiya politicheskikh otnosheniy* (The Sociology of Political Relations). Edited and introduced by Fedor M. Burlatskiy. Moscow: Progress, 1979. Translated from the Polish.

Winn, Gregory F.T. "Western and Soviet Systems/Social Sciences Approaches to International Affairs: An Introductory Comparison," *Behavioral Science*, vol. 26, no. 3 (July 1981), pp. 281–93.

Yakovlev, Aleksandr. *Ot Trumena do Reygana. Doktriny i real'nosti yadernogo veka* (From Truman to Reagan. Doctrines and Realities of the Nuclear Age). Moscow: Molodaya Gvardiya, 1985. Second edn.

"Voprosy teorii: Imperializm – Sopernichestvo i protivorechiya" (Problems of Theory: Imperialism – Rivalry and Contradictions), *Pravda*, 23 March 1984, pp. 3–4.

Yegorov, S.A. "K voprosu o sovremennoy metodologicheskoy evolyutsii politologii S.Sh.A." (On the Question of the Contemporary Methodological Evolution of US Political Science), in Sovetskaya Assotsiatsiya Politicheskikh Nauk. *Politika mira i razvitiye politicheskikh sistem* (The Peace Policy and the Development of Political Systems). Moscow: Nauka, 1979, pp. 247–56.

*Politicheskaya sistema, politicheskoye razvitiye, pravo: kritika nemarksistskikh politologicheskikh kontseptsiy* (Political Systems, Political Development, Law: A Critique of Non-Marxist Political-Science Concepts). Moscow: Yuridicheskaya Literatura, 1983.

Yermolenko, D.V. "Sociology and International Relations: Some Results of the 6th World Sociology Congress," *International Affairs*, no. 1 (January 1967), pp. 14–19.

*International Relations in the Era of the STR*. Moscow: Novosti, 1973.

"Sociology and Problems of International Conflict," *International Affairs*, no. 8 (August 1968).

"Sotsiologicheskiye issledovaniya i mezhdunarodnye otnosheniya" (Sociological Research and International Relations), *Voprosy Filosofii*, no. 1 (January 1971), pp. 75–86.

*Sotsiologiya i problemy mezhdunarodnykh otnosheniy* (Sociology and Problems of International Relations). Moscow: Mezhdunarodnye Otnosheniya, 1977.

"Vozmozhnost' primeneniya matematicheskikh metodov" (The Possibility of Applying Mathematical Methods), *Mirovaya Ekonomika i Mezhdunarodnye Otnosheniya*, no. 11 (November 1969), pp. 89–91.

"Yevropa v mirovoy politike 1980-kh godov" (Europe in the World Politics of the 1980s), *Mirovaya Ekonomika i Mezhdunarodnye Otnosheniya*, no. 2 (February 1984), pp. 3–10.

Zamkovoy, V.I. *Kritika burzhuaznykh teoriy neizhbezhnosti novoy mirovoy voyny* (A Critique of Bourgeois Theories of the Inevitability of a New World War). Moscow: Mysl', 1965.

Zhurkin, V.V. and Primakov, E.M. *Mezhdunarodnye konflikty* (International Conflicts). Moscow: Mezhdunarodnye Otnosheniya, 1972.

Zimmerman, William. *Soviet Perspectives on International Relations 1956–1967*. Princeton: Princeton University Press, 1971.

Zuyeva, K.P. *Vopreki dukhu vremeni. Nekotorye problemy teorii i praktiki mezhdunarodnykh otnosheniy v rabotakh Raymona Arona* (Against the Spirit of the Times. Some Problems of the Theory and Practice of International Relations in the Works of Raymond Aron). Moscow: Nauka, 1979.

# Index

RH M / 01030TS

WW LYNCH